D0536540

# From Crime to Crime

# From Crime to Crime

RICHARD HENRIQUES

HODDER &
STOUGHTON

First published in Great Britain in 2020 by Hodder & Stoughton
An Hachette UK company

3

Copyright © Richard Henriques 2020

A CIP catalogue record for this title is available from the British Library

Hardback ISBN 978 1 529 33348 0
Paperback ISBN 978 1 529 33349 7
eBook ISBN 978 1 529 33350 3

Typeset in Bembo MT by Palimpsest Book Production Ltd, Falkirk, Stirlingshire

Printed and bound by Clays Ltd, Elcograf S.p.A.

Hodder & Stoughton policy is to use papers that are natural, renewable
and recyclable products and made from wood grown in sustainable forests.
The logging and manufacturing processes are expected to conform to the
environmental regulations of the country of origin.

Hodder & Stoughton Ltd
Carmelite House
50 Victoria Embankment
London EC4Y 0DZ

www.hodder.co.uk

*To my wife, Toni*

# Contents

# Introduction:

## A Fisherman from Madeira

THIS IS NOT a memoir. It is not about me, but about the criminal cases I have been involved in, either as counsel or judge, and the lessons I have learned from them. Our entire criminal justice process is in crisis and the subject of much justified public criticism. Years of underfunding, ignoring reviews, and ministerial incompetence have driven me to write this book. The system is struggling to face the demands placed upon it.

My intention is to demonstrate how the justice process has worked through the prism of cases with which I have been closely associated. I chose the title because each case concerns a crime of varying magnitude and long-term significance. They will show, I hope, how these diverse crimes have been prosecuted, defended and judged at different times in the past forty years.

A career for me in the law seemed a rewarding inevitability, given the strong legal thread running through the Henriques family history. During the Spanish Inquisition, the family lived in Spain and Portugal, before fleeing the Iberian Peninsula via Madeira to the Caribbean. My great-great-great-grandfather, Jacob Henriques, was born in Kingston, Jamaica in 1758. His grandson David, born in Kingston in 1804, emigrated to London thirty years later, and David's sons settled in Manchester in 1865. I was amused to read in a tabloid newspaper during the trial of Dr Shipman that I was described as the grandson of a fisherman from Madeira.

My grandfather, Edward Henriques, was in fact an engineer and a colonel, who chaired Salford magistrates for a number of years. His elder brother Henry was a QC who appeared in several capital murder trials on the Northern Circuit, and his cousin Sir Basil was chairman of East London Juvenile Court for nineteen years. My father, Cecil, and maternal uncle Randle Baker both practised at the Bar on the Northern Circuit.

I was fascinated with the criminal courts from an early age. I was aged ten when the Blackpool poisoner Mrs Merrifield was convicted of murder and hanged at Strangeways. I read every word of the trial, including the sentencing remarks of Mr Justice Glynn-Jones. We lived in Blackpool at the time and the case made a great impression on me, not least when shortly after the trial, the defence counsel Jack Nahum QC visited our home, as did the stunningly accomplished Rose Heilbron QC, who had recently secured the acquittal of a man charged with murder whilst committing a burglary. I soon knew exactly what I wanted to do in life.

A key period was a gap year between school and university spent in a solicitor's office in Fleetwood. The Lancashire town was then a bustling port with more than its fair share of violent misconduct. I attended courts and helped to prepare cases. I also sat behind and observed the leading criminal practitioners at Blackpool Quarter Sessions and Lancaster Assizes.

I was called to the Bar in 1967 and found the perfect pupil master in my father's chambers in Manchester. Ian Webster was a busy and talented criminal practitioner, who taught me how to communicate with all levels of the criminal justice system. Everyone in and around court mattered to Ian, and he mattered to them. He was able to persuade defendants, in a kindly manner, how hopeless their cases were whenever it was appropriate. He was similarly persuasive with juries when cases permitted it. I am much indebted to him.

Pupillage offered an opportunity to observe the great men

and women of the Northern Circuit in court. My fellow pupil, who joined chambers one month before me, was Daniel Brennan. In 2009, Dan, having been ennobled, was asked by *The Times*, 'Who has been the most influential person in your life in the law?' He replied, 'The great advocates of my time on the Northern Circuit. Patrick Russell for the art of the understatement. Christopher Rose for the powerful and short cross-examination. George Carman for captivating a jury and Mick Maguire for courage under fire.'* Dan and I were observing the same advocates at the same time and reaching the identical conclusion.

I have noted over the years that students, pupils and young members of the Bar rarely sit in court watching 'the great advocates of the day'. They would be well advised to do so. Whilst agreeing with Dan, I continued to be influenced, not only by those more senior than me, but also by my contemporaries: Rodney Klevan for his deployment of humour, David Poole for his polished and measured use of language, Brian Leveson for his preparation and attention to detail, Peter Openshaw as an immaculately fair minister of justice, and Peter Wright for his power in cross-examination.

No case conducted by me as junior counsel merits a place in this book. The low point was losing thirteen consecutive careless driving cases. The high points were being led by each of those celebrated advocates named by Dan Brennan. I saw more of George Carman than the others; we both grew up in South Shore, Blackpool, and our families knew one another well. I had canvassed the possibility of George becoming my pupil master, but my father, for good reason, was less than enthusiastic. By coincidence, when I bought a flat in Manchester, George lived only a hundred yards away.

* *The Times*, June 2009, quoted in the Supplement to the *Northern Circuit Directory* by His Honour David Lynch.

George was a senior junior at the time and became a regular drinking companion. To his credit, he was generous with his advice and tended to display more interest in my careless driving cases than in his own, very well-paid, personal injury cases. Even at that time, George's consuming ambition was to become a High Court judge. He appeared to do everything in his power to render that ambition unattainable. He gambled, usually black-jack, to an almost destructive degree, frequented most of the lowest dives in Manchester and regularly drank to the point of incapacity. More than once he failed to arrive at court when a case had been adjourned overnight during a trial. The bad oyster excuse wore very thin.

That George became the most sought-after and successful advocate of his generation was attributable to his formidable intellect, his determination to win every case, his ability to communicate attractively with every jury, and a lot of luck. I was fortunate to spend time with him at an impressionable age.

In April 1986, I was engaged in a planning application when our chambers clerk, Trevor Doyle, telephoned me: 'Congratulations, boss, you and I are going places!' He had opened the letter indicating that I was to be appointed Queen's Counsel.

Instant elation was soon replaced by the realisation that for the first time in eighteen years I had no pending work. The panic was fortunately short-lived. At my celebration party the following day, a supportive Blackpool solicitor and friend, Peter Lawson, arrived with a brief several feet high to defend an alleged fraudster at the Old Bailey; the trial to commence within days of my swearing-in ceremony, and expected to last for several months.

My exhilaration did not last long. Medical reports began to arrive and the defendant was not in good condition. 'He may not survive the demands of a lengthy trial,' said one report. In due course I wrote to the Attorney General, Sir Michael Havers, who agreed to enter a *nolle prosequi*, a procedure that brought an immediate end to the prosecution and thus to my immediate prospect of earning a living.

I returned to Manchester to be greeted by Trevor with the words, 'Birmingham riots, sir,' as he pointed to several cardboard boxes full of lever-arch files. The case dragged on through the summer of 1986. On its completion, I was sent to Leeds to defend a serial rapist, a case lasting for several weeks. I recall sitting in a shabby hotel bedroom as paper peeled from the wall, wondering whether taking silk had been such a good idea.

Fortunately, a fascinating case was just around the corner . . .

# QUEEN'S COUNSEL

# Chapter 1

## The Murder of Julia Avery

B RIEFS FIND THEIR way to counsel in a variety of ways often unknown to the recipient. The brief in *The Queen v. Mitchell Robinson* in Worcester Crown Court was a good example. I had never visited Worcester and as I perused the back sheet, I wondered how a firm of solicitors in that city had come to brief me. Trevor Doyle could shed no light on events, save to say, 'You are gaining a reputation, sir.'

My instructing solicitor was Joe Kieran, senior partner of Kieran and Co., the leading criminal firm in Worcester. Joe is from Liverpool, read law at Liverpool University, and was articled in that city; on becoming qualified, he looked at a map of England and decided that Worcester was the ideal location to set up his own practice. His instincts proved fruitful and some twenty years later, Joe had developed a thriving concern.

The case of Mitchell Robinson was extraordinary, with characteristics untypical of this respectable shire city and far more consistent with gangland activity in his native Liverpool or in Manchester. The case called for Queen's Counsel from the Northern Circuit and Joe's cousin, a recent circuit junior, had kindly recommended me.

Mitchell Robinson had the perfect alibi. He was in police custody when his partner and mother of his baby daughter, Julia Avery, was strangled in the early hours in their bedroom. The prosecution asserted that he had deliberately brought about his own arrest by committing a robbery in a chip-shop queue, having arranged for an associate, Noel Brown, to kill Julia. They asserted that Robinson had insured Julia's life for £150,000, which constituted a clear and compelling motive. Three days after the murder, he had pressed the insurance company for immediate honouring of the payment. Further, they alleged that days before the murder, Robinson had taken Julia for a car ride in the country and deliberately driven into a telegraph pole, in an attempt to kill her and benefit from the insurance policy.

They alleged that Martin Evans, a friend and associate of Mitchell Robinson, had assisted in the planning and had been at the murder, overseeing the killing. They also relied on a statement of Mitchell Robinson, in which he implicated both Brown and Evans in the plot to kill Julia, whilst exculpating himself. On the first day of the trial, Brown pleaded guilty to murder, leaving Robinson and Evans to stand trial on their own.

Martin Wilson QC opened the case for the prosecution, describing the murder being staged to look like a burglary and frenzied sexual attack. So violent was the assault that the main strut on the base of the victim's bed had been broken. Julia's body had been stripped and her underclothes torn before she was placed at the foot of the stairs. The killer had stamped on her neck to make sure it was broken. Neighbours had heard breaking glass, fifteen minutes of violence, and male voices.

The first two witnesses spoke of Robinson's attempts to recruit someone to kill Julia. They were forcefully challenged and demonstrated to be of dubious background and character.

A succession of pretty young girls then gave evidence, telling of sex sessions with Robinson in the days before and after Julia's death. One of them had been given a fur coat. Another had married shortly before the trial.

On the day before Julia's death, Robinson had visited Redditch, some twenty miles from Worcester, where he purchased a bala-clava helmet, woollen gloves and a pair of training shoes.

Noel Brown was the critical witness. He was now aged eighteen, described later by Chief Superintendent Cole as 'a huge, illiterate youth, whose only interests in life were fitness and the martial arts. He was dim-witted and immature.' Brown was in the witness box for four days. He described killing Julia in every detail. He said that on the evening of the murder, Mitchell Robinson provided him with the clothes he was to wear and gave him the key to the back door of his home. Brown then said he set his alarm clock for 1.00 a.m. and claimed that he met Evans outside Julia's house. He had no wish to go through with the plan, but was forced to do so.

Cross-examining Brown was a considerable challenge. Brown's limited intelligence was his greatest strength. The jury may well have concluded that Brown lacked the reasoning power to fabri-cate a version of facts that implicated two innocent men in Robinson and Evans. A difficulty for Brown was that on arrest, within twenty-four hours of the murder, he denied any connec-tion with the event, asserting that he was at home asleep at the time of the murder. This problem was counterbalanced, however, by the fact that some weeks later, he voluntarily surrendered himself to the police, admitted killing Julia, and then made a lengthy detailed statement that was consistent in every detail with his sworn testimony.

Mitchell Robinson was also in the witness box for four days. His defence was simple: he had no part in the murder. His arrest was not contrived, he had planned nothing with Evans, and Brown was a callous killer; insuring Julia's life was a responsible act and neither the sum assured nor the modest premiums were excessive. He said that the car crash was a genuine accident, and the statement he made implicating the others was false, and was made to show how easy it was for innocent men to be charged.

Over the four days, Mitchell Robinson stood his ground and defended himself robustly.

Martin Evans was also in the witness box for four days and asserted that he was involved neither in the planning nor the killing. He claimed that Brown had admitted to being the killer within twenty-four hours of Julia's death. He did not believe him then, but when details of the killing appeared in newspapers, he realised that Brown must have been responsible. Whilst he did not immediately report the matter to the police out of loyalty to Brown, pressure placed by the police on his friends and associates drove him to persuade Brown to give himself up. He added that Robinson had offered him £40,000 to kill Julia some months before her death, but he had not taken the proposition seriously. Evans maintained that Brown had implicated him because the police had put pressure on him to do so.

The jury retired for a day and a half before convicting Robinson. They were unable to reach a verdict in Evans's case and, on a retrial, he was acquitted. Robinson was sentenced to life imprisonment. The trial judge, Mr Justice Boreham, described him in his sentencing remarks as a cruel, calculating and cynical manipulator, and the minimum term was fixed by the Home Secretary at twenty years.

I was shocked to learn that he remains in custody to this day, having served some thirty-three years. I am, of course, unaware of the contents of any report placed before the parole board. I can only assume they indicated that Robinson remained a continuing danger to the public, not least Noel Brown, who was detained for life, but was too young for a minimum term to be fixed and regained his liberty some time ago.

From the time I first went to Winson Green Prison for a consultation with Mitchell Robinson until the day he was sentenced, I found him to be a model client. He was polite, charming and most co-operative. He was a young man with considerable ability. His undoubted success with young women was easily explained: he was good-looking, physically very fit, and extremely fluent. He held his own with leading counsel over days in the witness box facing a weight of evidence.

There were no possible grounds of appeal and I so advised. The recommendation made was very much less than it would have been under current guidelines.

# Chapter 2

## The Murder of Annette Wade

IN AUGUST 1989, my brother-in-law and his wife, both then professors at a Canadian university, were visiting my wife Toni and me at our house near Blackpool. We had gone to the theatre in Manchester and on our return home at approximately 11.00 p.m., a police officer was waiting at our front door. I instantly feared all manner of bad news and invited him inside.

He was no stranger. Over the years, Detective Chief Inspector David Belcher and I had been engaged in several cases both as friend and foe. He readily accepted my offer of a drink, having assured me there was no bad news to impart. He told me that an arrest had been made and a man had been charged with the murder of Annette Wade, a crime committed within two miles from my home. The case had received nationwide publicity for several days and I was well aware of the facts thus far publicised.

DCI Belcher then said, 'I have a problem. I want you to prosecute the case, but the CPS have in mind someone else.'

I explained that the briefing of counsel was a matter for them and for them alone. He then explained that knowledge of the locality would prove vital, as there had been numerous sightings of the suspect in and around Poulton-le-Fylde, my local village, and that his alibi was that he was at Blackpool Pleasure Beach. I asked him not to give me any further information that might prevent me accepting the defence brief. He said he was pleased to hear that I had not yet been briefed by the defence, and his first task tomorrow would be to go above the CPS solicitor with whom he had been dealing and speak to John Bates, the chief Crown prosecutor for Lancashire. The following lunchtime, Trevor Doyle told me I had been retained to prosecute John Geoffrey Heeley.

Annette Wade was nine years old on 18 July 1989. About 3.15 p.m., her parents collected her from her school in Poulton-le-Fylde and, on returning home, Annette changed out of her school uniform into casual clothing. She seemed to her mother to be agitated and several times asked her if the time was 4.00 p.m. At 3.55 p.m., Annette left the house by bicycle, saying that she was going to play with friends.

At 5.15 p.m., two men were fishing on farmland close to playing fields. They heard noises indicating that someone was moving around in a nearby hedgerow, before seeing smoke rising from it and a man disappearing through a gap into an adjoining field. The fishermen went to investigate and saw part of a bicycle under a fire that had become too large to extinguish. They notified the farmer on whose land they were fishing, and together they took several containers of water to dowse the fire. They moved the bicycle and branches and then saw the outline of a child's body. They called the police.

The post-mortem examination revealed three stab wounds to Annette's neck and a further stab wound to the left side of her chest. There were clear indications of serious sexual assault and the cause of death was the direct result of the stab wounds.

Within a few yards of the body was a barbecue set, a tin of baked beans, a tin of hamburgers, an empty wine bottle and a pair of Doc Marten boots. It was clear that someone had been living rough in an area close to the fire. A major police investigation began and they soon established that John Geoffrey Heeley had been living rough with a campfire and makeshift tent in that very location from 12 July to 18 July. He had purchased provisions at nearby shops and on 16 July had threatened two young boys and a young girl with a knife, telling them to play elsewhere.

At 7.00 p.m. on 17 July, the day before the murder, some five witnesses saw Heeley speaking to Annette near to some swings on nearby playing fields. One of those witnesses saw Heeley appear to give Annette some money. Later that evening, Annette's mother found that she had sixty pence in her possession and asked her about it; Annette said a school friend called Jennifer had given it to her.

At 8.00 p.m. that evening, three girls saw Heeley by those same swings. He spoke to them and said he was watching the legs of young girls playing netball in a nearby sports field. He said his name was 'Murcock'; his mother's maiden name was Murcott. The girls noticed that he was wearing a very distinctive 'Borgia' ring. Subsequent enquiries revealed that a similar ring had been stolen earlier that morning in a nearby burglary, together with a green Metro car.

On 18 July, the day of the murder, there were numerous sightings of Heeley in and around Poulton-le-Fylde. At 12.45 p.m., he had his hair cut in the centre of the village. He arrived with a ponytail and left with a crew cut, significantly altering his appearance for identification purposes. He then went into the Post Office, where he obtained a British visitor's passport in the name John Geoffrey Heeley, clearly planning his escape. Between 1.45 p.m. and 4.15 p.m., some ten witnesses saw Heeley on the playing fields adjacent to the murder scene.

Meanwhile at 4.30 p.m., Annette told friends she had been to meet someone who had not been there, and she was returning to meet him. She said he was a 'special friend', who was a man and his name began with 'H', and she had to go over some fields. A witness saw Annette riding her bicycle across the playing fields and a further witness saw Heeley crouched down by the swings as Annette was swinging on them.

At 4.35 p.m., a witness heard a muted scream as he walked

by the hedgerows and presumed it was merely some children playing.

At 5.20 p.m., Heeley was seen leaving the farmland carrying a rucksack and afterwards noticed by various witnesses in the locality, before getting into the green Metro stolen the previous day at the same address where he stole the 'Borgia' ring. Between 6.30 p.m. and 8.00 p.m., Heeley was observed by witnesses in Blackpool and at 11.00 p.m., he picked up a hitchhiker on the M6 motorway service area at Keele. He drove to Toddington Services, where he placed diesel fuel into the petrol-driven car, causing a breakdown on Finchley Road, north London, where he parted company with his hitchhiker and the Metro car.

At 12.30 p.m. on 19 July, the day after the murder, Heeley boarded a cross Channel ferry from Dover to Boulogne, returning on 26 July, when he was arrested and brought back to Blackpool. He was confronted by a volume of evidence.

The cans and bottle of wine found near the murder scene bore his fingerprints. The boots found nearby had been purchased by him from a second-hand shop in Blackpool; his fingerprints were also on the Metro car and on his passport application form. On his arrest, he had in his possession a recorder bag of a type in use at Annette's school. When shown the bag, a classmate of hers was able to identify the bag as positively belonging to Annette, because it had a small hole three inches above the label; she had discussed this hole with Annette previously.

When interviewed by the police, Heeley asserted that he had been on holiday for two weeks, even complaining that 'this has ruined my holiday'. To every other question, Heeley chose to make no comment.

Further work was carried out and the police discovered that Annette's body had been wrapped in a patterned material before being set alight. A small section of that material had not been burned away. In the last bedroom that Heeley had occupied before living rough, one curtain was missing, and the pattern on the remaining curtain matched the material recovered from the fire. The conclusion was inescapable that Heeley had removed one curtain from that bedroom and used it to wrap Annette's body. The defence contended that it was common material sold nationwide, but the single missing curtain was more than a coincidence.

The trial took place in Liverpool before Mr Justice Kennedy. Defence leading counsel was Rhys Davies QC, a future Recorder of Manchester, and both the judge and my opponent were of the very highest calibre. Whilst the prosecution had an overwhelmingly strong case, many of the witnesses were children and the level of emotion was extreme. Police officers were concerned that the ordeal of giving evidence might overwhelm them. Indeed several parents, conscious that Annette's murder had greatly affected their children, were reluctant to allow them to give evidence, but eventually did so.

One unusual event deserves a mention. The jury requested a view of the murder scene and thus the judge, counsel and jury travelled by coach from Liverpool to the Fylde coast. At the scene, the jury foreman asked his fellow jurors to stand by him and then he said prayers. For everyone, it was a most moving and very sad occasion.

The trial made me more conscious than I had been previously of the difficulty that all witnesses face in giving evidence. Remarkably, the children were magnificent and compelling witnesses, particularly Annette's friends, who had more reason than most to be distraught. By contrast, some of the adults who purported to have seen Heeley in the village did not know their left from their right and appeared to suffer from a form of stage fright. Murder trials in Liverpool are invariably very well attended and this was no exception. The evidence, however, was overwhelming and understandably Heeley chose not to enter the witness box. He was sentenced to life imprisonment with a whole life order.

This was a most important case in the development of my career in silk. Notwithstanding the strength of the case, murders of children where guilt is denied present particular difficulty and attract nationwide publicity. Emotions run very high and more often than not young children are called as witnesses, as they were in this trial, and as they would be later in the trial of Venables and Thompson.

I was blessed with a particular advantage as an advocate. My son Daniel was a few months younger than Annette and of similar age to several of the witnesses. Understanding and communicating with that age group on a daily basis made my task much easier.

# Chapter 3

## The Trial of Leonard Newsham

IN 1989, I was briefed to defend the alleged prime mover in the most successful bank robbery ever committed in the United Kingdom. My opponent prosecuting was the future president of the Queen's Bench Division, Brian Leveson QC. The facts were remarkable.

At 6.00 p.m. on 14 September 1988, Roger Ball, the manager of the National Westminster Bank, Fishergate, in Preston, left the bank and went to his car. He was confronted there by two hooded gunmen and was gagged and blindfolded, before being driven to a phone box in Bolton-le-Sands. He was forced to phone his wife Jean and instructed her to let himself and his abductors into their Morecambe home, where they lived together with their thirteen-year-old daughter, Vanessa.

Roger Ball was then taken to his home and, together with the two gunmen, was let in by his wife. There followed a lengthy ordeal for all three members of the family, who were held prisoners at gunpoint. Jean Ball, however, showed a remarkable sense of Lancastrian hospitality, offering her captors some food, including apples and oranges, which both gunmen devoured whole, including cores and peel, a detail that would prove to be significant.

At about 4.00 a.m., the gunmen announced that it was time to leave. The Ball family had remained in their sitting room or kitchen all night, at gunpoint throughout. They were then bound, hooded, and placed in the boots of two vehicles, before being driven thirty miles to a disused building off Fishergate, close to the NatWest Bank. There they were kept hostage.

At 8.30 a.m., Roger Ball was taken to the bank and forced to open up, under threat that his wife and daughter would be shot if he failed to cooperate. As each member of staff arrived at the bank, they too were taken hostage. In all, sixty-two members of the bank staff were detained at gunpoint whilst the gang removed banknotes and coins from the vaults. More than £500,000 in notes and two and a half hundredweight of coins was taken, together with foreign currency and travellers cheques. Mr Ball was ordered to tell his staff that if they raised the alarm, his wife and daughter would both be shot.

When one of the gunmen shouted at Mr Ball, he had a speech impediment, causing him to shout 'Wodger' rather than 'Rodger', and when he ordered staff into the vaults, he shouted 'faults' rather than 'vaults'. He also had a Liverpool accent.

The alarm had already been raised by members of the public who found the bank closed. Some twenty police marksmen were summoned and initially they went to the wrong NatWest branch. Eventually they reached the correct building, but the robbers were able to escape, having dug up some bollards outside Preston railway station and taking an alternative route that avoided Fishergate, where the marksmen waited in vain. It soon became clear that at least three robbers had participated: two were in the bank and a third was guarding Jean and Vanessa Ball.

The Lancashire Constabulary were dismayed at the outcome. A £50,000 reward was advertised and there was considerable publicity, including a *Crimewatch* reconstruction, in the hope of both recovering the proceeds and bringing the robbers to justice.

Months later, an observant detective of the Merseyside Police, DC Moorcroft, was walking along a street in Liverpool when he saw two men eating a whole orange. He had read the crime report, including the fact that one of the robbers had a Liverpool accent and a speech impediment. He spoke to Leonard Newsham and to his companion Jimmy Gibson, and watched as they continued eating the whole orange, including the peel. In due course, Merseyside Police's undercover team kept Leonard Newsham under surveillance, but not before Jimmy Gibson was shot in the head and found dead in the street.

The Lancashire Police spoke to Leonard Newsham about the death, but unknown to the force, the Merseyside Police surveillance team then followed him from Preston police station back to Liverpool to the grounds of Fazakerley Hospital, where they watched him dig up a package containing £6,900 in used bank notes that could be traced to the robbery. A further package was recovered containing two balaclavas linked to fibres found in the vehicle that had been abandoned in Morecambe. Unsurprisingly, Leonard Newsham was arrested and charged with robbery.

I read the brief with more interest than optimism. At consultation in Risley Remand Centre, I was anxious to test my client's ability to say both vaults and Roger, bearing in mind the robber's asserted speech impediment. He licked his lips, stared at the ceiling, and in rapid fire delivered, 'Vault, vault, vault, vault, vault, vault,' before I stopped him and asked him to say it only once.

He started afresh, 'Vault, vault, vault, vault . . . ,' so I interrupted and asked him to say Roger.

Once more, he licked his lips, stared upwards, and began, 'Nodger, Nodger, Nodger, Nodger, Nodger . . . ,' until I halted him, pleading, 'Once only, please!'

He burst out, 'Mr Enreex, I practise for five hours a day. I promise it will be all right on the night.'

We left the consultation even less optimistic than before, having concluded that on balance we could continue to represent him, his speech rehearsals not amounting to a confession of guilt.

The first witness in the trial was Roger Ball. I cross-examined him quite firmly, but I believe fairly, and he was followed into the witness box by his wife Jean. I then received a message from Mr Newsham: 'Please be nice to Mrs Ball, she's a very nice lady.'

I had no option but to ask the judge for a short break. I explained to Mr Newsham that I was professionally embarrassed and that none of us could continue to represent him. He readily understood and pleaded guilty. His concern for Mrs Ball was his principal point in mitigation and he was sentenced to thirteen years' imprisonment. The prosecution sought to persuade the Attorney General that the sentence was unduly lenient, but they were unsuccessful.

Unfortunately, Leonard Newsham took matters into his own hands. Whilst on home leave from Sudbury jail, he committed a raid on the home of a businessman and his family and was given a further twelve years' imprisonment to run consecutively.

# Chapter 4

## The Murder of Julie Christian

IN 1992, I defended Ian James Thomas, who was charged with the murder of his girlfriend and cohabitee, Julie Christian. I led an experienced and able junior, David Boulton, a future circuit judge and a good friend. Rodney Klevan QC prosecuted. It was a fascinating trial, not so much a who done it, but did he do it. On receipt of the brief, it appeared that two young girls, aged nine and seven, had seen the victim alive and well at a time when the prosecution asserted that she had already been murdered. Most curiously, those two girls were then prosecution witnesses.

Julie Christian lived with the defendant Ian Thomas at 3 Teilo Street, Toxteth, in Liverpool. The prosecution alleged that between midnight on Saturday 11 November 1990 and about 1.00 p.m. on Sunday 12 November 1990, Ian Thomas killed Julie Christian within their home, and that between 6.00 p.m. and 11.00 p.m. on the Sunday, he hid the body under bags of household waste in the alley behind their house and set fire to it.

The times are of critical importance in this case. Julie was alive about midnight on Saturday, when she spoke to her sister Sally on the telephone. At 1.00 p.m. on the Sunday, a debt collector named Mr Kamara called at 3 Teilo Street, by which time the prosecution alleged that Julie had been killed and that Ian Thomas was very distressed and significantly affected by the event.

Vital to the defence case was evidence from a ten-year-old girl, Emma Duffy, who lived nearby at 7 Teilo Street. Emma gave evidence that she, then aged nine, was accompanied by a seven-year-old friend, Sarah Skelland. Emma described seeing Julie walking from her home about 3.00 p.m. on the Sunday, more than two hours after the prosecution alleged that the defendant had murdered her. In both a trial and in a retrial, Emma gave her evidence in a clear manner, expressing confidence both as to the recognition of Julie, whom she knew well, and as to the time and date when a brass band had passed by, an occasion confirmed by independent evidence.

At a trial fourteen months after this sighting, however, and at a retrial four years after the sighting, Sarah was unable to recollect the event, notwithstanding the existence of a note written by a police officer and signed by Emma's parents describing Emma's sighting of Julie at 3.00 p.m. on the Sunday. For reasons we will examine later, neither jury was made aware of the existence of that very significant note. The defendant was convicted of murder.

This question arose in three separate appeals, namely: 'If both girls then aged ten and eight, rather than Emma only, had given evidence that they had seen Julie alive at 3.00 p.m. on the Sunday, might it have affected the jury's verdict?'

## The Prosecution Case

The defendant and Julie had cohabited for some time and, according to Julie's family, appeared to get on well together. They were in debt, however, which placed a strain on the relationship; they had rows and sometimes came to blows.

### Saturday
The defendant and Julie visited her grandmother's house, where he did some decorating. They returned to Teilo Street, where they found a card from a debt collector, which prompted a row

leading to Julie remaining at home whilst the defendant joined her family at a public house. He stayed with them for about forty minutes. No member of Julie's family observed any mark or injury to the defendant's face or hands. During the evening, Julie telephoned her sister Sally; she was very upset and told her about the debt collector's card. Julie phoned Sally again about midnight, saying she was no longer upset and would phone again on Sunday.

*Sunday, 1.00 p.m.*
Mr Kamara, the debt collector, arrived at 3 Teilo Street. According to him, the defendant came to the door dressed in a T-shirt and shorts and looking very upset. His hands were shaking and his mouth was quivering. He told Kamara to wait outside for a few minutes and then came out and asked him to drive to the next street, saying that he did not want his family to know about the debt.

*Sunday, 3.00 p.m.*
A brass band passed the end of Teilo Street and Emma Duffy, aged nine, said she was playing outside her home at 7 Teilo Street with Sarah Skelland, aged seven, when she saw Julie leave No. 3 and turn left towards a T-junction with High Park Street. She said Julie was wearing a black skirt and jacket and had a shoulder bag. She then saw a man whom she had not seen before walking behind Julie along Teilo Street and turning left into High Park Street after her.

*Sunday, 3.30 p.m.*
The defendant visited a B&Q store in Speke and purchased some decorating materials. He made a timed purchase at 3.30 p.m. According to the defendant, he visited Julie's grandmother before

returning home about 6.15 p.m. He then took the dog for a walk, washed the back yard and at about 7.15 p.m. set off for Julie's sister Sally's house, where he had arranged to meet Julie.

*Sunday, 6.50 p.m.*
A witness living in Elwy Street, which runs behind and parallel to Teilo Street, smelled an unusual sickly odour coming from the direction of Teilo Street. The prosecution asserted that this was the first indication of a fire in the alley behind No. 3 and of Julie's body being burned.

*Sunday, 8.00 p.m.*
The defendant arrived at Sally's house, saying that he was expecting Julie to be there, having arranged to meet her there when he last saw her at about 2.00 p.m. Sally rang various members of her family trying to locate Julie. According to Sally, the defendant expressed no concern as to where Julie might be, but he then said he would go home and look for her. A friend of Julie's took him to Teilo Street and left him there for about forty-five minutes, before returning and taking him back to Sally's house about 11.00 p.m. The prosecution case was that the defendant had an opportunity at this time to stoke up the fire.

*Monday, 0.01 a.m.*
Just after midnight, a nearby resident was conscious of what she described as a horrid, acrid smell of burning. Others began to notice it on the Monday morning and throughout the day.

*Monday, 1.30 a.m.*
The defendant was driven back to Teilo Street by Brian Lloyd, together with Sally, her boyfriend Brian Cummings, and Pat Gandy. On entering No. 3, they were met by a sweet sickly

smell, and the defendant observed that children had been burning rubbish. The house was very tidy. Sally wanted to know what Julie had been wearing and the defendant looked in the wardrobe and straight away said that a black jacket and skirt and a blue tracksuit were missing, together with a pair of court shoes. The defendant and Brian Cummings remained at No. 3 for the night.

*Monday, 8.45 a.m.*
Refuse collectors called to collect household waste from the alley. They saw burning rubbish at about the spot where Julie's body was found two days later, but because it was burning, did not remove it.

*Monday, 10.00 a.m.*
The defendant and his mother returned to No. 3 and the defendant went through an entry leading from Teilo Street to Elwy Street, permitting him to look into the alley.

*Monday, 11.00 a.m.*
Several residents by now had become conscious of a smell of burning. A Mrs Corkhill saw a smouldering pile of rubbish in the alley and her husband threw water on it. They did not notice a body burning.

*Monday, 4.15 p.m.*
A boy found a handbag, later identified as Julie's, some distance away from No. 3 in a waste area known as Diggers Park.

*Monday, 6.00 p.m.*
Sarah Skelland's mother told the defendant that her daughter had seen Julie whilst playing in Teilo Street on Sunday afternoon.

*Monday evening*
There was an organised family search for Julie, and Cummings again spent the night with the defendant at No. 3.

*Tuesday early hours*
The defendant and Cummings walked to Julie's grandmother's house following a phone call from Julie's father. Julie's grandmother insisted that the defendant should notify the police of Julie's disappearance. He did so at 5.45 a.m. Police officers observed marks on the defendant's face. Local residents continued to be aware of a terrible burning smell throughout the morning.

*Tuesday, 11.20 a.m.*
The defendant spoke to one of the refuse men, Mr Jackson, asking him if he had seen anything unusual and told him that the police had found a handbag, make-up bag and shoes on some waste ground. At that time, no such items had been handed in to the police or notified to them.

*Tuesday, 11.35 p.m.*
Police were handed Julie's bag found the previous day at Diggers Park.

*Tuesday, 1.00 p.m.*
Dr Baker examined the defendant at the police station and found four marks on his face, which he assessed to be two to four days old. They were scratches above the left eyebrow and on his left temple and a scratch and a red mark on his nose. He also had bruising on his chest and some older marks on his hands. The defendant explained the marks to his face as a cat scratch and the injury to his hands being caused by contact with a wall whilst decorating. Dr Baker was not able to exclude those

explanations, but said that an alternative explanation was scratching by a human hand.

*Tuesday, 3.30 p.m.*
Julie's make-up bag was found by police at Diggers Park.

*Tuesday evening*
The smell continued. Sometimes there was merely smouldering, sometimes burning, as if replenished with more rubbish.

*Tuesday night*
The defendant spent Tuesday night with his parents. A resident whose home backed onto the alley heard what sounded like two people carrying something and turning into the alley and in the direction of No. 3. The prosecution alleged this was a replenishing of the fire.

*Wednesday morning*
The defendant returned home briefly to No. 3. According to residents, the fire was still alive and then smoking badly.

*Wednesday, early afternoon*
The defendant made a statement to the police explaining the marks to his face as resulting from banging against some railings while decorating and the marks to the back of his hands as a result of grazing against a house wall on the previous Friday or Saturday.

*Wednesday, 3.00 p.m.*
Julie's purse was found in a lay-by.

*Wednesday, 3.30 p.m.*

Julie's body was found in the alley. Mr Corkhill, when dousing the fire and stirring it with a stick, had found the body in the fire. She was very small and the fire had further reduced her body size.

The body was so badly burned that the pathologist, Dr Burns, could not determine the time or cause of death. He could exclude shooting, stabbing, beating, strangling and poisoning, but drowning or suffocation were possible causes. She was dead before being placed in the fire and the fire had been built around her.

Dr Davidson, a forensic scientist, found that the fire debris was mostly domestic rubbish. Julie had been wearing black briefs and both parts of a dark blue tracksuit. There were also in the fire some fragments of a dark jacket with yellow paisley lining, black socks, and a blue pullover. He could not say whether she had been wearing any of these items. There were no traces of any shoes and he could see no indication of a fire accelerant. Also recovered from the fire was some burnt fabric with an inner mesh lining, apparently from a garment of the same type as two pairs of nylon shorts found in a drawer in the bedroom at 3 Teilo Street. The defendant subsequently acknowledged that he had three pairs of shorts at the time.

Dr Davidson also examined 3 Teilo Street. It was very clean and orderly, having been cleaned within the previous two days. At the top of the stairs were hanging some bathroom mats, a carpet, and a dressing gown, freshly washed and still damp, and there were wet clothes in the washing machine and a wet mop. There was no blood staining or sign of a struggle.

Mr Douglas Leitch, from the Strathclyde Fire Brigade, an expert in the examination of fires, said the condition of the body was consistent with it having been destroyed over a period from Sunday to Wednesday. The fire would require stoking more than once during that period. Rigor mortis had already set in when the body was placed in the fire. Normally rigor starts to develop some six hours after death.

### Wednesday, 10.30 p.m.

The police informed the defendant that Julie was dead and that her body had been identified. He broke down and cried. The police arrested him for murder. He said he had not done it.

### Wednesday, midnight

Dr Messing examined him. The injuries to his face were all consistent with having been caused five or six days earlier. They were not consistent with having been caused in the course of decorating, but were consistent with a scratch from a human hand; however, there could have been many causes. The marks on his hands were more consistent with human scratches than an abrasion from a wall. The mark on his chest was not consistent with having been struck by a ladder as the defendant had claimed.

Whilst in police custody, the defendant was interviewed seven times in all. He repeatedly denied killing Julie. He said the injuries to his hands and face were caused whilst decorating, that one of the marks on his face was a cat scratch and another a spot, and the marks on his chest were caused by carrying ladders.

## The Defence Case

In summary form, this was Ian Thomas's evidence:

> On the Saturday afternoon Julie and I visited her grandmother where I did some decorating. We returned home around 7.15 p.m. when we found a card from the debt collector stating that he would return the following day at 1.00 p.m. This resulted in an argument between us which turned into a row. As a result

Julie did not want to go with me to meet her family in the public house, so I went alone. I already had marks on my face and hands, caused in the way I described to the police. After meeting her family I returned home about 10.15 p.m. and my relationship with Julie was then back to normal. We went to bed about 3.00 a.m. On Sunday we woke about midday. The debt collector arrived about 1.00 p.m. I was not wearing shorts but jeans. I told Mr Kamara to wait in his car because I did not want him looking at property in our house. I went to tell Julie who it was and then went and got into his car. I was apprehensive but not shivering or shaking. I asked him to drive to the next street to discuss the debt and he did so.

Around 2.00 p.m. on the Sunday I left No. 3 to buy some decorating materials at B&Q. Julie said she might go to visit her grandmother and meet me later at Sally's house. I bought the materials as shown on the receipt at 3.30 p.m. I then went to Julie's grandmother's house and returned home about 6.15 p.m. I assumed Julie had gone to her sister Sally's. I took the dog for a walk and washed the yard because there was dog excrement in it. I left to go to Sally's about 7.15 p.m. arriving about 8.00 p.m. When Julie was not there, I got a lift home from Kenneth Maidment. I then became very worried about Julie's whereabouts and took part in searches as described by her family. I was able to tell Sally on the Sunday night which clothes were missing by looking in the wardrobe. I did not tell the refuse man Mr Jackson at 11.20 a.m. on the Tuesday that items belonging to Julie had been found. I have told the police how I sustained my injuries. I did not murder Julie.

## The First Trial

This took place in January 1992 before Mr Justice Waterhouse. Both Emma and Sarah, now aged ten and eight, were listed as prosecution witnesses. This was a strange decision as their evidence clearly undermined the prosecution case. If they saw Julie at 3.00 p.m. on the Sunday, the defendant could not have killed her prior to Mr Kamara's visit at 1.00 p.m. There were, however, potential advantages for the defence. If they were called by the prosecution, I could cross-examine them, and put leading questions to them. Further, if called by the prosecution, it could not be suggested that they were witnesses dredged up by the defence and rehearsed by defence solicitors.

The disadvantage was that Emma could not be shown and asked to read her statement by the defence before she gave her evidence, and Sarah could not be shown the note by the defence and have it read to her before she gave her evidence. On balance, the defence team as a whole were more than happy that the two witnesses most helpful to the defence case were prosecution witnesses.

The situation changed rapidly. Rodney Klevan QC, prosecuting, appreciated the difficulty he faced and told me that he intended to tender the two girls as witnesses. It had clearly been a mistake to include these two girls in the list of prosecution witnesses. This meant that I could cross-examine both girls, as I have said, but critically, neither had been given the opportunity to refresh their memories from the relevant documents.

Accordingly, I applied for both girls to be shown those documents before they gave their evidence. In Emma's case the judge concurred. However, since Sarah had not made a written statement, but the police had interviewed her three days after Julie's disappearance with notes being taken by the police officer and signed by her mother as correct, the judge refused my application that Sarah should read the notes. He expressed the view that in the case of so young a child, it would not be appropriate for her to be shown an *aide-memoire* before giving evidence.

Emma gave her evidence in an immaculate manner and I was able to extract from her in cross-examination a clear recollection of seeing Julie leaving her home at 3.00 p.m. on the Sunday as the band passed the end of Teilo Street, coupled with the fact that she was being followed. The detail accorded with the narrative above.

Sarah, on the other hand, was very clearly distressed when she entered the court. I renewed my application that she should be shown the notes. Again the judge refused, expressing himself somewhat forcefully. Sarah entered the witness box, but could remember very little of her original account. She could not recall when she last saw Julie or even being questioned by the police. I could make no useful headway and terminated my cross-examination by observing that I had taken the matter as far as I could. Having twice asked for permission to show the notes to Sarah, a third application would in my judgement have certainly failed; it would also have further distressed Sarah and shown disrespect for the judge's two earlier rulings, and in all likelihood have alienated the jury.

The jury convicted Ian Thomas and he appealed against conviction on the sole ground that the judge wrongly disallowed the applications for Emma to be shown the signed notes of her interview. In allowing the appeal and ordering a retrial, Lord Justice Russell said that 'had the notes been put to the witness, it may be that her memory would have been refreshed and she would have been able to fill in the gaps which her evidence undoubtedly left.' A retrial was ordered.

## The Retrial and Appeals

Unfortunately, the retrial did not take place until October 1994, some four years after the alleged murder. Lord Justice Russell had made his views very clear, namely that the two girls should never have been prosecution witnesses and accordingly at the retrial it was anticipated that both would give evidence for the defence.

Emma did so and gave her evidence in accordance with her witness statement and her evidence at the first trial. Sarah, however, in the presence of her parents and outside court, indicated to our solicitor that she had no recollection of events nor of the police interview, despite being informed of its contents. Consequently, there was no purpose in calling her and I chose not to do so. For the second time, Ian Thomas was convicted.

He appealed again and I represented him on this occasion before a constitution presided over by Lord Justice Rose. The ground of appeal was that the decision of the prosecution at the first trial to treat both Emma and Sarah as prosecution witnesses had effectively deprived the defence of interviewing and treating them as defence witnesses. The cumulative delay had deprived the appellant of a fair trial. The argument failed effectively on two grounds. Firstly, the notes of Sarah's interview were hearsay and thus inadmissible. It would be unthinkable to allow an appeal based on inadmissible evidence. Secondly, there was a strong circumstantial case and Emma's evidence had been rejected by both juries.

For a third time, in 2002, Ian Thomas appealed pursuant to a reference by the Criminal Cases Review Commission based on fresh evidence. I had by this time been appointed to the Bench and Michael Mansfield was instructed to conduct the appeal, together with my friend James Gregory.

Before dealing with the fresh evidence, they sought to canvass again the fact that Emma had been wrongly treated as a prosecution witness to the prejudice of the defence. Together with cumulative delay, it was submitted that this amounted to an abuse of process. The court, presided over on this occasion by Lord Justice Auld, concluded that there was no new argument and that any submission at the second trial that there had been an abuse of process would properly have failed.

Two witnesses had come forward in response to a television

programme, *Clear My Name*, asserting that they had seen a dead female body on waste ground some 500 yards from Teilo Street on the Tuesday afternoon, suggesting that Julie had not been murdered within Teilo Street. The two male witnesses were nine and seven at the time of their observation. The court found that their evidence lacked credibility and that the presence of an evil-smelling fire burning in the alley behind Teilo Street over the three days after Julie was last seen alive, and in which her badly burned body was eventually discovered, rendered the significance of any purported observation of a body on the Tuesday wholly irrelevant.

It was not a realistic possibility that a killer, whether the appellant or another, would have initially deposited the barely concealed and naked body of Julie in a derelict garden some 500 yards from her home and then, while the hunt for her was on, returned the body to an alley behind her home, re-clothed it and then put it on the fire. As it transpired, Ian Thomas did not have a car and could not drive. Any argument in support of this ground of appeal was manifestly hopeless.

A further ground was argued by Michael Mansfield, namely that fresh scientific evidence indicated that the body may have been placed on the fire about twelve hours before its discovery and that the cause of death should not have been limited to suffocation or drowning. The severity of the burns made it impossible to exclude a head injury or stab wounds. The court readily rejected this ground. The jury's verdict turned on the identity of the killer and not the method of killing, and the eye or nose witness evidence as to the duration, intensity, and smell of the fire prevailed over speculative evidence of fire experts, as each acknowledged in their evidence.

Lord Justice Auld concluded the third judgment rejecting Ian Thomas's third appeal thus:

We have referred more than once to the strength of the circumstantial evidence of the appellant's guilt . . . We mention in particular: the serious argument between the appellant and Julie on the Saturday night; the nature and timing of the appellant's injuries and his differing and unconvincing explanations for them; the appellant's appearance and behaviour on Sunday at 1.00 p.m. when Mr Kamara the debt collector called and his subsequent lie as to what he had been wearing at the time; the appellant's washing of the bath mats, tidying of the house and washing of the back yard; the appellant's conduct thereafter in seemingly establishing an alibi; his immediate ability on the Sunday night to identify which of Julie's clothes were missing; his delay in reporting Julie's disappearance to the police; the evidence of the fire and the nauseous smell emanating from it over the next three days; his opportunities to replenish the fire; and his curious conversation with Mr Jackson on the Tuesday morning.

I have set out the above passage as an indication of the thorough and detailed work typical of the Court of Appeal (Criminal Division). However, Ian Thomas may continue to believe that he has been most unfortunate. Had the two girls been defence witnesses at the first trial and been taken through their evidence from time to time in advance of the trial, a jury may well have had difficulty rejecting the real possibility that Julie was alive at 3.00 p.m. on the Sunday and was being followed by an unidentified man.

Both girls knew Julie well. She lived two doors away from Emma. The band did pass by at 3.00 p.m. and the band leader gave evidence to that effect. Julie did have clothes that matched Emma's description and Sarah had told her mother that she had seen Julie whilst playing in Teilo Street on the Sunday afternoon. A jury would not have considered whether the two girls might have been mistaken.

They might also have asked themselves whether the defendant

might have staged Julie's appearance on Teilo Street by arranging for some other female to dress in Julie's clothing and come out of No. 3 as the band passed, thus creating the illusion that it was Julie. Any such female would have needed to be very small in order both to fit Julie's clothes and to mislead the two girls. A jury may have found difficulty in reaching a guilty verdict.

Ian Thomas was unfortunate in a second respect. At the time of both his trials, the notes of Sarah's interview were hearsay and thus inadmissible in evidence. The Criminal Justice Act 2003 rendered those notes admissible in evidence. Had either trial come after the operation of that Act, the notes would have been admitted in evidence.

A further matter exercised both my mind and that of the prosecutor, Rodney Klevan. The wet bath mats and carpet, and the likely cause of death, indicated to the prosecution that Julie was either drowned or suffocated during a domestic row. Rodney told me that if the defendant provided a credible version of facts justifying a verdict of manslaughter on the grounds of provocation, the prosecution would give it most careful consideration.

That message was communicated, of course, but no such admission was forthcoming. Indeed, throughout both trials and both appeals that I conducted, Ian Thomas remained consistent and resolute in his denial of guilt.

# Chapter 5

## The Trial of Derek Hatton and Others

JANUARY 1993 MARKED the commencement of the trial of Derek Hatton, former deputy chairman of Liverpool City Council, and two fellow councillors together with a tailor and a builder, at Mold Crown Court, having been transferred from Liverpool. I was briefed to defend John Nelson, who was Chairman of the Planning Committee during the earlier dates covered by the indictment. Hannah Folan had succeeded John Nelson as chair of planning, John Monk was Hatton's tailor and Roy Stewart, a builder, completed the line-up.

The allegation arose from city council activities in the 1980s. The prosecution alleged inter alia that the city had been defrauded by the defendants issuing licences to Mr Monk for the use of two small bombsites owned by the council as temporary car parks, together with the alleged criminal disposal of other council property. After an eight-week trial before Mr Justice Waterhouse, all five defendants were acquitted, Stewart having been discharged at an earlier stage through a lack of evidence.

Derek Hatton was a national figure. The Trotskyist group Militant had been in control of Liverpool City Council through much of the 1980s. Militant claimed that cuts to the Rate Support Grant for the city were unfair and argued that £30 million had been 'stolen' from Liverpool by Margaret Thatcher's government.

In 1983, the Militant-led Labour party took control of the council, and a year later launched its Urban Regeneration

Strategy to build many thousands of houses, seven sports centres, new parks and numerous other works, as well as cancelling 1,200 redundancies planned by the previous Liberal administration, and creating 1,000 new jobs. They abolished the position of Lord Mayor and sold the ceremonial horses. In 1985, the council joined the rate-capping rebellion, and passed an illegal budget in which spending exceeded income, demanding that central government made up the deficit.

At the Labour Party Conference in October 1985, Neil Kinnock attacked Militant, referring to the 'grotesque chaos of a Labour council, a Labour council, hiring taxis to scuttle round the city handing out notices of redundancy to its own workers . . . I tell you – and you'll listen – you can't play politics with people's jobs and people's homes and people's services.'

Throughout Kinnock's speech, Hatton repeatedly shouted 'lies' from the balcony, prompting anti-Kinnock booing from hard-left supporters. Inevitably, all the major news channels carried this drama, whilst in interviews Hatton continued to denounce Neil Kinnock. In 1986, Hatton was expelled from the Labour Party. Unsuccessful appeals followed by some forty-seven councillors, ending in March 1987 when the Law Lords dismissed their appeals with £242,000 costs.

In 1990, Operation 'Cheetah' was launched by the Merseyside Police and critics of Militant expected a punitive outcome. By 1993, however, some of the heat had passed. The resulting trial proved to be a damp squib, but that was not apparent on receipt of the brief. Derek Hatton remained a hugely controversial figure. Other counsel in the case were most highly regarded and this was in many ways the most challenging brief I had received.

Murder cases often proved simple and intellectually undemanding. The present brief necessitated an understanding of local government practice and procedure and some comprehension of political nuance. Remarkably, the Bar, certainly in my time, showed little or no interest in political discussion. Political silks no longer existed and whilst organisations such as the Society of Labour Lawyers attracted members, the robing room was essentially non-political. Those with strong political views tended to keep their own counsel.

None of the counsel briefed in *Hatton and Others* shared the political views of the defendants, so far as I know; all were briefed for legal expertise. The Bench is necessarily non-political and I have never questioned the observance of that convention. In theory, Lord Chancellors had the opportunity of loading the Bench with political supporters. In the cases of Lords Mackay, Irvine, and Falconer, all of whom were to consult me on appointments, I never detected the slightest hint of political bias or favouritism in relation to their appointment of any candidate.

Brian Leveson QC was briefed to prosecute and the trial judge was Mr Justice Waterhouse. Weeks before the trial and subsequent to two pretrial hearings, Brian returned his brief, his clerk indicating that a clash of cases made it impossible for him to conduct the trial. Before leaving the case, Brian made an important strategic decision. He decided to place Hatton last in the indictment, in order to prevent his conducting the defence with other defendants merely adopting his lead.

The consequence of this decision was that I represented the first named in the indictment and Hatton, defended by Rodney Klevan QC, was last named. This was a very significant move from my perspective. Counsel for the first in an indictment must make the running. The burden of my task was considerably increased.

Brian's departure resulted in Alan Rawley QC, a Western Circuit silk, being briefed for the prosecution. This was a daunting task to inherit at very short notice. He was most ably assisted by Andrew Menary, the present Recorder of Liverpool. Alan was not fazed by the task and the prosecution were in no way disadvantaged.

The defence was surprisingly simple. Every act asserted to be criminal was actioned by committee, minuted and voted upon, or made pursuant to delegated powers by local planning officers. There was no evidence before the jury as to valuation of the prospective car parks and, in any case, it was necessary to raise funds as a matter of urgency as the city approached bankruptcy. Any tendering process would have been too slow and the price agreed with Mr Monk was competitive.

For the duration of the trial, Alan Rawley, Michael Maguire, Rodney Klevan and I stayed in the St David's Park Hotel, near Mold. Dinner was always a most enjoyable occasion. For every Northern Circuit tale, Alan produced the Western Circuit equivalent. Rodney was now circuit leader and a non-driver, and it fell to me to drive him to Bar Mess events for local barristers in Manchester, Liverpool, Preston and Carlisle. Listening to Rodney's speeches at Bar Mess was no hardship; he was a most polished after-dinner speaker, specialising in one-liners.

It was during one of these journeys that Rodney asked if I had considered applying to succeed him as circuit leader and assured me that I would have his support. Rodney was only in his second of four years as leader, but the seed had been sown and I was able to observe and admire a highly respected man performing a demanding but most rewarding duty.

The trial took an unusual course. Cross-examination of the council officers was left to me and Tim King QC, Hannah Folan's counsel. We introduced various minutes, established that alleged criminal acts had been minuted and voted upon by various committees, discussed with officers, and so on. Rodney Klevan did not ask a single question during the prosecution case. All defendants chose to offer no evidence.

The final and closing speech was Rodney's. It was a tour de force and the best I ever heard, although I doubt any transcript exists. It was a thesis on the development and progress of political theory from Greek civilisation, via the Roman Empire, the French Revolution and into modern times. He ridiculed our state's response to his client's ideals, asking rhetorically whether Mr Hatton had actually erected a guillotine outside the Town Hall in Dale Street. Militants had come and gone, as had numerous other political parties over history. They had failed and been despatched, not in the courtroom but at the ballot box, in accord with established and civilised democratic process. At the conclusion of Rodney's speech, when the jury retired to their room, the sound of applause could be heard in the courtroom.

It came as no surprise when the defendants were all acquitted. Whilst not subscribing to Derek Hatton's then political views, I have no doubt as to the accuracy of the jury's verdicts. From a personal standpoint, this was an important case.

# Chapter 6

## The Murder of James Bulger

ROBERT THOMPSON AND Jon Venables were the youngest children to stand trial for murder in the twentieth century. Aged eleven, they stood trial in the Crown Court, sitting at Preston, Lancashire, on 1 November 1993. They were alleged to have abducted a two-year-old boy, James Bulger, from his mother in a Liverpool shopping precinct, to have taken him to a railway line, and subjected him to a prolonged and terrible attack, killing him before placing his body on the railway line.

I was a little surprised to be retained by the prosecution as leading counsel for the Crown. I was not yet circuit leader, nor had I been a member of any Liverpool chambers. The case had received worldwide publicity and whilst I was now a circuit silk of some seven years' standing, there were others more senior and well established who would have welcomed this brief. In one respect, however, I was well qualified: my son Daniel was twelve years old and cross-examination of the two boys seemed likely to be a critical part of the case.

Thompson was defended by David Turner QC, a local man, in only his second year in silk, and Venables by Brian Walsh QC, then Leader of the North Eastern Circuit, a future Recorder of Leeds and a pre-eminent silk of some seventeen years' standing. The trial judge was Mr Justice Morland, then Presiding Judge of the Northern Circuit, a Liverpool man with great energy and presence and well versed in the criminal law.

The trial process began with David Turner submitting in the

absence of the jury that the judge should stay the proceedings on the grounds that massive media publicity had rendered a fair trial impossible. He produced numerous newspaper articles, the content of which was highly critical of the two defendants. It is fair to say that the material produced was as supportive of such an application as it is possible to conceive. Brian Walsh leant powerful support to the submission and I detected a distinct feeling of unease on the benches behind me, including the press benches, with the *New York Times* and Canadian and Australian agencies all present. An untimely end to the proceedings would have been worse than inconvenient.

I submitted that any prejudice that may have been created could be negated by a strong judicial direction warning the jury not to be influenced by anything that they had seen, heard, or read, and I continued, 'Never in the history of criminal trials has any trial been stayed on the basis of adverse publicity prejudicing a fair trial. In any event, the real issues in the case are not affected at all by the publicity, as the real issue the jury will have to try is between the accounts of the two defendants. There is nothing which poisons the case of defendant A over B, or vice versa. There does come a point when lambasting by the press can become counterproductive, and we apprehend that twelve fair-minded jurors seeing two eleven-year-olds in the dock will deal with their cases as juries must always do, on the evidence.'

I was to be faced myself with similar submissions whilst I was on the Bench some years later, most especially in the cases of the Leeds United footballers, the Morecambe Bay cockle pickers, the shooting of Jean Charles de Menezes, and the plot to blow up a number of transatlantic airliners. On each and every occasion, the trial proceeded and the convictions withstood any appeal. The airline case, however, was taken to the European Court of Human Rights in July 2015. In *Abdulla Ali v. United Kingdom*, it was held that unfavourable pretrial publicity was unlikely to violate a suspect's right to a fair trial, provided suffi-cient time had elapsed between the media coverage and the trial and the judge gave adequate guidance to the jury.

Mr Justice Morland accepted the defence submission that the media coverage suggested by innuendo that the defendants were guilty, but indicated that he believed a fair trial was possible, and said that he would direct the jurors in the clearest terms when they retired to put out of their minds anything that they may have read seen or heard outside the court about the case or its background.

Before the jury returned to court, there was further legal argument concerning photographs the prosecution wished the jury to see of James's body. David Turner submitted that photo-graphs showing James's tiny head on the railway line should be removed from the jury bundle: 'Even to those of us regularly in these courts, these are emotive and distressing. We submit that a jury could be emotionally involved by these photographs and we submit that they should be removed.'

I responded, 'Very great consideration was given to the selec-tion of photographs. Many were more distressing than these. The cause of death was multiple blows to the head and this is the sight that a person inflicting those blows would have had at that time.' The photographs were admitted.

## The Prosecution Case

These were my opening words:

James Bulger was two years and eleven months old when he died. He was the only child of Ralph and Denise Bulger and they live in Kirkby. They always called him James and we will refer to him as James throughout this trial. He died on Friday, 12 February this year. In short, these two defendants abducted James from his mother in a shopping precinct in Bootle. They walked him some two and a half miles across Liverpool to Walton, a very long and distressing walk for a two-year-old toddler.

James was then taken onto a railway line and subjected to a prolonged and violent attack. Bricks, stones and a piece of metal appear to have been thrown at James on that railway line. He sustained many fractures of the skull. Death resulted from multiple blunt force injuries to the head. There were several lacerated wounds. At some point James's lower clothing was removed. His body was placed across a rail on the railway line and sometime later his body was run over by a train, which cut his body in two.

The pathologist concludes that death occurred prior to the impact of the train. The prosecution alleges that the two defendants acting together took James from the precinct and together were responsible for causing his death. Both defendants are now eleven years of age. On Friday, 12 February, they were both ten years, six months old, both being born in August 1982. Notwithstanding their ages, it is alleged that both intended either to kill James or at least to cause him really serious injury and they both knew that their behaviour was seriously wrong.

Not only is it alleged that they both abducted and murdered James, but that they attempted, prior to abducting James, to abduct another two-year-old boy. He was in the same shopping precinct three hours earlier. That attempt failed because the boy's mother saw one of the defendants beckoning to follow him. She called to him, thus preventing any abduction.

I related in more detail the events of that day – how the defendants played truant, how they visited a number of shops and stole some modelling paint that was later daubed on James. The jury were shown the CCTV pictures of James being led away and the long march from Bootle to Walton was detailed with the accounts of numerous witnesses who had seen James being led along their streets, including several who had enquired as to what was going on. Everyone was fobbed off with a lie, usually that they were taking their little brother home.

The jury were told of James's blood being found on Venables' shoes and that marks on James's face closely matched the shape of the laces on Thompson's trainers, consistent with a kick to James's face. Further, blue paint daubed on James's body, clothing, and left hand matched a tin of modelling paint found nearby.

I then summarised the very lengthy interviews of both boys. Thompson blamed Venables from beginning to end of eight forty-minute interviews. In the early stages, he asserted that Venables alone had perpetrated the abduction saying, 'You will find out in the end it was him that took the baby.' By the fourth interview, Thompson admitted that together they had taken James to the railway line, saying that Venables had thrown paint from a tin of modelmaker's paint into James's eye, making him cry.

He went on to say, 'Jon might have hit him in sly, because Jon is sly.' Later he remarked, 'Ask Jon. I never touched him. Why would I want to hurt a little boy? How do I know what Jon done?' He claimed, 'Jon threw a brick in his face and he just fell on the floor,' and 'I never touched the baby. I wouldn't touch him.' He also alleged, 'Jon then hit him again. He picked up a big metal thing that had holes in and hit him again. Then he hit him again with a stick and then threw him in the nettles. He hit him with a stick in the face.'

By the end of the seventh interview, he was saying, 'James was knocked out and wasn't moving. He was lying on his back over the railway track. I was trying to see if the baby was still alive and he wouldn't move. I got my ear against his belly and he wasn't moving.' In the eighth and final interview, he maintained, 'I didn't touch the baby. I tried to get him off the railway track. I lifted him up around the belly. Then I put him back because I was going to get full of blood.' He added, 'Jon threw

49

bricks at him and hit him with a stick. He threw a battery at James and hit him in the face.' Asked why, he replied, 'Because he felt like it. I told him I was going, because he kept on hitting him.'

I turned to Venables' interviews. He began with a total denial, turning to his mother who was present, saying, 'We never got a kid away, Mum, we never got a kid. You think we did, we never.' When told by the police that Robert had admitted seeing James in the Strand shopping centre, Venables replied, 'We never, we never.' He later claimed that Robert had taken James and left him in the road, saying that he had left Robert on his own till he came back to Walton.

'I never killed him, Mum. We took him and left him at the canal, that's all.'

In due course he alleged that Robert had said, 'Let's get him lost outside, so when he goes in the road he'll get knocked over.'

'I said, "It's a very bad thing to do, isn't it."'

Venables then and in subsequent interviews sought to put all the blame on Thompson, accusing him of slamming James down, putting a bump on his head, throwing paint in his face and throwing a brick in his face, and then hitting James with a steel bar. He admitted throwing small stones at James, because he didn't want to throw bricks, and had missed James with some of them. James had fallen down, but kept getting up again, and that was when Robert hit him with a steel bar. In his final interview, he said, 'I think he was moving, because the bricks on top of him were moving about.' He agreed he had kicked James in the face on the railway line.

The evidence commenced with some non-controversial witnesses who had seen the defendants in and around the Strand shopping precinct in the hours preceding the abduction. Mrs Power then gave evidence speaking of the attempt by the two defendants to abduct her son. The public may well have forgotten that the jury failed to reach a verdict on that count and were discharged from doing so. A retrial would have served little purpose, but seeing Mrs Power in the witness box was a moving experience. She had no doubt that what she observed was an attempt to take her little boy away and she was none too impressed with David Turner's suggestion that her account had been coloured by subsequent publicity.

She was an impressive witness and it must be the case that the jury were preoccupied with consideration of the more grave allegation and the volume of evidence relevant to the abduction and murder of James. Should Mrs Power feel let down by our criminal justice process, I could well understand. The enormity of the murder allegation had diminished the import of the earlier attempted abduction.

Denise Bulger's evidence was read to the court by Henry Globe, my junior. Henry took silk the following year and became Recorder of Liverpool in 2003, before being appointed to the High Court Bench in 2013. Shortly thereafter he became Presiding Judge of the North Eastern Circuit, an appointment that I had greatly enjoyed in the years 2001–04. Henry is a perfectionist and it was a great comfort to know that all the nuts and bolts of a substantial case were being meticulously overseen. Our instructing solicitor was John Brighouse, a senior Crown prosecutor, whose assistance throughout was invaluable. Administratively, every possible step was taken to ensure a seamless presentation of the case.

Denise Bulger's statement had spoken of their visit to the butcher's shop. James was by her side as she was being served. She then looked down and he was gone. She panicked, ran out of the shop, ran to the security office, looked around, but couldn't see him. She went frantically into neighbouring shops, but could not find him. She asked people if they had seen him and nobody had. She then returned to the security office and reported him missing. The call to the police was timed at 4.22 p.m. on that Friday afternoon. It was almost forty-eight hours later that the Bulger family received the dreaded news that James had been found and that he had been murdered.

There followed a phase of the case that was more disturbing than I had anticipated and destructive of any slight chance either defendant might have had. The walk from Bootle to Walton taken by the defendants with James in tow took them through a residential area where most of the roads are named after Oxford colleges. There was Balliol Road, Oriel Road, Merton Road, together with Keble, Wadham, Hertford, Exeter, and Worcester all being represented. I almost felt ashamed perusing the map looking for other colleges when such moving evidence was at hand.

Thirty-eight witnesses had observed this unusual threesome on its way from Bootle to Walton and not only saw them, but sought to intervene. Everyone who spoke to the boys was fobbed off with calculated lies, which were varied by the defendants to fit each individual situation. To some they were with their little brother, to others they were simply taking the toddler home, to one they had found him by the Strand and they were taking him to Walton Lane Police Station. This witness was about to intervene and take James herself, but one of the defendants insisted, 'It's all right. We will take him to the station.'

Much of this evidence was challenged by the defence. It was put that their accounts were inaccurate and that they had been influenced by what they had read and heard of the case. Such suggestions were robustly rejected time and again. These were independent, honest and decent witnesses, many of whom were visibly distressed by the realisation that an intervention by them would have saved James's life. This was not evidence of which they could be mistaken, nor could they ever forget such a tragic event.

Worse was yet to come for the defendants. The last witness to see James alive was a fifteen-year-old girl, who saw James being pushed towards the road by the railway bridge in Walton

Lane. She then saw one of the boys pick James up and carry him across his body like a baby towards the railway embankment. At the time, all she could hear was laughter. Thereafter evidence was called of the defendants' movements after the killing. They went to the video shop and went on an errand to collect an unreturned video. The following day they spent some three hours at the video shop and their behaviour seemed quite normal.

## Expert Evidence

Dr Alan Williams, the Home Office pathologist, gave evidence. He found forty-two injuries on James's body, fifteen of them to the front of his face. The cause of death was the result of multiple head injuries. He concluded that there were at least thirty separate blows to the body. The majority were due to heavy blunt objects and given the amount of brick dust at the scene, bricks were one likely implement. A pattern on James's face was consistent with a kick from a shoe. The imprint on the face matched the way in which the laces had been tied on Thompson's trainers.

This was demonstrated to the jury by the use of an overlay taken from the laces placed on top of a photograph of the mark on James's face. It was a most effective way of demonstrating to the jury that Thompson must have kicked James in the face, so detailed was the mark on the face and so marked was the correspondence with the laces and the D-rings through which they were threaded.

The compelling effect of this exhibit was demonstrated when David Turner suggested that the bruising might have resulted from James falling onto the trainer, a theory that received no expert endorsement. When that suggestion was put to a forensic scientist, Philip Rydeard, he expressed the opinion that 'the bruising on James Bulger's face is entirely consistent with a kick or a blow with a shoe with the distinctive components which are found on Thompson's shoe.'

Further scientific evidence was called linking the paint found on James with the tin of paint found at the scene and paint found on the clothing of both defendants. Of particular significance was a small handprint on Venables' jacket, a print attributable to a small hand covered in blue paint.

The prosecution next called two psychiatrists, Dr Eileen Vizard, who had interviewed Thompson, and Dr Susan Bailey, who had interviewed Venables. Thompson had on legal advice declined to be interviewed by any psychiatrist acting on behalf of the prosecution, thus making it more difficult for the prosecution to establish that he understood that what he did was seriously wrong. We knew, however, that he had been interviewed by Dr Vizard on behalf of the defence and that the defence did not intend to call her. The conclusion was obvious and accordingly we asked Dr Vizard to attend court and interviewed her, and decided to call her as a prosecution witness, there being no property in a witness.

Thompson's counsel were far from pleased, but realised that any objection would fail. Dr Vizard stated that Thompson knew the difference between right and wrong and on the balance of probabilities, would have known the difference on the day of the killing. He would have recognised that it was wrong to take a child from his mother, wrong to cause a child injury and wrong to leave an injured child on a railway line. Whilst he was suffering some post-traumatic stress, there was no evidence that any existed prior to the killing and there was no evidence of any abnormality of mind at the time of the killing. His present difficulties involved a constant preoccupation with the crime scene causing poor sleeping and eating patterns.

David Turner was anxious to prepare the ground for not calling Thompson to give evidence and asked whether his post-traumatic condition would affect his understanding of court procedures and his ability to give evidence. Dr Vizard replied that despite these symptoms, he was able to answer questions perfectly well and was able to be spontaneous.

Dr Bailey gave evidence that Venables, too, would have known that it was wrong to take a child from his mother and to leave him injured on a railway line. He was of average intelligence. She agreed with Brian Walsh that any discussion of the events that were the subject of the indictment caused Venables to burst into tears, and thus he could not talk about these matters in any useful way. It was obvious that neither defendant would give evidence.

We then called teachers from the boys' school, who gave unchallenged evidence that children at their school were specifically taught the difference between right and wrong and children understood that it was wrong to strike another child with a weapon when they entered school aged four or five. The headmistress stated that both boys would know that it was wrong to take a child from his mother and to strike a three-year-old with a brick.

The prosecution case concluded with the jury listening to the tape-recorded police interviews, which lasted in excess of twelve hours. These were played unedited in full over loud-speakers in open court, with both defendants in the dock listening to each blaming the other. The very plain distinction between the two was that Thompson denied his guilt throughout and appeared to be tough and resolute. Venables broke down, however, and his version of events was closer to the truth than his co-accused. As anticipated, both defence counsel announced that they intended to call no evidence.

Closing speeches for the prosecution are by convention much shorter when the defence call no evidence. Nevertheless, there remained a task in hand and an obligation to summarise the prosecution case, and to anticipate any plausible defence argument. I submitted that a child half the age of the defendants would know that what they did was seriously wrong, and it was clear from their interviews that each knew that abducting and killing a child was seriously wrong. Thompson had said, 'I never hit the baby. I wouldn't touch him.' Venables had said, 'It's a very bad thing to do, isn't it.' The unchallenged evidence of the psychiatrists and the schoolteachers was conclusive.

I submitted that a manslaughter verdict in either case would grossly understate the gravity of this crime. Far more than some harm was intended. At least really serious harm was intended. This was a murderous, prolonged attack on a small, defenceless child. If ever a crime was committed jointly and together, then this was the crime. Did one rain thirty or more blows on James's body while the other looked on with no active encouragement?

My concluding words were these: 'This was a very bad thing to do. Both these boys certainly did it and both these boys certainly knew it. We submit that their guilt is proved on all three counts.'

## The Defence Case

David Turner had prepared his opening remarks with due care. 'The sorrow and the pain of Denise Bulger and her husband dominate this trial. Those of us who have children must find the depth of their grief unimaginable. As I address you, I can only hope to reflect the dignity that has been shown by the Bulger family in this harrowing trial. When the news of young James Bulger's death became known on St Valentine's Day this year, the city of Liverpool missed a heartbeat and the nation was shrouded in grief. This case is not the tragedy of one family, but three families – a tragedy for the Bulger family, yes, but also for the families of Jon Venables and Robert Thompson.'

David is by nature an extrovert and a consummate performer. He was a member of Cambridge Footlights and lead singer of 'Prestons', the Northern Circuit Band. He was the junior silk by some distance and preceding Brian Walsh in a cut-throat defence was a daunting task. His performance was confident, loyal to his client, and beyond any fair criticism. He conceded that Thompson had played his part in taking James onto the railway track, but the attack on James was carried out from start to finish by Venables, who eventually confessed to police, 'I did kill him', but did not say, 'We did kill him.' Thompson had asserted over many hours that he played no part in the attack, yet conceded that he did play a part in covering the body with bricks.

Brian Walsh was a most imposing advocate and Venables' case could not have been enunciated with more style. 'The prosecution say Robert Thompson is a liar, who lied from beginning to end. I regret to say we agree. He lied to put the blame on Jon Venables and shuffle it off himself.' He described Thompson as unprincipled and callous, and whilst Venables had shown genuine remorse for James's death, Thompson had shown none. Venables had lied but eventually told the truth, whilst Thompson had waged a consistent campaign of lies. 'He was the sort of person who would only admit something if you caught him in the act.'

Jon Venables had deliberately missed James with bricks and thrown only small stones, not wanting to hurt James. He had given an excellent description of the difference between murder and manslaughter. If Venables was guilty of any crime, it was manslaughter and not murder.

## Summing Up

The summing up was meticulous and has never been the object of any criticism. No appeal was ever lodged in this case. The judge told the jury that between the ages of ten and fourteen, a child was exempt from criminal responsibility unless the prosecution could prove that the child knew when committing the offence that it was really seriously wrong. He told the jury that to convict them both, they had to be sure that both took an active part in the offences, the question being, were they both in it together? To find both boys guilty, they would have to be sure that whichever of them inflicted the blows to James's skull, both intended at that time that James should either be killed or suffer really serious harm.

The judge supplied the jury with a document entitled a 'route to verdict' that contained some twenty questions, a resolution of which would produce verdicts according to law.

Listening to the summing up, I was carrying out my responsibility of identifying any possible errors of law or fact to ensure correction before the jury retired and, as expected, there were none. At the same time, I was more than interested to discern the view the judge may have taken of the facts, should that be possible from the tone or content of his summing up. Judges are, of course, meticulously careful to ensure that a jury reaches a verdict on its own view of the facts. One passage, however, gave some insight into the judge's own view:

'This was not a single throwing of a stone or brick, but involved a number of blows to the-skull of a two, nearly three-year-old boy. You will consider why James Bulger was stripped of his shoes, socks, trousers, and underpants when he was attacked, and why the body was moved from one part of the track near the wall to the other line. Was that to suggest that the child had been subject to some form of assault, possibly by an adult, and then run over by a train? Was that to conceal or attempt to conceal the true cause of death?'

## The Verdicts

The jury retired at midday with six verdicts to consider. In the afternoon during their retirement, counsel acting for Associated Newspapers asked the judge to lift the order forbidding the naming of the defendants in the event of their being convicted. Counsel for both defendants opposed the application.

On behalf of the prosecution, and on instructions, I supported the application, submitting that publicity is in itself a deterrent to those who may be minded to commit grave crimes. Young children hearing about these events and seeing that others are known as A and B may themselves wonder if they commit crime, whether they can do so under the shield of such anonymity. In argument, I contended that the public had a right to know who had committed such terrible acts. The judge indicated that he would await the verdicts before making his ruling.

Plans had been made for the jury to spend the night in a hotel, but shortly after 5.00 p.m., the jury returned to court. They had not reached a verdict on Count 1, the alleged abduction of Diane Power's son, but had reached verdicts on the remaining counts. The judge said he would take those verdicts and when the verdicts of 'Guilty of murder' were returned, there were audible sounds of approval from the area of the courtroom reserved for the family and friends of James. The jury were then asked to continue their deliberations on Count 1, but after some forty-five minutes they had failed to reach even a majority verdict, and they were discharged on their return.

David Turner chose to say nothing in mitigation, whilst Brian Walsh told the judge that Jon Venables wished through him to say sorry to James's mother, a further indication of contrition.

Mr Justice Morland then proceeded to pass sentence: 'The killing of James Bulger was an act of unparalleled evil and barbarity. This child of two was taken from his mother on a journey of over two miles, and then on a railway line battered to death without mercy. Then his body was placed across the railway line so that it would be run over by a train, in an attempt to conceal the murder. In my judgement your conduct was both cunning and very wicked.'

He then ordered them to be detained during Her Majesty's pleasure. The defendants were taken below. The judge continued: 'How it came that two normal boys of average intelligence committed this terrible crime is very hard to comprehend. It is not for me to pass judgement on their upbringing, but I suspect that exposure to violent video films may in part be an explanation.'

The judge lifted the anonymity order and the media were thus at liberty to name both defendants. It seemed that a very long stay in secure units, followed by young offender institutions and ultimately prison, awaited both boys. The practice of announcing the minimum term in open court had not yet come into being. The trial judge wrote to the Lord Chief Justice with his recommendation as to the minimum time to be served. Mr Justice Morland specified eight years in each case. Lord Taylor increased this to ten years and Michael Howard, then Home Secretary, raised it again to fifteen years. This further increase appears to have been in response to public pressure expressed in petitions and certain newspapers.

In 1997, the House of Lords quashed the fifteen-year tariff on the grounds that fixing minimum terms should be a judicial function rather than political. The end result was that both boys were released from custody in June 2001, when both were aged eighteen. They have new identities and High Court orders protecting their anonymity for life.

## Legal Criticism

The trial process, the sentencing, and the granting of anonymity has divided public opinion in the most acute fashion. Sir Louis Blom-Cooper QC, a leading silk in public and administrative law, a distinguished academic, and a deputy High Court judge for many years, published an article in the *Independent* in November 1993. He wrote:

Finding out what happened on the fateful day of James Bulger's murder, and the circumstances leading up to it, would have been better achieved by a public enquiry, without the grinding mill of the criminal process – arrest, interrogation, criminal charge, committal for trial and months later, the trial itself. Since the two killers would be bound in any event to be placed in the care of the local authority – which would mean being kept in secure accommodation until they were adults – there was little purpose in resorting to the criminal process to achieve the same result.

Sir Louis went on to contend that the age of criminal responsibility was too low. 'First, it does not displace the criminal trial for dealing with this age group. Second, it fails to deal with the problem of immaturity.'

I do not agree with either of Sir Louis's contentions. A public enquiry would not have been preceded by a formal interrogation conducted pursuant to the Police and Criminal Evidence Act 1984 and thus critical evidence simply would not have existed. More significantly, failure to prosecute these boys would have resulted in civil disorder. Several hundred were present jeering and shouting as the defendants were driven away from court on the evening of their conviction at a venue some thirty miles from Merseyside, where feelings were at their strongest.

Speaking to the *Guardian* in 2003, David Turner spoke of 'the hatred of the people of Liverpool for the two boys', saying: 'They loathe them and I believe that if they ever came back to Merseyside, their lives would be at risk.'

I concur with that observation, which gains support from the decision of Dame Elizabeth Butler-Sloss in January 2001 in the Family Division, when she granted them anonymity for life once they were freed, with new identities. She said she was 'convinced that their lives are genuinely at risk as well as their physical safety if their new identities and whereabouts became public knowledge'. Of the highest significance, however, is consideration for James's parents and his family. The import to them of convictions in a criminal court is inestimable. The effect upon them of a failure to prosecute would be traumatic.

Sir Louis's real point is that the age of criminal responsibility is too low in this country and is out of step with a number of European countries, which fix the age of criminal responsibility at thirteen or fourteen. He cites the recommendation of the Ingleby Committee, who recommended a raising of the age from eight to twelve. In 1963, the Children and Young Persons Act had fixed the age of responsibility at ten.

In one respect, my experience is more extensive than that of Sir Louis. I have been involved in one capacity or another in criminal trials in Manchester and Liverpool for almost fifty years. At present, nine-year-olds are frequently used to deliver drugs, or more rarely firearms, and they are sent out on shoplifting expeditions. In the present case, the evidence of the boys' headmistress was that children of four or five would know that it was seriously wrong to stone a young child to death. Sir Louis gives precedence to the interests of violent children ahead of their wholly innocent victims.

His views were expressed in the immediate aftermath of the trial and having regard to changes in arrangements for the trials of vulnerable defendants introduced in response to the decision of the European Court of Human Rights in December 1999. It may be that Sir Louis is now less critical of the way in which the guilt of violent children is determined.

Sir Louis's final criticism of the criminal justice process was aimed at the trial judge, when he said: 'Mr Justice Morland was unable to resist the temptation, to which judges commonly succumb, to deliver a homily. His view that the murder of James Bulger disclosed "unparalleled evil" was out of place. So was his allusion to the possible effect on the boys of a particular video nasty – the investigating officer had taken a contrary view.'

Again, I disagree. I appeared in 106 murder trials as counsel defending and prosecuting in almost equal measure and I have no recollection of a judge failing to say something to a defendant prior to sentence concerning his view of the facts of the case, notwithstanding the fact that the only sentence available was one of life imprisonment. In due course, the tariff would fall to be considered by both the Lord Chief Justice and the Home Secretary, and the defendant and the public, including the victim's family, were entitled to hear sentencing remarks that encapsulated both aggravating and mitigating factors.

On any view of the facts, once murder was proven, this was an evil act or series of acts and it was without parallel in the judge's experience. As to the effect of the video, the judge attributed the effect as no more than 'possible', something that those responsible for the boys' rehabilitation thereafter were advantaged by hearing. This was an opinion the judge was entitled to express and he quite properly did so.

A question that overhung this trial was indeed the relevance of the video *Child's Play 3*. In it, an obsessed doll called Chucky comes to life in a military academy, abducts the youngest cadet, and tries to kill him under the wheels of a fairground ghost train. However, it is Chucky dressed in toddler's dungarees, his face splattered with blue paint, who is badly mutilated. This video was the last to be rented by Venables' father before the killing.

The prosecution had to decide whether to adduce evidence of this video as part of our case. On one view, it was highly probative of a planned and premeditated killing. The boys had stolen some paint that very day, which was very similar in colour to the paint that was splattered on Chucky's face in the video. A railway featured in both events, as did a toddler. Chucky died after being splattered with paint and having his face mutilated, as did James. An argument that the boys were re-enacting *Child's Play 3* was clearly tenable.

Police officers regarded the video as a red herring; there was no certain proof that either boy had seen the video and Venables' father was adamant that they had not. Anyway, the police took the view that there was a sufficiency of evidence to establish both intent and participation, and for that reason we decided not to include the video as part of our case.

In December 1999, the European Court of Human Rights ruled that the 1993 trial had been unfair, in that the proceedings violated the right to a fair trial, and they awarded costs and expenses of £15,000 to Thompson and £29,000 to Venables.

However, the criticism by the Strasbourg Court was limited. In two critical respects, they rejected arguments advanced on the boys' behalf. They rejected the claim that they were too young to comprehend criminal responsibility, stating that 'the age of ten could not be said to be so young as to differ disproportionately to the age limit followed by other European States'. Secondly, they rejected the argument that a three-week-long public trial in an adult Crown Court with attendant formality subjected the boys to degrading treatment in breach of Article 3 of the Human Rights Convention.

Their criticism was:

> the formality and ritual of the Crown Court must at times have seemed incomprehensible and intimidating for a child of eleven, and there is evidence that certain of the modifications in the court room, in particular the raised dock which was designed to enable the applicants to see what was going on, had the effect of increasing their sense of discomfort during the trial since they felt exposed to the scrutiny of the press and the public. There was psychiatric evidence that, at the time of the trial, both applicants were suffering from post-traumatic stress disorder as a result of what they had done to the two-year-old, and that they found it impossible to discuss this with their lawyers. They had found the trial distressing and frightening and had not been able to concentrate during it.

I found the criticism of the height of the dock floor somewhat harsh. The height of the floor was lifted by no more than one foot and without this the boys could not have seen out, thereby giving rise to an alternative complaint. The possibility of the defendants sitting outside the dock alongside their counsel was impractical, due to the public animosity towards them. They would not have been safe.

Whilst the Strasbourg Court acknowledged the special measures taken in view of the applicants' ages, they nevertheless concluded that the trial was unfair. The Court could not overturn the convictions, nor does the judgment suggest that would be an appropriate response by our domestic courts. With the benefit of hindsight, I now accept that alternative arrangements would have been more appropriate, but at the time of the trial I had no apprehension that any improvement could be made, and I am sure that defence counsel would have spoken up vociferously had either felt their client was being treated unfairly.

Mr Justice Morland was fastidious in ensuring that the most appropriate arrangements were made for the defendants. We sat school hours with no session exceeding forty-five minutes. The boys were not locked in cells below the courtroom and they were accompanied throughout by social workers, and almost always by counsel and/or solicitors. Indeed, one feature of the case was memorable. Junior counsel for Thompson, Richard Isaacson, and his solicitor, Laurence Lee, took the unusual but commendable step of taking their own Nintendo Gameboy computer games to play with and against Thompson to put him at ease and to relieve the tension.

In the robing room at the end of a day, Henry Globe and I would ask our opponents how their clients were and we heard nothing to cause us any anxiety, nor any suggestion that might improve matters for the defendants. I am certain it crossed none of our minds that we were participating in an unfair trial.

How then could better and fairer arrangements have been

made? Lessons have been learned and should a similar trial now be ordered, provisions first introduced in 2000 as an instant response to the Strasbourg judgment, and thereafter refined in a series of practice directions, will result in a very different scenario.

The principal changes are these:

The proceedings should if practicable and subject to appropriate security arrangements be held in a courtroom in which all participants are on the same level or almost the same level. A family member should if practicable be able to sit with an accused throughout, and in any event a supporting adult should be available throughout the proceedings.

Every step of the proceedings should be explained to the accused by his legal representatives. A timetable which takes account of a defendant's ability to maintain concentration should be formulated with regular and frequent breaks. Consideration must given to a defendant giving evidence by live link if it is in the interests of justice. Wigs and gowns should not be worn.

A small number of members of the public should be allowed to attend, perhaps those with an immediate and direct interest in the outcome of the trial. The number of reporters attending the trial should also be restricted. In such cases an audio and, if possible, a video link to an adjoining courtroom should be provided. Steps must be taken to ensure that a defendant attending court is not exposed to intimidation, vilification or abuse.

The courtroom in Preston was one of the largest in the land and most imposing. It has been referred to as the 'Old Bailey of the North'. There is seating for approximately one hundred members of the public and seats for thirty-four journalists had been reserved. In addition, the case was transmitted by infra-red audio link to a nearby office block, where numerous other media representatives could listen. It is no exaggeration to say that media interest was worldwide.

No child standing trial will ever face a similar situation. Crowds were regularly in the street behind the court jeering and shouting as the defendants were driven from court. This will be prevented on any future occasion. Would these changes and absence of wigs and gowns and a small level courtroom have made any difference to the verdict? I am sure it would not, having regard to the course that the trial took. I had anticipated a very different course of events.

Before the trial commenced and having read the papers, I expected that having regard to the strength of the evidence placing both boys at the scene, and both participating, that both defendants would admit the killing, but seek verdicts of not guilty and blame everyone in sight, not without a degree of justification. I thought that verdicts of manslaughter might possibly be the outcome, but not verdicts I could support.

Both boys could reasonably claim a deprived, even abused childhood. Thompson's father was said to be an aggressive alcoholic, who punished his children, including Robert, with sticks and belts. He abandoned his family for another woman and his wife had turned to drink. It was said that she fought with other women in public houses and occasionally with men. Robert's situation was giving the authorities much concern prior to the killing and the whole family were well known to Social Services and a major irritant to neighbours. Robert, aged ten, was often out after midnight.

Venables' upbringing was little better, if at all. His parents had split up when he was three. His mother was a regular visitor to public houses, leaving three young children alone unsupervised. Jon became unruly, kicking and punching other children, and provoking the family Rottweiler to bark at other young children. Both boys were habitual truants from the same school and both had been placed in the year below their contemporaries, not by reason of any lack of intelligence, but because of non-attendance. In the two years before this killing, Thompson was recorded as having missed 250 half days. Whilst at school, their conduct gave much cause for concern.

Finally, there can be little doubt that both boys were exposed to numerous potentially harmful videos, not only in the video shop where they spent much of their time, but also at Venables' father's house, where Jon spent a few days each week. His father had rented over 400 videos in the few years before James was killed.

It was apparently open to these two boys to say to the jury, 'This is the way society has brought us up. We have been deprived of any proper upbringing, of all moral guidance, of an education, and of any responsible supervision. We have been exposed to numerous damaging videos to such an extent that our understanding of criminal responsibility has been substantially reduced. Having treated us in this irresponsible way, society now seeks most unfairly to convict us of murder.'

There were two possible impediments to this line of defence. Firstly, both boys denied participation. Their defence was 'I played no part in the killing', and thus ill-treatment was irrelevant, as their case was that they had done nothing wrong. The terrible fate of Stefan Kiszko, who spent sixteen years in prison for a murder he did not commit, demonstrated the futility of running two inconsistent defences; namely, I was not there, but if you reject that contention, I was receiving medical treatment at the time, which makes it unlikely that I would commit this crime.

This difficulty presents itself in many murder trials, often when the killer has disposed of the body and asserts that someone else committed the murder. If the jury are sure the defendant was the killer, in essence he is precluded from asserting that he was provoked or lost control or was of diminished responsibility, or even that the killing was in self-defence.

One of an advocate's most difficult tasks can be to explain to a defendant that if he did kill the deceased it may not amount to murder, since he may have grounds for reducing murder to manslaughter, or even a claim of self-defence. It can be a difficult path for an advocate to take. It may cause a loss of confidence, not only by the defendant but also by the solicitor or even junior counsel, but on occasions such an approach is critical. In the present case, both defendants might have been advised that admitting participation would permit them to blame their upbringing and exposure to videos, with some possibility of a favourable verdict.

The other possible impediment was the absence of a psychiatric opinion that either defendant was of diminished responsibility. The law is that psychiatric support is a practical necessity for such a defence to run. With a full admission of participation and full disclosure of a dreadful upbringing, a psychiatrist may have concluded that a defendant was of diminished responsibility, whilst a jury might well decide that the child whose case they were considering was *doli incapax* (unable by reason of his age to appreciate the seriousness of his admitted conduct).

That is not my view of the case. I am satisfied that this was a premeditated murder, beginning with the theft of the blue modelling paint, followed by an unsuccessful abduction attempt. The abduction of James from his mother's side, having once failed, was opportunist and daring. Thereafter there were numerous opportunities to abort the venture, as thirty-eight witnesses testified.

Far from repenting, both defendants lied at will and with consummate skill to ensure that James was taken to his death. The many striking similarities with *Child's Play 3* establish that the long walk was undertaken to reach a railway line, known to the defendants, so that the demise of Chucky could be replicated by the killing of James. A large crowded courtroom, wigs and gowns, and an elevated dock made no difference to a verdict that I remain sure was correct.

Sentencing has always seemed a far more difficult problem. Mr Justice Morland had in mind a minimum term that would avoid the defendants facing a transfer to an adult prison; an approach that was both pragmatic and responsive to the mitigation available, in particular the deprived upbringing and the exposure to violent videos. On the other hand, eight years as a minimum term gave an appearance of wholly underestimating the gravity of this crime, as indeed did Lord Taylor's recommendation of ten years.

Were the sentence to be passed today, the trial judge would have the considerable advantage of the Sentencing Guidelines introduced in 2003, which provide a starting point of twelve years as the minimum term for murders committed by those under seventeen years of age. The judge must then consider both aggravating factors and mitigating factors. In my judgement, the aggravating factors as identified in the guidelines are, firstly, that there was a significant degree of planning or premeditation. The theft of the blue paint, the abduction, and the long walk provide a basis for an adverse conclusion, yet many would contend that this was not a classic planned murder and such planning was not significant. In my view, however, there was a degree of planning sufficient to aggravate the circumstances for the purposes of sentence.

In addition, the guidelines identify as relevant: the vulnerability of the victim, mental or physical suffering inflicted before death, and dismemberment of the body. On any view, the aggravating factors outweigh the mitigation and were these facts to be replicated today, I would anticipate a minimum term in the region of and close to fifteen years.

From the perspective of James's family, minimum terms of any dimension must appear derisory. To them there is no semblance of retribution, nor indeed justice, in events as they have unfolded. In reality James had his whole life taken from him, whilst the two defendants enjoyed one-to-one tuition in circumstances far superior to those they would have experienced but for this crime. They have had hundreds of thousands of pounds of public money spent upon them and have been granted anonymity to allow them to enjoy a full adult life as educated free men, absolved by their new identities from the disgrace that necessarily attaches to those who commit grave crime.

I have seen James's mother more than once on the television and I sympathise with her unreservedly. I have observed similar responses time and again both from families of murder victims and also from families of those killed by acts of dangerous driving. No sentence can adequately recompense a bereaved and loving family. Sentencing in such cases is one of a judge's most demanding tasks, none more so than in the present case. The Sentencing Guidelines for murder have assisted judges to a considerable degree, protecting them from over-emotional responses and providing a degree of consistency.

Every time I see a three-year-old, thoughts of James are rekindled, as indeed they are as I drive into Liverpool through Bootle, or out of Liverpool through Walton. No one who played any part in this trial will ever forget such a tragedy.

# Chapter 7

## The Case of Haase and Bennett

I N 1995, I received the brief to defend John Haase, who intended to plead guilty to a substantial conspiracy to import Class A drugs. Rodney Klevan QC was briefed to defend his nephew and co-conspirator, Paul Bennett. The case was in Liverpool Crown Court before Judge David Lynch.

My instructions indicated that both Haase and Bennett would admit leading roles in an international drug-smuggling operation, which originated in Turkey. It involved a major heroin shipment worth approximately £18 million destined for Liverpool. They were arrested in October 1993 and they both became registered as police informers and entered into a similar arrangement with Customs and Excise.

The criminal proceedings against them were delayed, so that they would have every opportunity to obtain and divulge useful information whilst in custody. They had links with a number of major gangsters and stated their intention to exploit their connections to provide information and thereby obtain a reduction in sentence.

My instructions disclosed that between October 1993 and August 1995, a substantial volume of vital information was provided relating to major criminal activity. No less than twenty-eight substantial firearms seizures were made on the basis of the information. The seizures were of sub-machine guns, assault rifles, handguns and shotguns. The most important seizure of firearms included 9mm automatic pistols that were found in

Holyhead; information from Haase and Bennett indicated that these weapons were destined to be sent to the Republic of Ireland at an extremely sensitive time during the peace process.

Further information identified a handgun attributed to a prisoner in Strangeways Prison, Manchester, who was facing a murder trial. In all, police recovered some 150 firearms, including AK-47 and M16A2 assault rifles, Czechoslovak sub-machine guns, shotguns, 1,500 rounds of ammunition and Semtex explosive.

Information supplied by Haase and Bennett as registered police informers was not limited to firearms and explosives. A number of substantial drugs seizures were undertaken and our clients also provided significant information about several professional criminals who operated in the Merseyside area. All the information supplied by our clients had been obtained by them whilst on remand in custody.

My instructions made it clear that none of the information given to the police or Customs and Excise could possibly be disclosed in open court. This was a situation that courts were fully prepared for and not unfamiliar with. Many defendants give assistance to the police or other law enforcement agencies in the legitimate expectation that their sentence will be discounted to reflect the degree and usefulness of the information.

This principle, well established in 1998, has been further regulated by the Serious Organised Crime and Police Act 2005. It is now recognised that the appropriate level of discount for significant assistance is between one half and two-thirds of the sentence that would otherwise have been passed. Only in the most exceptional case would the level of reduction exceed three-quarters. That mathematical expectation was in existence in 1998. Present arrangements are more formal and involve a written agreement between defendant and prosecutor, but as my instructions disclosed, Messrs Haase and Bennett had given quite exceptional and valuable information and could expect a discount in excess of two-thirds.

On the day of the hearing, everything proceeded as anticipated. David Turner QC prosecuted, and he and I attended the chambers of Judge Lynch, together with Rodney Klevan QC, our solicitor Tony Nelson and a senior customs officer. David Turner explained the full circumstances and required the officer to take the oath and to confirm both the nature of the information given and the value of it. Rodney and I had minimal roles to play. No facts were in dispute and Judge Lynch was fully appraised of the law including appropriate levels of discount.

He told us that absent any assistance, he would have passed sentences of eighteen years, but having regard to the exceptional assistance given by the defendants, the appropriate sentences to be served would be five years. In order to achieve this outcome, and to ensure that no publicity was given to the assistance, the judge would pass a sentence in open court of eighteen years and write to the Home Secretary indicating that, by reason of the assistance, the defendants should serve the equivalent of a five-year sentence.

Mitigating was an unusual experience. We could not under any circumstances utilise the exceptional assistance given to the authorities. The slightest hint of this would have put our clients and conceivably ourselves in the greatest danger. Indeed, the judge was assured by the prosecution that the defendants were in such danger that upon release they were to live in South America under new identities. Furthermore, the lives of customs officers who were still working undercover would be put at risk if the assistance was to become public knowledge.

Apart from pleas of guilty, there was little else to say and as earlier indicated, Judge Lynch told both Haase and Bennett that they were sentenced to eighteen years' imprisonment. We visited our clients in the cells and assured them both that the judge would write to the Home Secretary and they could expect to serve the equivalent of a five-year term. The judge was as good as his word and he wrote to Michael Howard recommending that he 'exercise the royal prerogative' on account of information that the pair had given, which had led to the seizure of a large volume of illegal firearms.

The judge was obliged to accept the evidence of the prosecuting authorities. He had no private investigators to send out to verify that the assistance was genuine, whereas the Home Secretary, whose final decision it was, had all the resources of the Home Office to inquire into the matter. Since both men had been in custody on remand for a considerable period, the equivalent of a five-year sentence was served after a further eleven months and on 4 July 1996 both men were released.

Upon their release, both men returned to their homes on Merseyside and within days were reported to the police as escapees, their neighbours believing, not unreasonably, that they were serving eighteen-year sentences. It was, of course, impossible for the police to explain the fact that both Haase and Bennett were free men. To have done so would have breached the confidentiality of the arrangement, and apparently put both men in instant peril. It became inevitable that the public and the media would seek an explanation.

I arrived home one evening and the headlines on the television news carried the story of the release of the two men after a matter of months, having been sentenced by Judge Lynch to terms of eighteen years' imprisonment and apparently released with his concurrence. I had not given the case a moment's thought since the sentence was passed. The judge was entrapped in the same way as the police and unable to explain the events.

The Home Office could have stated without any difficulty that the decision to release the two men was taken by the Secretary of State, and not by the judge, as indeed it was. This may have been politically inconvenient and inconsistent with Michael Howard's soundbite 'prison works', but initial silence on his part and the overall presentation by the media cast doubt on the competence and/or integrity of the judge. My instant thought as I watched the television news was that Judge Lynch had been left out to dry.

As one of the few to know the reality of the situation, I felt both aggrieved and intensely uneasy. It was obvious that many intelligent members of the public would suspect corruption within the justice process. For a considerable period, unanswered speculation prevailed.

Haase set up a security company called Big Brother, based in north Liverpool, which was a front for organised crime and involved running guns to Scottish gangsters. In 2001, he was jailed for money laundering and serious firearms offences for a term of thirteen years.

Without any explanation for the early release of both men, Peter Kilfoyle, the MP for Walton, campaigned for an investigation. In March 2001, he was granted a half-hour adjournment debate in the House of Commons at which he brought up the subject of Haase and Bennett, and specifically the damage done to the people of Liverpool by them being allowed back onto the street after such a short period of time in prison.

During 2003, it was widely reported that a drug dealer and associate of the two heroin smugglers, who was a cousin of Michael Howard and openly boasted of his relationship with him, had received a bribe of £400,000 from Haase that was to be passed onto the Home Secretary. Later on, it was established that there was no substance in the rumour.

In May 2004, Peter Kilfoyle again raised the matter in an adjournment debate having visited Haase in prison at HMP Whitemoor earlier. Haase had provided Kilfoyle with a sworn affidavit. In that document, Haase explained that all the seizures made by the authorities of guns, explosives and drugs had been planted by him and his associate Bennett, in order to effect a reduction in their sentences.

In that affidavit he said:

When me and Bennett got nicked we had over 50k of brown heroin which is worth £1.150m. Bennett already had a couple of hundreds of thousands of pounds of cash and so did I so we had plenty of money. No favours were done. We paid for everything, machine guns, AKs, hand pistols. When we were first getting the machine guns they were 2k, but later on, when we were getting them in 10s, the price was reduced. I can confirm that some of the guns which I bought had originated from a police depository – that is they had been confiscated by the police in previous crimes. A lot of them were coming in from Eastern Europe, especially the AKs. All the guns were spot on. I was getting them and telling people where to put them so that I could inform Customs and Excise where they could be found. It was con all the way, but for some reason they were delighted to get guns off the streets.

The next one was one of the big ones they were all drooling at. Someone went to Ireland, got an address over there, newspapers and pubs, cigarette stumps, all bits and pieces. A car we bought in Liverpool, that was booked through the travel agency in Alder Hey, booked onto the Holyhead ferry, thousands of pounds of ammunition on it, rifles etc, that was parked in Holyhead car park, newspapers and cigarette stumps in the car, and the keys were left in the back wheel. The car was full of rifles and thousands of pounds worth of ammunition. We told the customs about it, MI5 sat off and observed the car for three days before they hit it. The cache was planted by me and Bennett to give the impression there was an IRA connection. This was a total fabrication.

In the affidavit, Haase claimed that he paid hundreds of thousands of pounds to the cousin of Michael Howard, but this was subsequently proved to be a lie.

Having read this affidavit, in a further adjournment debate in May 2004, Kilfoyle concluded by saying:

I cannot believe that everyone touching on this case missed the obvious. To a simple-minded lay person such as myself, there can be only two possible conclusions. The first is that Customs and Excise, the Prison Service, the Police, the Judiciary and the Home Office were all duped by Haase and Bennett. The alternative is that there was, at some stage, some truth in the allegations that bribery played a part in securing Haase and Bennett's release. I do not want to believe that. All my instructions say that is not possible. Yet I also find it difficult to believe that no one within the system smelled a rat in the way which the gun stashes were set up. I just hope that today the Minister can throw some light on this sordid saga, so that I can explain to my constituents why it is that these people were allowed out.

Having signed the affidavit, it was inevitable that events would catch up with Haase and Bennett. In November 2008, in the Crown Court at Southwark, both were convicted after a trial of conspiring to pervert the course of justice. Haase was sentenced to twenty-two years' imprisonment and Bennett to twenty years.

Judge Lynch gave evidence at the trial. He explained that he was very impressed with the information given to him about the gun caches, the weapon seizures and the other matters, particularly in the light of what was then increasing gun crime in Merseyside during the 1990s. He had been assured on oath that the information was genuine and accordingly acted on established principles in substantially discounting the appropriate sentence for a grave case of drugs importation. The role of prosecution witness must have been most uncomfortable and highly unusual for a retired judge, not least since the ultimate decision to release the two men lay with the Secretary of State.

The jury rejected the submission of the defendants that the contents of the affidavit were false and that the information given to the police and Customs and Excise was true. Haase and Bennett appealed against their sentences. The Lord Chief Justice, Lord Judge, in rejecting their appeals, said this:

> It is worth emphasising that the criminality here was not merely the sophisticated conspiracy by professional criminals which led investigating officers and, on the basis of their assessment, the sentencing judge and ultimately the Secretary of State, to believe that a major discount from the appropriate sentence has been earned by the appellants. The criminality went much further. The conspiracy, run by the appellants from prison, depended on accomplices who were outside the prison to obtain possession of and then travel with firearms to different locations to deposit them where the police would eventually find them on the basis of the information fed to the police by the appellants (who will have been fed the information to give to the police by the accomplices who had deposited the guns). The handling of such a weapon on each occasion was in itself a serious offence which merited a significant sentence of imprisonment. The conspiracy offence alleged against the appellants therefore encapsulated very grave criminality indeed.

It follows that this elaborate and almost certainly unique conspiracy, initially successful, was ultimately self-defeating. There is no doubt that the Home Secretary, judge, counsel, solicitor, police and Customs and Excise were all comprehensively duped by two men operating from a prison cell. Whilst there have been numerous cases of gangsters running major crimes from within jail, the present facts outflank all others for their ingenuity, detail, and initial success. Had Haase and Bennett left Merseyside and laid low elsewhere, they may well have retained their liberty.

The availability and use of mobile phones in jail is a constant source of public concern. From time to time attempts are made to block phone signals at certain jails or on specified wings, but with limited or no success. Blocking signals may prove a serious handicap in emergencies and to prison officers. In the last twelve months, 10,643 incidents were recorded in UK prisons where mobile phones were discovered. The trend appears now to install in-cell phones in twenty prisons in England and Wales in order to 'tackle the flow of illegal mobiles and reduce tension on wings'. I fear that the reality of the situation is that if comprehensive and determined efforts were made to rid prisons of mobile phones, prison riots would promptly follow. The same may also be said in relation to drugs.

It may be of interest that recent episodes of the television drama *Line of Duty* touch upon the recycling of firearms recovered by police and subsequently stolen from a police depository. Haase and Bennett were not short of either plans or the ability to execute them. Their preparations in relation to the firearms seizure at Holyhead, namely planting of Irish newspapers, cigarette butts and addresses in the vehicle, in order to dupe investigators into the false conclusion that the arms were intended for the IRA, was typical of the thoroughness of their work. The thought that the numerous arms seizures may have been planted by the defendants themselves never crossed my mind.

After the affair became public, a number of 'wise after the event' police officers told the *Liverpool Echo* that they had doubted that the information was genuine. Yet not one of them raised any suspicion with the authority before the die was cast. When giving evidence at Southwark, Judge Lynch told the court that if anyone had raised the slightest suspicion that even one gun had been planted by or on behalf of the defendants, he would not have asked the Home Secretary to consider exercising the royal prerogative.

My abiding thought on the case is one of condolence with Judge Lynch. He entered the Circuit twelve months after me and I know him well. He enjoys the very highest reputation both as a judge and a Circuiteer. He will have asked himself time and again whether he could have taken some alternative course, such as adjourning sentence whilst further enquiries were made. I was well placed to observe events and have not the slightest reservation as to the course he adopted. It was wholly in accord with established procedure then in force.

As advocates and as judges, we are all liable to be deceived from time to time. Judge Lynch has the consolation of being deceived by the most remarkable series of ploys effected from within prison cells and being in the best of company when misled.

David Lynch is a wonderful example to all entering the profession. Few begin their working life as the office boy in a solicitor's office, take an external LLB, become a circuit judge, a Bencher of their Inn and a Doctor of Philosophy. David is Remembrancer of the Northern Circuit, welcoming every new member, giving lectures on circuit history, traditions and ethics. Over his lifetime he collected a magnificent library, principally made up of biographies of the great men and women of the Law. He has donated this library to the Royal Courts of Justice, where it stands as the Lynch Library.

# Chapter 8

## The Trial of Dr Harold Shipman

THROUGHOUT MY TIME at the Bar I had avoided working in August. It was a time for the beach somewhere in Europe, but August 1998 was very different. I had started a lengthy murder trial in Manchester at the beginning of June and a less than speedy opponent had caused the trial to run into August. Terri Creathorn, our admirable senior clerk, informed me that she had arranged a consultation one Thursday evening in Ashton police station at 5.30 p.m. She said that a doctor had been charged with forgery and the Crown Prosecution Service wanted me to act for the prosecution.

This seemed a less than thrilling proposition and I questioned whether a case of forgery really called for a QC to prosecute it. I certainly did not fancy a sunny summer evening in Ashton police station. However, very little escaped Terri's attention. She had anticipated my reluctance and had asked Tony Taylor, the chief Crown prosecutor, why he required a senior silk to prosecute a case of forgery. She was told that he believed it was the tip of the iceberg and very much a case that I should accept. There were no papers as yet and they wanted a preliminary discussion about the way ahead. It sounded interesting.

Consultations with QCs invariably take place in chambers and not in police stations, and as I drove to Ashton, my thoughts of the Mediterranean and a Sardinian beach clashed with the drab suburban scene. A surprise awaited me. I was greeted by a senior Crown prosecutor, Robert Davies, a man

I knew well and liked. He was energetic and enthusiastic, and we worked well together. He introduced me to Detective Superintendent Bernard Postles, of whom I cannot speak too highly; in his mid-forties, immaculate, intelligent, and a man with authority. In turn I was introduced to Detective Chief Inspector Mike Williams and Detective Inspector Stan Egerton, who were both to prove themselves consummate professionals. A number of junior police officers were also present and it was obvious that something more than a forgery investigation was afoot.

Bernard Postles came straight to the point: 'We believe we are investigating a doctor who is a serial killer.' It was early August and they had recently exhumed the body of Kathleen Grundy, whose will they suspected had been forged by Dr Shipman. They thought she had been poisoned, and tissue samples had been sent to the forensic science laboratory for analysis. Her fingerprints had also been taken to exclude contact with the will, and the results were being awaited. A number of problems had arisen and my assistance was sought.

The *Manchester Evening News* were taking an intense interest in the case and there was concern that disclosures by them might make a fair trial impossible. Many of Shipman's patients held him in very high regard and believed that he was innocent and being unfairly targeted. Some relatives were objecting to exhumation and advice was sought as to the appropriate action to be taken by the police.

Of particular concern was the fact that Shipman continued in practice and if the police theory proved accurate, further murders could not be discounted. The scientific results were urgently awaited, but in the meantime, there was insufficient evidence to arrest Shipman on suspicion of murder. Adding to the difficulties was that earlier in 1998, a police inquiry into Shipman's conduct carried out by a Detective Inspector Dave Smith had found nothing untoward.

It was agreed that in the event of a positive finding at the forensic science laboratory, an immediate arrest should take place and steps taken to ensure a replacement locum, as Shipman was a sole practitioner. The laboratory should be asked to give absolute priority to this investigation. Relatives of the deceased should be requested not to speak with the media and reasons given to them, and relatives of those deceased who were buried should be told of the necessity for exhumation as soon as the Kathleen Grundy report was received. Any decision to exhume was the exclusive responsibility of the coroner.

It was an intense and productive consultation, and this was a team that I would enjoy working with. Regular meetings would be essential and as I drove home, I realised that taking on such a case was ample consolation for missing a few days on the beach; in fact, I was excited at the prospect. At this stage, however, any case against Shipman was based upon the gut instinct of experienced police officers and the evidence of experts was still awaited.

On 26 August, Michael Hall, a forensic document examiner, informed the police that in his opinion Mrs Grundy's signature on the questioned will had been forged and the will had probably been typed on a portable typewriter seized from Shipman's surgery.

On 28 August, Julie Evans, a forensic scientist, informed the police that the levels of morphine present in Mrs Grundy's body were consistent with levels that had previously been known to have caused death by morphine overdose.

The time had clearly arrived for Shipman to be arrested, but Bernard Postles was determined that his team should be perfectly prepared for what were certain to be difficult interviews. Shipman had been interviewed on 14 August, but only in relation to background detail, and on that occasion, he was not arrested and had dealt with enquiries confidently and without apparent difficulty. Post-interview, Shipman had returned home and to his practice. The police had informed the General Medical Council of the position in August, but were told that they could do nothing until Shipman was convicted of an offence.

Bernard Postles was confident that Shipman would not be so foolish as to commit murder at this time and thus Shipman went to the police station by appointment with his solicitor, Ms Ball, at 9.00 a.m. on 7 September, when he was promptly arrested on suspicion of the murder of Mrs Grundy, of attempting to obtain property by deception, and of forgery. He was finger-printed and made a facetious comment as to the rank of the officer taking his prints, thereafter displaying an arrogance ill-befitting his predicament.

He carried this arrogance and condescending manner into the interview, which he appears to have regarded as a contest with intellectually inferior police officers. Detective Sergeant John Walker and Detective Constable Mark Denham had mastered their brief and at the conclusion of the interview, Shipman was charged with all three offences. He was held overnight in a cell and appeared before Tameside magistrates' court the following morning, when he was remanded in custody.

In the meantime, Robert Davies had briefed junior counsel to assist me and they were well chosen. It is rare for three counsel to appear for the prosecution in any criminal trial, but as Robert had anticipated, this was of abnormal complexity.

Peter Wright was at that time an exceptionally busy and able junior. He took silk the following Easter and thus two QCs prosecuted, an unusual but not unique event. Peter went on to become a Senior Treasury Counsel, the first ever to be appointed from outside London. He appeared before me several times and has prosecuted a number of very high-profile cases, not least the plot to blow up transatlantic aircraft in mid-flight, and fraudulent expenses claims by MPs. Peter remains at the Bar as one of its foremost practitioners.

Our second junior was Kate Blackwell, then some five years'

call, of great ability and of inestimable value in a team that I was proud to lead. She is now in silk with a fine practice and four children.

Robert had a formidable task in assembling a team. He required a handwriting expert in relation to the forged will, a typescript expert to prove the use of the typewriter, a toxicologist, a chemist, a pharmacist, and an anaesthetist to deal with the morphine, its detection, its use and effects. He also needed pathologists, a clinical cardiologist, and physicians to deal with the nine exhumed bodies and to meet the defence argument that they died of natural causes. An expert in computer science was required to analyse the contents of Shipman's computer and an expert in telephone communication to examine his phone records, even a trichologist to scrutinise hair samples from the deceased.

A critical and most valued member of the team was a GP, Dr John Grenville. He was highly qualified and had studied the medical records of each victim, which had been compiled by Shipman. His role was to explain the medical history of each victim and he was to express the opinion that in every case there was nothing in the patient's history to explain her sudden unexpected death. Both he and the relevant pathologist gave evidence in relation to each victim as we came to them, with the effect that Dr Grenville entered the witness box fifteen times. His manner was ideal for the task. He was modest, quiet, unassuming and on top of his subject, in total contrast with the defendant.

Dr Grenville had a secondary task. He sat alongside Peter Wright behind me and attended at every conference, ensuring that we had instant and well-informed facts and figures on any topic the defendant might raise. He made a lasting impression on all within the court; he was a doctor whom we would all have treasured. In one coffee break, he observed rather drily that when Shipman was not killing his patients, he was an extremely competent and caring doctor. He was able to make that judgement having reviewed numerous medical records.

As the weeks passed, and the formidable team of sixty police officers examined every sudden and unexpected death amongst Shipman's patients, it became clear that as prosecutors we would have to make a selection of the most suitable cases to place in the indictment. A criminal trial must be manageable and controlled. Ten counts was generally considered to be an appropriate and maximum number of allegations of murder, although every case turns on its own facts. We were conscious that there was likely to be an abundance of expert evidence and were anxious not to overwhelm the jury.

At the same time, we needed sufficient counts to demonstrate Shipman's methods and to show that there was only one possible explanation for the number of sudden deaths amongst his patients. The nine cases where the bodies had been exhumed were straightforward and were plainly to be in the indictment. A number of cases where cremation had taken place also merited consideration. We selected six cases. None of those six victims was terminally ill, all had died in Shipman's presence, and the deaths were sudden and unexpected.

In some the medical records had been altered post-death and in others Shipman had visited his patient's home without any phone call to the surgery, notwithstanding Shipman's assertion to the contrary. The selection meetings were far from easy, involving as they did over one hundred possible cases, substantially less than the eight hundred and eighty-eight considered much later by Dame Janet Smith in her enquiry.

During one of the selection meetings, it became clear that Bernard Postles was having great difficulty with certain relatives who wished to know what was being done about their relative. 'My mother has been murdered and what are you going to do about it?' was a frequent cry. Many were distraught and Bernard was concerned at the activities of certain media representatives who were taking a close interest. Not unreasonably, he feared the headline, 'Police Not Interested in Murder', followed by an article that would make it extremely difficult for Shipman to have a fair trial in which fifty or so complainants asserted publicly that a member of their family had been murdered and the police had done nothing about it.

Rosemary West's trial had recently come close to being stayed by reason of grossly prejudicial media comment. Appreciating Bernard's concern, I ventured a solution. 'Please assemble all the difficult relatives in a lecture hall and I will explain the reasoning behind our selections, and the necessity to limit in number the cases we can prosecute.'

Bernard looked me in the eye and said, 'Sir, I could not guarantee your safety.'

Eventually, we agreed that every family should be seen independently, and a full explanation given as to why other cases had been selected in preference to theirs and the reasoning behind it. In the event of any family not accepting the explanation from a police officer, we as counsel would see them. This was a bitter pill for many families to swallow and we are most grateful that they did so.

In due course the case was listed in order for the defendant to plead and for the judge to fix the venue and the trial date, and to give directions for the service of documents. This hearing took place in Liverpool before Mr Justice Douglas Brown. For the first time I met my opponent, Nicola Davies QC.

The briefing of Nicola Davies was a disappointment to the silks on the Northern Circuit. From the day of my first consultation, speculation was rife that a significant defence brief was in the offing and at the Criminal Bar such briefs are highly prized and much coveted. Nicola spent the majority of her time away from the criminal courts. Her practice was rather more sophisticated, dealing with clinical negligence cases and high-profile inquiries including the Bristol heart surgery inquiry, the Cleveland child abuse inquiry, and the BSE inquiry. She had also defended in a number of criminal trials involving doctors and dentists. In reality, the Northern Circuit silks had to concede that Nicola Davies was well qualified for the task in hand.

She was, however, anxious to ensure that she was ably assisted by a junior who was an acknowledged expert in the criminal law and she asked the advice of a leading criminal silk, David Calvert-Smith QC. David recommended Ian Winter, also from London, and he was an inspired choice. Shipman was a most difficult client during the trial; on more than one occasion he threatened to dispense with counsel, and on another he was determined to remain in the cells. Ian Winter played a vital role in assisting Nicola to manage Shipman and ensuring that his defence at least appeared to run smoothly. It was no surprise that Ian took silk a year or so later.

Within a few days of recommending Ian to Nicola, David Calvert-Smith was appointed Director of Public Prosecutions and soon afterwards found himself responsible for the prosecution of Dr Shipman. Indeed, he came to the trial and sat behind me more than once, well able to observe the defence team he had inadvertently helped to assemble.

Mr Justice Douglas Brown ordered that the trial take place in Preston on 5 October 1999. He also ordered that the defence must serve any expert evidence they may wish to rely upon at least six weeks prior to the trial date. As the six-week date approached, we were increasingly confident in the prosecution team that our case was watertight, and expected at any time to receive psychiatric reports raising a defence of diminished responsibility, which if successful would reduce the crimes of murder to manslaughter. How wrong we were.

## Defence Expert Evidence

Six weeks prior to trial, we received a substantial volume of expert evidence. The defence solicitor was Anne Ball of Hempsons, a firm that acts on a regular basis for the Medical Defence Union, which provides insurance cover for medical practitioners, including representation in criminal proceedings. As will become apparent, Anne Ball did everything possible to assist Shipman in a highly professional and skilled manner.

The first report served upon us was from a distinguished professor of clinical cardiology. In relation to every deceased, he provided a quite plausible cause of death. In one, 'A cardiac cause cannot be ruled out,' in another, 'There could have been a plaque fissure and platelet thrombosis which caused death,' and yet another, 'There was mild to moderate coronary artery disease which might be sufficient to cause myocardial ischaemia (shortage of blood to the heart). This would then lead to a serious and possibly fatal arrhythmia.'

He advanced an alternative cause of death for all nine deceased. However, he was not alone.

A consultant respiratory physician at a London teaching hospital said this in relation to Mrs Melia: 'I consider the Crown pathologist's conclusion that she died from morphine poisoning to be an over interpretation of limited evidence. I consider the alternative diagnosis of lobar pneumonia to be reasonable in that pre-existing lung disease will both increase susceptibility to pneumonia and increase the chance of it proving fatal if it occurs.'

In relation to Jean Lilley, he said, 'I do not agree with the Crown pathologist Dr Rutherford that it is unlikely that fibrosing alveolitis could reasonably be considered to be material to her sudden and unexpected death.' In relation to Mrs Adams, he said, 'It is plausible that she could have developed rapidly progressing bronco pneumonia with hypoxaemia and thereby provoked a sudden disturbance of cardiac rhythm, which caused sudden death.'

A further two consultant forensic pathologists, both attached to London teaching hospitals, produced comprehensive reports advancing an alternative cause of death other than morphine poisoning for each of the nine deceased whose bodies were exhumed.

Then a distinguished professor of chemistry wrote a report, stating, 'The reports prepared by the prosecution tend to give the quite false impression that the drug analyses in the nine deaths offer proof that morphine was the cause of death.' Of those embalmed, that is six of the nine, he wrote, 'Formaldehyde, the embalming solution, may clinically change one drug into another and affect the concentration of the drug detected.' It seemed that cardiologists, physicians, forensic pathologists and chemists were united in support of Shipman.

The best was yet to come from a forensic toxicologist. 'The concentration of drugs in the body may change after death as the result of the breakdown of the drug either by chemical processes or by the action of the micro-organisms associated with putrefaction. For example, it is possible that codeine could be converted to morphine after death.' The proposition was floated that codeine, which is found in Lemsip and many other non-prescription medicines, may convert to morphine after death. Was this then the answer: none of the ladies was injected with morphine, but each had taken Lemsip or something similar before they died of natural causes?

Worse was to follow from the consultant forensic toxicologist: 'The structure of the drug Pholcodine, a drug available in the UK without prescription as a cough suppressant, is such that it could possibly be converted into morphine by the action of micro-organisms.' And then: 'A comparatively small amount of kaolin and morphine mixture remaining in the body after death may by these several processes indicate an abnormally high reading of morphine some time after death.'

Next was head hair. The prosecution relied on tests to show that not one of the deceased had any history of drug abuse. Those who use opiates have traces in the hair canal that can be detected by gas chromatography. The defence served evidence from a professor at Heidelberg University indicating positive findings, where the prosecution had found none.

The receipt of these several reports with six weeks in which to respond to them created a degree of alarm at the Crown Prosecution Service offices, but Robert Davies was equal to the task. Each and every assertion was dealt with, and it became clear that a scientific battle would be joined. The prosecution would call twelve scientists and the defence had served evidence from ten scientists. As events unfolded, the battle was to prove illusory.

## The Prosecution Case

The trial commenced on 5 October 1999. The trial judge was Mr Justice Forbes. Thayne Forbes's background was in construction and before appointment to the High Court he was for a short time an Official Referee in the Technology and Construction Court. He was now in his seventh year on the High Court Bench and had shown himself to be a very safe pair of hands, and it was easy to see why he had been entrusted with this trial. His style in court was reserved and non-interventionist, but there was a quiet authority and a very necessary attention to detail. He was able to put a number of very nervous witnesses at ease and from counsel's viewpoint, we could not have had a more considerate judge. In retirement, he has chaired the Al-Sweady Inquiry, which took the best part of five years. It came as no surprise when I read: 'The judge was credited with a thorough job.'

Proceedings began with Nicola Davies making three applications. As she made the first, I had a sense of déjà vu. Six years earlier in the same courtroom I had opposed an application to stay proceedings on the grounds that the two young killers of James Bulger could not have a fair trial by reason of the 'unremitting, extensive, inaccurate and misleading publicity about the case'. It was the same crowded courtroom, several press representatives were the same, as were the ushers and the court manager, along with a similar lack of credulity concerning the facts as they unravelled, and a corresponding response from me: the public were entitled to know.

The publicity was not sensational – one hundred and thirty-six deaths were investigated, close to the one hundred and fifty claimed by the papers. The papers were entitled to report these events and most of the publicity was accurate and responsible. The jury would decide the case on the evidence they saw and heard in court and would be so directed.

The outcome of the first application was the same.

The second application was to sever the charges so as to make three separate trials. The first would relate solely to Kathleen Grundy, as it was the only case where the prosecution were able to allege a motive, namely money. The second case would relate to those deceased who had been buried, as there was evidence as to their mode of death, specifically morphine poisoning. The third would relate to those deceased who were cremated, as there was no physical evidence as to their mode of death. The argument was that a single trial would overburden the jury, it would take several months and involved fifteen victims, six hundred witnesses and eight thousand exhibits, all against a complicated medical background.

I responded by submitting that this was no more than an attempt to emasculate the prosecution case. All fifteen murder allegations were highly probative of one another. The prosecution had already taken drastic steps to ensure that the indictment was not overloaded. The jury could only reach a proper conclusion by hearing the case as a whole. Again, the application failed.

The third application was to rule a volume of evidence referred to as 'Volume Eight' as inadmissible. That volume referred to Shipman's treatment of twenty-eight patients, most of whom had died. Shipman had prescribed morphine in large quantities and after their death he had taken away their remaining ampoules and instead of destroying them, he had kept them. On some occasions, he prescribed morphine even after a patient had died, and at other times, he prescribed morphine to patients with no need for it and kept the morphine for his own purposes.

The argument was that by introducing the evidence of numerous other deaths, it would portray Shipman as having committed more murders than those with which he had been charged. At most, it was said, the pattern of stockpiling was that of an addict and not a murderer.

I responded by submitting that it was essential to prove that Shipman had access to the drug morphine, despite the fact that he had removed himself from the Controlled Drugs Register following his conviction for unlawful possession of pethidine in 1977, when he became addicted to the drug pethidine. Absent this evidence, it would be open to Shipman to assert that there was no evidence he was ever in possession of any significant volume of morphine. The prosecution did not allege that he murdered any one of the patients referred to in Volume Eight. Again this application failed and two days of court time had passed.

On 11 October, I opened the case to the jury. These were my opening words:

> The defendant is a general practitioner. The prosecution allege that he has murdered fifteen of his patients by administering to them substantial doses of morphine or diamorphine very shortly before they died, thereby causing their death. Nine of the fifteen were buried, six were cremated. The bodies of those buried were exhumed. Tests carried out on the blood, liver or muscle

of each established a significant presence of morphine within their bodies. None of those buried, nor indeed cremated, were prescribed morphine or diamorphine. All of them died most unexpectedly. All of them had seen Dr Shipman on the day of their death. There is no question in this case of euthanasia or what is sometimes called mercy killing. None of the deceased was terminally ill. The defendant killed those fifteen patients because he enjoyed doing so. He was exercising the ultimate power of controlling life and death, and repeated it so often that he must have found the drama of taking life to his taste.

Much has been written concerning the motive or lack of motive in Shipman's killings, Mrs Grundy apart. It is a common misapprehension that motive is an ingredient in the crime of murder; unhappily, many murders are without reason or motive. In others, the motive is known only to the killer. The prosecution need never prove a motive, although if they can identify one, their task in proving guilt is made more simple.

Dame Janet Smith wrote: 'If one defines motive as a rational or conscious explanation for the decision to commit a crime, I think Shipman's crimes were without motive. The psychiatrists warn me that it is possible that, in Shipman's own mind, there was a conscious motivation. All I can say is that there is no evidence of any of the features that I have observed, in my experience as a judge, that commonly motivate murderers.'*

For my part, I have concluded that, except for Mrs Grundy's case, the explanation is comparatively simple. Shipman enjoyed the thrill of killing his patients. It was not merely injecting them with morphine on the spurious pretext that he was taking blood, it was the subsequent drama of fobbing off the family, ensuring that no post-mortem took place, keeping control of the body, falsifying medical records, ensuring if possible that the body was cremated, and deceiving the undertaker and the coroner.

* *The Shipman Enquiry First Report*, Volume One.

Shipman was an expert in all these functions. He had achieved his purpose on some two hundred and fifteen occasions, if Dame Janet is correct, and that estimate is said to be a conservative one. Shipman must have enjoyed each episode, so often did he repeat it. He read crime novels by the score and had few if any leisure pursuits. He was a loner. Whilst some doctors with an hour or so to spare between morning and evening surgeries might go to the golf club, Shipman would go out and kill a patient.

My opening, which lasted for the best part of a day, dealt individually with each killing and, of course, the forgery. There was not an empty seat in court. The adjacent courtroom had an audio link, and the approaches to the court were dominated by television cameras and assembled crowds. It was an action replay of the trial six years before, taking place in the very court where I had spent most of my formative years. This was a home fixture, but very much more demanding than the trial of Thompson and Venables in terms of detail. Emotionally, however, there was little to choose between the two. Intense sympathy for James's family in one, and similar feelings for the many bereaved families in the other. Only sixteen murder convictions would satisfy the many relatives.

## The Fraudulent Will

Shipman's supporters were now merely his wife and two sons, who attended daily and were shown to their reserved seats shortly before the court sat. The initial intense support of his devoted patients had melted away as a grim realisation permeated Hyde. When I drove home that night, my thoughts were with those relatives who faced the ordeal of giving evidence.

More often than not, a daughter faced the trauma of describing the moment she discovered her mother, who had died suddenly and for no apparent reason. The daughter was then confronted by Shipman, who railroaded her into accepting that nothing would be achieved by a post-mortem. Only recently had the horrific realisation dawned that the man in whom she had placed such trust, often over many years, was a serial killer who for no comprehensible reason had taken her mother's life. Now the daughter faced a large, crowded court and the terrifying experience of giving evidence awaited by millions of people. There was real terror in the thought of breaking down and being unable to articulate an experience that few will ever know.

The prosecution began with Counts 1 and 2, the forgery of the will of Kathleen Grundy and the murder of Kathleen Grundy.

Shipman made many errors. Selecting Mrs Grundy as his final victim was one of them. Her daughter, Angela Woodruff, was a solicitor and a lady of considerable substance, though even she was described as looking drawn and distressed throughout her time in the witness box. It was easy to foresee the ordeal that awaited her. She would face the absurd suggestion made on behalf of Shipman that her mother was a drug addict and that her mother had disinherited her in favour of her doctor.

As Angela Woodruff entered the witness box, I knew that she required every assistance that an examining advocate can give. She visibly shook as she took a drink of water. Fortunately, there was an easy, albeit sad start to her evidence as she was taken through a bundle of photographs of her mother's home. Mrs Woodruff observed as an aside that she found it too painful to visit the house at present.

We moved to the moment she received the news of her mother's sudden death from the police in Hyde and her meeting with Shipman, when he told her that he had been to see her mother at her home on the morning of her death. Mrs Woodruff went on to say that she had been too distraught to remember what reason Shipman had given for visiting her mother at her home. Mrs Woodruff was then asked about her relationship with her mother and her mother's state of health.

These were easier topics and she spoke with great pride of her mother, describing her as amazing. They went for long walks together and after a five-mile walk, her mother would come in and ask where the ironing was. She was proud of her mother's contribution to civic life and to a number of charities, and of her relationship with her grandchildren, whom she adored. Nobody could have been further removed from a drug addict who had chosen to disinherit her family.

Turning to the will, Mrs Woodruff told the jury that since she qualified as a solicitor, she had conducted any necessary legal work on her mother's behalf. In 1986, she had drawn up Mrs Grundy's will, by which Mrs Grundy had made her daughter the sole beneficiary of her estate. After her mother's death, Mrs Woodruff became aware of the existence of what purported to be a new will and was immediately suspicious.

She visited the two patients of Shipman whose signatures appeared on the will as witnesses. Those meetings increased her misgivings and she reported her suspicions to the Warwickshire police where she lived. The Warwickshire police passed the investigation to the Greater Manchester police, who instantly realised that the doctor stated to be the beneficiary under the questioned will was the same doctor who had been the subject of a police investigation only a few months earlier.

The task facing Nicola Davies was immense, and she set about it in a measured but firm manner. It would have been so easy to alienate the jury permanently with a combination of aggression and a lack of sympathy. Nicola began by asking Mrs Woodruff about her financial situation and that of her husband, inferring that they were in no need of an inheritance. Both Mrs Woodruff and her husband had good incomes and Mr Woodruff had inherited over one million pounds from his father. She had put the family home in her husband's name to protect herself from being sued. Mrs Woodruff responded by saying that, even if her mother had come to the conclusion that she had no need for any inheritance, there were no circumstances in which she would have overlooked her grandchildren, whom she adored.

The suggestion was put gently that Mrs Woodruff was not seeing so much of her mother and there had been at the very least a cooling off in the relationship. Diary entries of Mrs Grundy were put to her daughter to demonstrate periods of no apparent contact. In a moment of some drama, Mrs Woodruff asked to look at her mother's diary and as she flicked through the pages, absolute silence prevailed in court. The issue was peripheral in the extreme, namely whether in 1998 Mrs Grundy had visited her daughter in Warwickshire as she had in previous years. When Mrs Woodruff found an entry that confirmed her mother's visit, she brandished the diary in victory. Mrs Grundy had taken a taxi to the station and there was proof of it.

As the cross-examination continued, Mrs Woodruff became more familiar with the process and more sure of her ground, particularly so when praising her mother and her role in civic life. When they last spoke a few days before Mrs Grundy died, she was talking of buying a new back door and changing her car. She would have given her old car to one of her grandsons, had he not been going to Japan. By the time Mrs Woodruff had completed her evidence, she had paid a fulsome and plainly accurate tribute to her mother.

In order to reinforce the description of Mrs Grundy, we called a number of witnesses to describe her contribution to life in Hyde. A charity shop worker, meals on wheels volunteers, and a former Mayoress all spoke volumes praising their great friend, who was a bundle of energy and loved by all. One such witness told of her pride in her family, that she often spoke of her grandsons, and one had got a job in Japan. She thought the world of her daughter Angela. During this passage of evidence, the mood of the court lifted somewhat until Mrs Clark, the former Mayoress and a very close friend, spoke of the day of the murder. They were due to meet at the lunch club and Mrs Grundy was always very punctual.

The evidence that Mrs Grundy was a healthy and energetic lady who loved her family could not have been stronger and so we moved to the alleged forgery. According to the will, Mrs Grundy had left all her property to Shipman and nothing to her daughter or grandchildren. The will stated that she wished to give all her estate to her doctor to reward him for 'all the care he has given to me and the people of Hyde. He is sensible enough to handle any problems this may give him.'

Mrs Grundy died on 24 June and on 28 June a letter was sent to Hamilton Ward Solicitors typed on the portable type-writer seized by the police from Shipman's surgery, the same typewriter used to create the questioned will. The letter purported to have been written by a friend of Mrs Grundy who had helped her to make her will, and it informed the solicitor of her death. It was signed J. Smith or possibly S. Smith. We were able to prove that Mrs Grundy knew no one with either of those names.

Brian Burgess was the solicitor at Hamilton Ward. His evidence was that the receipt of the 'will' was in itself a strange event, as Mrs Grundy was not a client of the firm, and his initial reaction was to put the document on the corner of his desk. When he learned of her death, he was instantly suspi-cious. It was manifest that this aspect of Shipman's criminality was destined to fail.

The two apparent witnesses to the will were similarly unhelpful to the defendant. Claire Hutchinson was a young mother, who indicated that her signature was a forgery. She did not think the handwriting was hers and explained how various letter forma-tions were inconsistent with her own. Paul Spencer was an unimpressive youth, who had sold his story to a tabloid and seemed to have only the vaguest recollection of any role in the creation of the document.

There followed the expert evidence relating to the will. Once the fingerprints of Brian Burgess, the solicitor, and his secretary had been eliminated, there was only one full print remaining, namely Shipman's little finger, and there was no print of Mrs Grundy. The will had been typed on Shipman's portable typewriter, as had the letter to the solicitors, and the signatures on the 'will' were described by a document examiner as crude forgeries. The importance of proving the forgery could not be overestimated. Not only did it prove a motive, it also destroyed Shipman's credibility, and we were satisfied at the conclusion of the forgery evidence that there was simply no answer to it; whatever scientific evidence we may be confronted with by the defence, the proof of forgery was a critical setback for Shipman.

Returning to the allegation of murder, Dr Rutherford was called to give evidence, one of nine visits to the witness box, as he had carried out post-mortems on all nine women who were buried. He was familiar with the witness box and is a man of style and authority. With a calm voice and an understanding of the need to assure relatives, he performed his task with respect for the deceased. He described Mrs Grundy as a very healthy woman with far fewer fatty deposits than could be expected in a woman her age. She did not die of old age or any natural cause. She had died of morphine toxicity.

Dr Grenville, our expert GP, having considered her medical notes, described Mrs Grundy as a fit, healthy woman. Although her notes described her as tired and generally unwell, that would not explain her sudden and unexpected death. He went on to describe how he would have conducted himself if he had been called to her home upon her body being discovered, which contrasted dramatically with Shipman's casual approach. He would ensure there were no suspicious circumstances and examine the body to confirm that death had in fact occurred; diagnosis of death is not always straightforward. If he found no pulse, he would look for a more central point, and might even contemplate resuscitation.

Finally, in relation to Mrs Grundy, we adduced evidence of unguarded statements by Shipman whilst in his surgery post Mrs Grundy's death. Realising he was about to be arrested, he broke down in the presence of District Nurse Marion Gilchrist and, in tears, said, 'I read thrillers and on the evidence they have, I would have me guilty. The only thing I did wrong was not having her cremated. If I had her cremated, I wouldn't be having all this trouble.'

On another occasion, about this time, he broke down in the presence of a patient, Lesley Pullford, saying, 'If I could bring her back and sit her in that chair, I would say look at all the trouble it's caused. I was going to say I don't want the money, but because of all this trouble, I will have it. We have had a meeting, the staff and I, and decided what to do with the money if we get it. We will have a week off each and on the anniversary of her death, give so much to old people's homes, and if anyone had a baby that day, give the money to a charity of their choice.'

It was these bizarre utterances that caused me to believe before the trial that there was a real possibility of Shipman admitting his guilt and advancing a defence of diminished responsibility, which would reduce the crimes from murder to manslaughter, if successful. Having observed Shipman in the witness box, however, I have no doubt that his arrogance, conceit, and contempt for those he considered to be his intellectual inferiors, coupled with his precious professional reputation, would in no circumstances permit Shipman either to confess his guilt or admit to an abnormality of mind.

The trial continued with Count 3, the alleged murder of Bianka Pomfret.

## The Burial Cases

*Bianka Pomfret* was a divorced lady aged forty-nine, living alone and with a long history of psychiatric illness. She was seen through her front window sitting on a settee by a support worker, who had come to visit her. She looked an unusual colour and the support worker thought she was dead and contacted her son. Subsequently, Shipman arrived and announced that Mrs Pomfret had died of a heart attack. He asked her son if he knew about the angina and he said he did not. Shipman said he had seen her earlier and she had complained of chest pains, and he had told her to make another appointment if they continued. He was abrupt in his manner and recorded that the principal cause of death was coronary thrombosis.

Shortly after her death, her psychiatrist, Dr Tate, contacted Shipman worried that perhaps his patient had committed suicide. Shipman assured Dr Tate that she died of a heart attack, saying she had been found with a 'thready pulse' by paramedics who tried to resuscitate her. He said that he had previously taken an ECG reading, but the result had been insignificant. The conversation was noted by Dr Tate, a note to which he referred in evidence. Shipman's problem was that the whole conversation was a lie. Mrs Pomfret was never treated by paramedics and he had never taken an ECG. He compounded his problems by altering her medical history with five false entries.

The computer examination unit established that a computer entry of 21 April 1997, showing that she did not attend the surgery, was deleted on 10 December 1997, the day of her death, with an entry: 'Chest Pain Vague? Angina smokes 40 plus per day'. In all there were five false entries, designed to show untruthfully that Mrs Pomfret had a history of angina. Dr Grenville's evidence was that without the five new computer entries, all made post-death, there was no evidence of her suffering angina or any form of heart disease. Dr Grenville would have contacted the coroner's office, stating that he was unable to give cause of death in a patient who was not seen at the time of her death. The five false computer entries, coupled with the lies told to Dr Tate, made this an unanswerable allegation.

*Winifred Mellor* was a widow, aged seventy-three, and there was an abundance of evidence that she was very fit and in the best of health. She died on 11 May 1998. Unbeknown to Shipman, he had been observed by Mrs Mellor's neighbour, Mrs Ellis, visiting Winifred Mellor's home at 3.00 p.m. She saw Shipman again about 6.30 p.m., when he called at her house asking if there was any way of getting into Mrs Mellor's home; as he could see her seated in a chair in her front room, but could not gain access.

Mrs Ellis had a key and she and her husband accompanied Shipman into Mrs Mellor's front room, where she was slumped in a chair. Shipman merely flicked her right arm by lifting her fingers up with his and then letting her arm drop, announcing, 'This lady's gone.' Mrs Ellis found his conduct callous and disrespectful of the deceased.

That evening, the family gathered together with Father Maher, in order that Mrs Mellor could be given the last rites. Shipman arrived at the house and announced that Mrs Mellor had suffered from angina, a condition he diagnosed in August 1997. This was a surprise to the family and, as in Mrs Pomfret's case, Mrs Mellor's medical notes were altered between her death and her body being discovered, to create the false impression that she had a pre-existing condition of angina. Similarly, Shipman lied to the family by telling them that Mrs Mellor had twice phoned the surgery on the day of her death. The itemised telephone records proved that no such phone calls were ever made.

As if those incontrovertible facts were not damaging enough, Father Maher's evidence was damning. He described Shipman as being 'very uncaring, extremely insensitive'; he was also very rushed and dismissive. He told of Shipman asking the family, 'Have you got an undertaker?' Father Maher intervened and said he would help the family with that, but Shipman took no notice of what he had said. This was one of several examples of Shipman endeavouring to keep control of the body and, if possible, ensure cremation rather than burial. Again, both pathologist and GP were united in the opinion that the cause of death was morphine toxicity, as indeed they were in every burial case.

*Joan Melia* was a divorced woman, aged seventy-three when she died on 12 June 1998. She lived alone. On the morning of that day, she visited Shipman's surgery and was prescribed some antibiotic tablets for a respiratory tract infection. She was accompanied on the way home by friends and told them that she expected a visit that afternoon at her home by Dr Shipman.

A friend, Derek Steele, stayed with her until 2.00 p.m. At about 5.00 p.m., Steele rang her and received no reply. He went round and let himself in, and he found Mrs Melia sitting motionless in a chair. He rang Shipman, who arrived and simply said, 'The tablets haven't had time to work.' He never examined Mrs Melia and issued a death certificate indicating that she had died from pneumonia.

When a few days later Mrs Melia's niece asked Shipman for an explanation, he said that he had considered sending her to hospital, but had decided that she could have died on the way to hospital and so advised her to go home to bed. Dr Rutherford in his post-mortem found that the lung disease present was minimal and not of sufficient severity to account for death. The presence of pneumonia was not confirmed and in his opinion the cause of death was morphine toxicity. In reality, the only explanation was that Shipman did visit as she had expected between 2.00 p.m. and 5.00 p.m. and injected her with a fatal dose of morphine, as confirmed by Julie Evans, the scientist.

*Ivy Lomas* was a widow, who was aged sixty-three when she died on 29 May 1997. She lived alone and her case differs from others in one material respect. She did not die at home, but died in Shipman's surgery. She was a regular attender there and, quite remarkably, Shipman himself was to say to Police Sergeant Reade, who was called to the surgery after Mrs Lomas's death, that he considered her such a nuisance that he had laughingly considered having part of the seating area reserved for Mrs Lomas, even mounting a plaque above a seat to the effect: 'Seat permanently reserved for Ivy Lomas'. Whilst she was a regular attender at the surgery, none of her complaints or ailments were life-threatening.

On the day of her death, she was out and about in the morning. Later in the afternoon, she told a neighbour that she was experiencing pain in her chest, but was in no great discomfort. About 3.30 p.m., she walked to the bus and from the bus to Shipman's surgery, arriving early for a 4.00 p.m. appointment. Dr Shipman arrived at 3.55 p.m. and within minutes activated the buzzer for Mrs Lomas to enter his room.

Carol Chapman was the receptionist on duty and shortly afterwards, she heard Mrs Lomas and Dr Shipman walk from his room to the treatment room. Some twenty-five minutes later, Shipman appeared looking tired and flushed, saying in a loud voice, 'I'm sorry about the wait. I've just had a problem with the ECG machine.' He then saw three further patients, before calling Carol Chapman into his consulting room.

He told her, 'I put her on the ECG machine, but there was nothing there.' He then said that Mrs Lomas had died despite his attempts at resuscitation. After that, Shipman simply continued seeing his patients, whilst Mrs Lomas lay dead in the treatment room. The emergency services were never called and no attempt was made to call any assistance. When Shipman did call the police, it was purely with a view to relations being traced and informed.

Sergeant Reade arrived at the surgery at 6.00 p.m. and Shipman immediately said that he was in a position to issue a death certificate, but was having trouble tracing and contacting the next of kin. Sergeant Reade left the surgery and contacted Mrs Lomas's son, who was unwell, and when the sergeant returned to the surgery, he learned that Shipman had contacted a relative and that funeral directors were on their way to remove the deceased.

At this stage, the sergeant asked Shipman for his account and Shipman gave a version that was very much at odds with Mrs Chapman's recollection. He said that Mrs Lomas had come in with a bronchial problem and he had shown her into the treatment room, so she could rest whilst he saw to other patients. When he returned to the treatment room, she had died. This account omits any mention of his spending twenty-five minutes with Mrs Lomas in the treatment room, and also makes no mention of the ECG machine.

Later that evening, Shipman saw Mrs Lomas's daughter at her mother's home, and gave to her yet a third version of her mother's final minutes. In this conversation, Shipman said that he asked Mrs Lomas to sit in the examination room whilst he examined another patient, and when he returned to her, she was blue around the mouth and had died of a massive heart attack. He certified the cause of death as coronary thrombosis.

Mrs Lomas was buried in Hyde Cemetery and when exhumed, samples revealed very high levels of morphine. Dr Rutherford found some minor lung disease and some coronary artery disease, but 'it was not uncommon in routine autopsy practice to find a similar degree in people who have died from other causes'. He had no doubt that the cause of death was morphine toxicity.

In this case, three computer entries all made post-death were highly incriminating. The first made at 4.57 p.m., shortly after her death, merely said, 'Seen in surgery'. The following day he made two further entries, one reading, 'Chest pain. Lots of problems at home clinically ct (coronary thrombosis)' and later, 'O/E dead'. The jury were asked to consider why Shipman failed to make all three entries together, given that he was aware of Mrs Lomas's death when he made the first entry.

Dr Grenville spoke with particular emphasis in this case, the events having taken place within a doctor's surgery, stating that if Shipman had thought that Mrs Lomas had a coronary thrombosis, he should have devoted his entire attention to her and should not have left her, except to make an emergency phone call. Resuscitation should have been attempted. An ECG recording would have added nothing to Shipman's clinical diagnosis and it would be very poor practice to spend twenty or twenty-five minutes having technical problems with the ECG machine, whilst the patient was in a critical condition.

Dr Grenville pointed out that Shipman never called for help. Cardiopulmonary resuscitation is difficult to perform alone and the success rate is increased if performed by two or more competent people. His behaviour in leaving Mrs Lomas to attend to three other patients was unusual to say the least. Further, no printout from the ECG machine was with her medical notes.

When Shipman came to be cross-examined, this case was to prove especially problematical for him, indeed as it transpired, quite impossible.

*Marie Quinn* was a widow aged sixty-seven when she died. On the day of her death, she was well and up and about. Around 2.00 p.m., she made two phone calls, one to a family friend in which she sounded chirpy, the other to her son John in Japan, in which there was no mention of feeling unwell. Some six hours later, Shipman phoned Ellen Hanratty, a close friend of Marie Quinn, informing her that Mrs Quinn had died. He said that Mrs Quinn had phoned the surgery saying that she was unwell. He had gone to her home and found she had had a stroke. When Mrs Hanratty asked if he had admitted her to hospital, he replied that it was too late for that. Shipman asked for permission to have the body removed and asked Mrs Hanratty to contact Mrs Quinn's son John.

Some two hours later, John Quinn telephoned Shipman from Japan and was told that his mother had phoned the surgery about 6.00 p.m., saying she thought she had suffered a stroke and she was paralysed down one side of her body. He told her to leave the front door on the latch and he would come up and see her after the end of evening surgery. He had arrived thirty minutes later to find her in the back kitchen, 'breathing her last'.

Shipman's account of Mrs Quinn's death is demonstrably false. Telephone billing shows that no phone call was made from Mrs Quinn's home to the surgery. Anyhow, it defies belief that no call would be made to the emergency services if a person living alone suffered a stroke causing paralysis down one side. Further on Shipman's account, Mrs Quinn, notwithstanding her stroke and partial paralysis, had been able to make a phone call from her front living room, open the front door, and then make her way to the rear kitchen. In reality, her door was such that it could not be left on the latch and Shipman already had a key to the house. Shipman issued a death certificate giving the cause of death as: 1. (a) Cerebrovascular accident (b) Arteriosclerosis (c) Hypertension, 2. Scleroderma.

John Quinn returned from Japan and spoke with Shipman, who explained that scleroderma, a hardening of the skin, causes a progressive narrowing of the arteries leading to kidney damage and eventual failure. The disease had caused hypertension in the final year of her life and the actual cause of her death was a stroke. When John Quinn questioned why Shipman had not come sooner, or arranged for his mother to be hospitalised, Shipman assured him that nothing more could have been done for her. Had she survived, he said, she would have been in hospital paralysed with no quality of life whatsoever, merely waiting for an inevitable second stroke.

Mrs Quinn was buried and later her body was exhumed, and as in all such cases, tissue samples contained a very high proportion of morphine indicative of a rapid death. Dr Rutherford concluded that the stated cause of death did not correlate with the pathological evidence. Scleroderma was not confirmed at autopsy and, even if it had been, would not pose a threat to life. He was satisfied that the cause of death was morphine toxicity.

Dr Grenville examined Mrs Quinn's medical record and could find no evidence of either arteriosclerosis or hypertension. The jury were left to consider why Shipman had visited her home, when it was proven that no phone call had been made.

*Irene Turner*, a widow, was aged sixty-seven when she died. She had a complex medical history, including a heart attack in 1994 and breast cancer successfully treated that same year. On 10 July 1996, she had recently returned from holiday and was being occasionally sick. Her daughter suggested she ring Shipman's surgery, which she did, and the following day her son-in-law visited at 1.00 p.m. and found Mrs Turner in bed awaiting the doctor. Although unwell, she was in her usual good spirits. At 2.15 p.m. that afternoon, Mrs Turner got out of bed to call her son-in-law concerning some shopping he was to do for her.

At 3.25 p.m., a neighbour, Sheila Ward, observed Shipman visiting Mrs Turner and it appears that Shipman realised he had been seen, because he knocked on Mrs Ward's door and asked her if she would assist Mrs Turner to pack some belongings, as she would be going to hospital. Strikingly, he asked her to 'delay going over to Irene's for a few minutes'. The prosecution contended that in all likelihood Shipman had just injected Mrs Turner and was ensuring that Mrs Ward did not visit before Mrs Turner had died.

When Mrs Ward did go round five minutes later, she found the front door unlocked and discovered Mrs Turner lying motionless on the bed in her night clothes. Shipman had told Mrs Ward that he had to carry out some tests, and soon after she had found Mrs Turner, Shipman returned. He went into the bedroom, came out and said, 'I think the lady's dead.'

Mrs Ward asked, 'Was it cancer?' and he replied, 'No, it was diabetes.' He went on to say that if he had sent her to hospital, it would have been too late, remarking that from the test he had just done, there was a substance in her blood and her whole body had been affected by her condition. By the preceding Tuesday, it had been too late to deal with it.

Mrs Ward immediately contacted Mr Woodruff, Mrs Turner's son-in-law, who went to her home, where Shipman stated that there was no necessity for a post-mortem. 'With the amount of tablets that Irene was on, I'll be able to issue a death certificate.' He said that he had wanted Mrs Turner to go into hospital, but she refused. The prosecution asserted that was a clear lie, because Shipman had asked Mrs Ward to assist her to pack a bag as she would be going into hospital, and since she had died on his return, there was no opportunity for her to refuse. Further, there had been no contact with Thameside General Hospital with any view as to an admission.

The following day, a family friend, Albert Isherwood, called at Shipman's surgery to collect the death certificate. He asked Shipman to explain Mrs Turner's death. He said she died from a combination of diabetes and blood pressure and said it was known as ischaemic heart disease, whereby 'the veins in the arms and legs collapse and everything goes to the centre. Mrs Turner would have slipped away into a coma and died peacefully.' The death certificate signed by Shipman stated that the cause of death was circulatory failure, ischaemic heart disease, diabetes mellitus and hypertension.

Mrs Turner was buried and thereafter exhumed. Dr Evans again concluded from her examination of thigh muscle that death was due to a substantial dose of diamorphine, suggesting a rapid death. Dr Rutherford's examination revealed some degree of coronary artery disease, but having considered Dr Evans' findings, he concluded that death was due to morphine toxicity.

*Jean Lilley* was a married woman, the only deceased in this case to be so. She was fifty-eight years old and did not enjoy the best of health, having suffered with angina, arthritis and a lung condition, and received regular treatment from Shipman. During the last week of her life she suffered with a cold and her husband, Albert Lilley, persuaded her to arrange a home visit from Shipman.

Albert Lilley was a lorry driver, who left home at 5.00 a.m. on 25 April 1997. That afternoon he received a phone call on his mobile phone from Shipman, in which the doctor stated that he had been with Mrs Lilley for quite a while trying to convince her to go to hospital, but she refused because her husband was not at home. He went on to say that he would return after evening surgery when Mr Lilley would be home, but that it was too late. By that bizarre and circuitous route, Mr Lilley was informed that his wife had died.

Elizabeth Hunter was a very close friend of Mrs Lilley and lived in the flat above her. She had visited Mrs Lilley on the morning of the 25th and found her to be in good spirits, despite feeling tired and unwell that week. She was laughing and joking, and about 11.55 a.m., Mrs Hunter left her friend and returned to her flat. At about 12.10 p.m., she saw Shipman park his vehicle outside the address and walk towards Mrs Lilley's flat. She thought no more about it, but after some forty or fifty minutes, she became increasingly concerned about the length of time Shipman had been with Mrs Lilley. She decided to go and see if everything was in order.

As she walked down the stairs, she saw Shipman leaving Mrs Lilley's flat, only some six feet away, walking towards his vehicle. Mrs Lilley's front door was always unlocked and Mrs Hunter entered, shouting, 'It's only me, Mrs,' whereupon she saw Jean Lilley sitting motionless on the settee with one arm across her stomach and the other dropped down her side. Mrs Hunter immediately went outside to see if she could recall Shipman, but he had driven off.

She returned to find Mrs Lilley fully clothed, but her hand was cold despite the flat always being kept warm. Mrs Lilley was blue around the lips and Mrs Hunter attempted mouth-to-mouth resuscitation without success and then rang Shipman's surgery and was advised by a receptionist to ring for an ambulance, which she did. The ambulance arrived quickly and the paramedics examined Mrs Lilley. She appeared to them to have been dead for some time and blood had begun to settle.

Later that afternoon, Shipman arrived at the flat and Mrs Hunter instantly challenged him, saying, 'You must have known she was dead.' Shipman denied that he had known of her condition and explained that he had tried to get Mrs Lilley to go to hospital, but she had refused, the same line of defence that he had deployed in Mrs Turner's case. He went on to tell Mrs Hunter that he had intended to return to further attempt to get Mrs Lilley to go to hospital after the end of his surgery. Mrs Hunter expressed incredulity at her friend's refusal, knowing her as she did, but Shipman countered with the words, 'Well, she was very poorly and she had heart failure.'

Mrs Hunter became very distressed and described Shipman's manner as blasé and uncaring. He did not examine Mrs Lilley at all. When the paramedics arrived, according to them, Shipman gave an unusually deep explanation and details of Mrs Lilley's pulmonary history and stressed that there was no requirement for a post-mortem. On hearing that Mrs Lilley's daughter was due to visit, he seemed unduly anxious to leave before she arrived. He issued a death certificate giving the cause of death as heart failure, ischaemic heart disease, hypertension, fibrosing arthritis and hypercholesterolemia.

Mrs Lilley was buried and her body was later exhumed. Dr Evans found a lethal quantity of diamorphine in her body tissue, sufficient to bring about rapid death. Dr Rutherford found some narrowing of the arteries, but not of the severity to bring about sudden unexpected death. He had no hesitation in concluding that the cause of death was morphine toxicity.

*Muriel Grimshaw* was the ninth and final burial case. In those cases, there was no selection process by the prosecution team. Every body exhumed was found to have a lethal quantity of morphine within them. Mrs Grimshaw was a widow aged seventy-six years, in good health and an infrequent visitor to the surgery. On Sunday, 13 July, she had gone to church with her daughter and gave no concern as to her health. She had suffered a degree of arthritis and high blood pressure, but her condition was well managed and she had not visited the surgery for some six weeks.

About 9.00 a.m. the following Tuesday, 15 July, Mrs Ryan, a friend of Mrs Grimshaw, called at her home by arrangement so that they could go shopping together. There was no response, so Mrs Ryan returned to her own flat and telephoned, but again there was no reply. Mrs Ryan contacted Mrs Grimshaw's daughter, Ann Brown, who went immediately to her mother's and let herself in with her own key. She found her mother lying on her bed, fully clothed and motionless. She immediately contacted Shipman by phone and he attended a short time later. He made no bodily examination of Mrs Grimshaw, but commented, 'It was a good way to go.' He made no mention of any cause of death, but stated that there was no need for a post-mortem.

He later issued a death certificate stating that the cause of death was cerebrovascular accident, hypertension with a contributing factor of rheumatoid arthritis. The certificate bore a correction. The original date entered was 15 July, which had been altered to the 14th. It also bore a falsity, namely that Shipman had seen Mrs Grimshaw on 2 July 1997. The purpose of that false statement was to obviate the necessity for a post-mortem, as the doctor appeared on the face of the certificate to have seen the deceased within fourteen days of her death.

This was yet another case where an examination of the computer records produced damning evidence. Firstly, there was an entry timed and dated 14 July 14.06.24, reading, 'Seen in own home.' When Shipman spoke to Ann Brown, he made no mention of having seen her mother the day before she was found dead. The prosecution contended that it was inconceivable that he would fail to mention such a meeting, unless of course it had taken place and he had then murdered her.

The next incriminating entry was devastating and indefensible. It was made on 15 July at 13.14.36 and read, 'On Examination Dead. CVA (cardiovascular accident), hypertension, RA (rheumatoid arthritis) last seen 2/7/97 died 1800 14.7.97.' Since the body had not been discovered until the 15th, Shipman could not possibly have known when she died unless he had killed her.

Further, there is no entry in her medical records showing that she was seen on 2 July. Appointment sheets, a home visits diary, drug history details and all manual records were inspected and there was no record in existence showing that Mrs Grimshaw was seen on 2 July. This we submitted was clearly a falsified entry intended to create a false medical history, with a view to avoiding a post-mortem on the basis of a visit within fourteen days of death.

Mrs Grimshaw was buried and in due course her body was exhumed. Dr Evans made her invariable discovery and Dr Rutherford's findings did not correlate with the cause of death as stated on the death certificate. He again concluded that the cause of death was morphine toxicity.

The conclusion of the burial cases permitted a moment or so of reflection on the progress of the prosecution case.

Everything had thus far proceeded as we had anticipated. Both scientist and pathologist were unshaken in their findings; nervous relatives had come up to proof, and whilst the defence had chipped away at minor inconsistencies in recollection, no inroad of any significance had been made. Shipman was almost in permanent motion, scribbling notes and grabbing Ian Winter's gown furiously, emphasising points he wished to be made on his behalf. He was at his most animated when Dr Grenville was in the witness box, feeling no doubt that a professional colleague was showing a degree of disloyalty.

Shipman had no reason to be critical of those representing him. His defence was being conducted skilfully and elegantly in the face of a torrent of incriminating evidence. In the prosecution camp, the only lingering apprehension was the volume of expert evidence from highly qualified scientists and doctors advancing an alternative explanation for each of the deaths. All that, however, was some time away.

## The Cremation Cases

The cremation cases appeared, initially at least, to be somewhat weaker than the burial cases. There was, of course, no evidence of morphine toxicity, nor any pathological evidence. The evidence was necessarily circumstantial, an expression all too often deployed by defence advocates to denote weakness. However, good circumstantial evidence can be devastating. It does not rely on the truthfulness or accuracy of witnesses, nor in this case on resolving differences between experts; it relies upon a combination of proven facts.

In each of the six cases, the victims were far from terminally ill. In four of the six cases, Shipman admitted to being present at the death, in one the victim was found within half an hour of Shipman's visit and in the other Shipman contended he had found the deceased.

All six deceased were found sitting peacefully in a chair or on a sofa. In no case had Shipman been called on account of a sudden deterioration in the health of the deceased. In only one case had a phone call to the surgery been made, despite Shipman's contention to the contrary, and post-death alteration of medical records was a regular theme.

*Lizzie Adams* was a widow, aged seventy-seven years, who lived alone. She was active and in a good state of health. She had been a dancing teacher and continued to dance on a regular basis with her dancing partner, William Catlow. She had a mild form of diabetes, which was diet-controlled, and she had recently returned from a holiday in Malta when she died. She had been feeling a little unwell with a cold when she returned home on Wednesday, 26 February 1997 in the early hours of the morning. Later that day, she received separate visits from her two daughters, who found their mother in good spirits but slightly under the weather.

On Thursday, 27 February, one of her daughters, Doreen Thorley, went shopping with her and found her again in good spirits, but with a sore throat and dry cough. Accordingly, the following day Mrs Thorley went to Shipman's surgery to collect a prescription that Mrs Adams had ordered by phone from the surgery. It was a prescription for Ceporex, a form of antibiotic.

On Friday, 28 February, Mrs Thorley phoned her mother at home. After some delay in answering, because she was hanging out washing, Mrs Adams told her daughter that one of the pills prescribed by Dr Shipman had nearly blown her head off. Mrs Adams phoned the surgery at 12.10 p.m. requesting a home visit because she felt poorly, the tablets were not agreeing with her, and she felt dizzy, sick and wobbly.

At about 2.00 p.m., William Catlow, Mrs Adams' long-term dancing partner, called at her home. The front door was open, which was unusual as Mrs Adams was very security conscious.

On entering, Mr Catlow saw Shipman standing in the lounge looking at Mrs Adams' collection of Royal Doulton figurines. Shipman immediately turned to Mr Catlow and said, 'Are you Bill?' and then said, 'Betty is very ill. I'm sending her away. I've called an ambulance.'

Mr Catlow rushed past Shipman into the living room and to Mrs Adams, and said that he thought she had fainted. Shipman bent over Mrs Adams and replied, 'She's gone. I'd better cancel the ambulance.' Mr Catlow asked if he was sure, because Mrs Adams was still warm and looked as if she was only asleep. Shipman went to the phone as if cancelling the ambulance, but this was a cynical charade. No phone call was made that day either summonsing or cancelling an ambulance. Shipman had been waiting for Mrs Adams to die when he was disturbed by Mr Catlow.

Shipman telephoned Mrs Adams' daughter, Doreen Thorley, who ran to her mother's home and observed that her mother seemed as if she was asleep. Her clothing was not disturbed and she held her mother's hand, which was still warm. Shipman told Mrs Thorley that her mother had died from chronic pneumonia and that a post-mortem was not required because he had attended her, and she should get in touch with the funeral directors. He gave the impression that as a daughter she should have seen her mother more often, an observation that Mrs Thorley found most hurtful. He told her to visit the surgery the following day to collect the death certificate.

Sonia Jones, Mrs Adams' other daughter, went to the surgery in order to ascertain the circumstances of her mother's death, bearing in mind her state of health upon return from her holiday in Malta. Shipman explained that her mother had only just managed to answer the front door to him because she was so ill and that he had to help her into the back room. He had called for an ambulance, whereupon he asked Bill if he would wait with Mrs Adams while he went to visit another patient around the corner, and that he would be back before the ambulance arrived.

He recounted the discovery of the death and that he then cancelled the ambulance before phoning Mrs Thorley. He said there was no need for a post-mortem, because he knew what was wrong with her. On the death certificate, he recorded that a neighbour and himself were present at the moment of death. Shipman told others that he had advised Mrs Adams that she should be moved to hospital, but she had refused.

Dr Grenville gave evidence, and without the toxicology evidence of Dr Evans and the pathology of Dr Rutherford, he was now centre stage. He began by pointing out that a natural death at home during a doctor's visit is an extremely rare event in the experience of most general practitioners. In the present case, however, the event was apparently most frequent. That single observation was possibly the most telling of much valuable evidence from Dr Grenville. He continued by explaining that bronchopneumonia does not bring about sudden death. The patient is very ill for a few hours before death and, in Mrs Adams' case, she had been out shopping the previous day and done a variety of household jobs on the morning of the day she died.

Shipman's treatment of her was anyhow inappropriate. Had she been as ill as he claimed to relatives, he should have called an ambulance immediately, and if she had been unwilling to go, he should have called her daughter. If Mrs Adams really had collapsed, he should have tried to resuscitate her, and it was obvious from all the evidence that he had made no attempt to do so. The stated cause of death, namely bronchopneumonia, was inconsistent with the observations of the witnesses, namely that Mrs Adams was sitting peacefully immediately after death. Patients who die of lack of oxygen due to very severe chest infection become distressed prior to death, whereas Mrs Adams appeared to be asleep.

In cross-examination Shipman's case was put, namely that he never mentioned calling an ambulance, but plainly there was little scope for a conclusion that William Catlow or Sonia Jones were mistaken on that issue. The similarity with Jean Lilley's case cannot have escaped the jury.

*Kathleen Wagstaff* was a widow, aged eighty-two, who lived alone in a first-floor flat. She was in excellent health for her age. On the morning she died, she had visited a building society in Hyde and made a withdrawal, and around lunchtime she went shopping. About 1.45 p.m., Carol Chapman, the surgery receptionist, saw Shipman leave the surgery. He gave no indication of where he was going.

In fact, he went to Mrs Wagstaff's flat later that afternoon and was seen to enter by Margaret Walker, who lived in the ground floor flat below. He rang the bell and Mrs Wagstaff came downstairs to open the door. She heard Mrs Wagstaff say, 'Fancy seeing you here.' She seemed surprised to see him, but greeted him and invited him in. Mrs Walker then went out, leaving her husband in the downstairs flat. Within half an hour, there was a knock on the door. It was Shipman. He identified himself and then said he had been to see Mrs Wagstaff and that she was dead.

Shortly afterwards, Shipman went to a nearby primary school and asked to speak to Angela Wagstaff. He told her that her mother was ill and that she had required a home visit. He said he was nearby when he received the call and so had visited her. He had gone to get his bag from the car and when he returned, her mother had died. She had not suffered. Shipman said he would see her at her mother's home. This was a terrible mistake by Shipman; Angela Wagstaff was not Kathleen Wagstaff's daughter, but her daughter-in-law. She ran to her own mother's home and there was her mother alive and well at the door. Shipman soon learned of his blunder. He rang his surgery and told Carol Chapman that Mrs Wagstaff was dead and that he had contacted her daughter at school.

Carol Chapman pointed out his mistake. In evidence, she confirmed that no call had been made to the surgery by Kathleen Wagstaff and no call had been made to Shipman's pager unit asking him to go to Mrs Wagstaff's home.

Mrs Wagstaff's son Peter was informed of his mother's death and went to her flat, where he found his mother slumped in a chair. Shipman told him that his mother had telephoned the surgery asking for a visit, and that the surgery had paged him. All that was untrue, as both the telephone billing and Carol Chapman confirmed. He went on to say that he had found Mrs Wagstaff looking ill, very grey, sweating and blue around the mouth. He had helped her upstairs and settled her in her chair.

He said that he had found that her pulse was 'thready', so he had called for an ambulance. He went to his car to fetch his bag and when he returned, he found that Mrs Wagstaff was slumped over and had died. He had checked her pulse and then cancelled the ambulance. Again, as in Mrs Lilley's case and in Mrs Wagstaff's case, telephone billing proved that there had been no call to the ambulance services. Shipman concluded by saying that she had died of a heart attack and had a heart disease of a kind that could carry you off quite easily. Mr Wagstaff was surprised, as he was unaware that his mother had any heart problem.

The death certificate issued by Dr Shipman gave the cause of death as: I. (a) Coronary Thrombosis (b) Ischaemic Heart Disease. Dr Grenville said that Mrs Wagstaff's records showed that she had been very healthy for her age and there was no sign of heart disease. There were two entries showing raised blood pressure, but no real hypertension. If Mrs Wagstaff had collapsed in the way Shipman claimed, he should have called an ambulance immediately, as every effort should have been made to resuscitate her.

This was a comparatively straightforward case. Yet again a fit and healthy woman died suddenly and unexpectedly during a home visit by a general practitioner, a very rare event. Shipman had lied about a call to the surgery, he had lied about a call to his pager unit, and he had lied about calling and cancelling an ambulance. He gave Peter Wagstaff an untrue account of his mother's medical history. There was no good reason for Shipman to visit Mrs Wagstaff that day. The only rational explanation for all these events was that Shipman called upon Mrs Wagstaff intending to kill her. There was no other explanation for her sudden death.

*Norah Nuttall* was a widow, aged sixty-four when she died. She lived with her son Anthony. She enjoyed good general health, although her medical records described her as obese and suffering from a number of chronic conditions, including breathlessness on exertion and oedema of the legs. She was, however, active and often went into Hyde to shop and meet friends, and was seen out and about on the morning of her death. She was killing time waiting to go to the doctor's, which she could do after 11.00 a.m. without an appointment; she said she had a cough and wanted some medicine. Her friend Anne Robinson recalled that she was not actually coughing and she looked well, happy in herself, and very smart.

Mrs Nuttall did visit the surgery and an entry appears on her medical record timed at 10.41 a.m., which reads 'acute wheezy bronchitis'. At 12.19 p.m., she telephoned a friend, Mary Oliver, telling her that she had been given some cough medicine. They chatted away and there was no indication that Mrs Nuttall was in any kind of critical condition; the call ended with her saying she was going to have a bit of dinner. At 2.00 p.m., her son Anthony returned from work and saw the cough medicine, and said his mother seemed no different to when he had seen her in the morning.

Shortly before 3.00 p.m., Anthony left the house. He returned thirty minutes later and was met by Shipman at the front door.

He was surprised to see the doctor, as his mother had never mentioned a home visit. Shipman said that his mother was not well and that he had called an ambulance. Anthony Nuttall went into the front room and saw his mother slumped in a chair, as if she was asleep. He kneeled in front of her and took her hands, gently shaking them to try and wake her up. Shipman then intervened and said, 'Oh, she looks to have taken a turn for the worse.' He appeared to feel for a pulse in her neck, before telling Anthony Nuttall that his mother had passed away.

He stated that he would cancel the ambulance, whereupon he went to the telephone and seemed to be doing just that. Yet again, this was a complete sham. Telephone billing proved that he had neither called nor cancelled an ambulance, which was confirmed by the Manchester Ambulance Service records. This was an action replay of both Mrs Adams' case and Mrs Wagstaff's case, involving identical lies by Shipman in all three cases.

Having been told of his mother's death, Anthony asked Shipman if he had spoken to his mother, and Shipman stated that she had complained of chest pains. He happened to be nearby when he got the call and had come round straightaway. This was also a repetition of the lie that he told in Mrs Wagstaff's case. There had been no call to the surgery and none from the surgery to Shipman's pager. No attempt was made to render any first aid or to resuscitate the patient. When Anthony expressed concern that no effort had been made to revive his mother, Shipman stated that there was nothing he could do, as he could see that his mother had died of ventricular failure.

Shipman recorded on the death certificate that the cause of death was: 1. (a) Ventricular failure (b) Congestive heart failure (c) Hypertension with the significant condition contributing to death being obesity. Dr Grenville said that Shipman's claim to have found Mrs Nuttall in a poorly condition did not tally with her son's description of her condition only minutes earlier. This was again a case of a sudden and unexpected death occurring during a home visit by a general practitioner, normally a very rare event.

Shipman's description of the death was not typical of ventricular heart failure, in which the patient would be gasping for breath and usually producing froth at the mouth and nose. If as Shipman suggested, Mrs Nuttall appeared to have stopped breathing, she should have been resuscitated, especially as she was only sixty-four, and two persons were present and thus able to attempt to do so. Dr Grenville's evidence, together with Shipman's multiple lies, rendered this a strong case.

*Pamela Hillier* was aged sixty-eight when she died; she was a widow and lived alone, but she had a busy active life and walked her dog several times a day. She had been diagnosed as having high blood pressure in 1995, which was treated successfully, and she continued to take medication for hypertension. She frequently participated in long walks with the family and worked part-time in a solicitor's office with her son-in-law when other staff were on holiday; she was an excellent typist and very competent. During the week prior to her death, unassisted, she stripped wallpaper off two rooms at her house and moved items of furniture.

About ten days before she died, she tripped over some loose carpet at home and injured her knee, causing some discomfort that did not interfere with her daily routine. On Monday, 9 February, she telephoned Shipman's surgery asking him to visit. When making the appointment for a home visit, the receptionist noted the painful knee and nothing more. Shortly after that appointment was made, Mrs Hillier was visited by her daughter, Mrs Jacqueline Gee, for about two hours. She found her mother 'very well' and left shortly before lunch.

At about 2.00 p.m., Mrs Gee phoned her mother but there was no reply. Later in the afternoon, she made several more attempts to speak to her mother and became worried. She contacted a neighbour of her mother, Peter Elwood, who had a key, and he agreed to visit Mrs Hillier. It was about 5.15 p.m. when he entered. He went upstairs to the first floor and saw Mrs Hillier lying on the floor on her back in the space between the bed and the dressing table. A packet of blood pressure tablets was on the bed. Mr Elwood checked for a pulse and could find none.

He fetched his wife and they tried resuscitation, but without success. Mrs Elwood phoned for an ambulance, which arrived within five minutes. Examination by a paramedic revealed no pulse and she was not breathing. He carried out resuscitation with the aid of a defibrillator, until death was confirmed. During the procedure, Shipman rang apparently out of the blue and asked the paramedic what the circumstances were, saying that he would attend shortly.

Shipman arrived with the ambulance crew still present. A member of the crew said, 'I think we ought to notify the police, it's sudden death at home,' to which Shipman replied, 'I don't see there's a need to do that.' This was yet again Shipman doing all he could in a case of sudden death to avoid a post-mortem taking place. When the ambulance crew had left, Shipman told Jacqueline Gee that the cause of her mother's death was a stroke. He claimed that this was apparent to him due to the way in which she lay, notwithstanding the fact that by the time he saw her, she had been lifted from the floor onto the bed.

He went on to say that he had visited at 1.30 p.m. and had told her to go upstairs and to take another tablet. He said this was not an unexpected death, as Mrs Hillier had a history of headaches and high blood pressure. When Mr and Mrs Gee raised the question of having a post-mortem, Shipman stated that there was no need saying, 'Let's put it down as a stroke.' They found Shipman very short in his answers, but accepted his proposal, as it was 'the word of a doctor'. They had observed that Mrs Hillier had been in the process of making a meal and working on her accounts, which were laid out on the table.

The following day, Mrs Hillier's son Keith and her daughter Jacqueline visited the surgery in order to discuss the circumstances of their mother's death. Shipman said that Mrs Hillier had suffered a massive stroke that had killed her instantly and that it was in keeping with her high blood pressure. Mr Hillier queried that, saying that he understood his mother's blood pressure was high, but not seriously so. Shipman then read out a series of blood pressure readings asserting that they supported his argument, but according to Mr Hillier, there was no significant difference between those figures and normality.

Shipman caused frustration to Mr Hillier by stating that his mother's blood pressure was not high enough to cause him concern, and yet he was completely sure that it had been high enough to kill her. Mr Hillier suggested that the only way to get a real answer was to have a post-mortem examination. Shipman responded by saying how unpleasant a post-mortem would be and insisted that it was unnecessary, because he was absolutely certain about the cause of death.

Eventually and with great reluctance Mr Hillier gave way, having become too upset to argue any further with Shipman. He and his sister left the surgery in possession of the death certificate, which recorded the cause of death as: 1. (a) Cerebrovascular accident (b) Hypertension. Shipman completed the cremation form by recording the time of death as 2.00 p.m., whereas the body was found at 5.34 p.m. He also put on the form that he saw her alive about thirty minutes before she died.

Of great significance in this case is the fact that between 3.31 and 3.37 p.m., Shipman created eight separate fresh and false entries on Mrs Hillier's medical record and deleted two genuine entries. All this was taking place after Shipman had killed her, but before her body had been found.

Unsurprisingly, the false entries related to fictitious visits to the surgery with high blood pressure readings. The result of those machinations was that on 5 February there were four entries on her record: two of them created on 5 February, apparently genuine entries, but two further entries for that date created on 9 February, clearly false entries designed to support a fictitious cause of death.

Dr Grenville expressed the opinion that having considered Mrs Hillier's medical records, the risk factors for a stroke or heart attack were negligible and he did not believe that the diagnosis of cerebrovascular accident was justified by what was recorded. If the backdated entries created on the day of her death were ignored, there was nothing in her medical record to suggest that Mrs Hillier's death was in any way attributable to high blood pressure. An autopsy was mandatory following her sudden and unexpected death.

Mrs Hillier was one of the fittest and most active of Shipman's victims. She died at or about the time of his home visit and the creation of a false medical history to support an innocent cause of death was most powerful evidence, particularly since the false entries were created between the home visit and the finding of the body. Shipman timing the death at 2.00 p.m. was one of many mistakes that he made. The greatest impact upon the jury was surely the manner in which Shipman applied emotional pressure on the family in order to avoid a post-mortem examination, in particular when he explained how unpleasant it would be.

*Maureen Ward* was the final case for the jury to consider. Although it was a cremation case and thus with no direct evidence of morphine poisoning, it was nevertheless a very clear case of murder. Miss Ward was a single woman, aged fifty-seven when she died. In 1992 she was diagnosed as having cancer of the right breast, which was successfully treated, and in 1997 she had a malignant melanoma removed from her abdomen. She was on twelve-month reviews and in January 1998, there was no evidence of any reoccurrence. Miss Ward lived alone at Ogden Court, a complex of sheltered housing for the elderly, in which Miss Ward had lived with her late mother.

On 17 February 1998, the day before her death, Miss Ward visited the surgery and Carol Chapman, the receptionist, remembered her being in good form and telling her about a cruise that she was looking forward to on 1 March. That evening, she rang a friend and gave no cause for any concern. The following morning, she met her friend Mary France for a coffee in Hyde town centre; the two were planning to cruise together, and Miss Ward appeared to be in the best of health and gave no indication to the contrary. After their coffee, Miss Ward carried a bin liner full of washing across to the laundry for her friend.

At 3.30 p.m. that afternoon, Shipman knocked on the front door of the warden of the complex, Christine Simpson, and told her that he had just found Maureen at No. 41 dead on the bed. He added, 'She did have a brain tumour, you know.' Mrs Simpson knew Miss Ward well and that disclosure came as a total surprise to her. They both went to No. 41 and Mrs Simpson asked Shipman how he had gained entry to the flat. He replied, 'She left the door on the snip, because she was expecting me.' Again, this was a total surprise to Mrs Simpson, because Ogden Court had a very sophisticated security system in operation and in all the time that she had been warden, she had never known the door to be insecure. There was an internal system enabling the door to be released from within the flat.

Shipman went on to explain that the reason for his call was to deliver a letter containing an appointment to see a consultant at Stepping Hill Hospital, a Mr England. In fact, this was a lie. No appointment had been made for Miss Ward to see anyone at Stepping Hill Hospital and Shipman had fabricated a reason for his having visited Miss Ward.

When Mrs Simpson entered the flat, she found Miss Ward on the bed lying straight, as though she had been placed there on the bed. Shipman did not touch the deceased or undertake any form of examination. An open tin of cat food, with a spoon in it, was in the kitchen next to an empty cat bowl, indicating that Miss Ward was disturbed by Shipman's arrival as she was serving the cat food. Arrangements were made for funeral directors to remove the body, but no police or ambulance were called, and a post-mortem examination was not requested by Shipman.

Within half an hour, Shipman had returned to his surgery, where he announced the death of Miss Ward to the receptionist, Mrs Chapman. He gave a wholly different account to the one he had given to Mrs Simpson. He stated, 'I was driving past the end of her street and could see an ambulance outside her flat, so I went. She had already been found and an ambulance had been called, but it was too late.'

Christine Whitworth, a close friend of Miss Ward, was greatly shocked by her friend's death and visited Shipman in his surgery to discuss what had happened. Shipman asserted that before Christmas 1997, Miss Ward had come to the surgery concerned that she had come round and had wet herself. Shipman said he had referred her to the optician's and there appeared to be some blurring in her eyes. He had secured a speedy referral for her to hospital and he had gone over to her home with the referral and found her dead in bed, and so had to fetch the warden.

Mrs Whitworth was greatly concerned that Miss Ward may have suffered, but Shipman assured her that death would have been very quick, because 'when cancer is secondary in the brain, it can cause the patient to pass out and she would have laid down on the bed feeling unwell and would have died.'

Shipman recorded on the death certificate that the cause of death was: 1. (a) Carcinomatosis (secondary in brain) (b)

Carcinoma breast. He stated on the cremation form that the time of death was about 3.20 p.m. on 18 February 1998. He also falsely stated that he had seen the deceased twenty-four hours before she died, and also misleadingly asserted on the form that the warden at Ogden Court was present at the moment of death. All this was to avoid any post-mortem.

This was another case where Shipman created a false medical history to support his purported cause of death. Less than one hour before Shipman pretended that he had discovered Miss Ward's body, he was creating false backdated entries on her record. The following false entries were made: 6 February, 'Complaining of headache. Feels off colour at times to see optician'; 17 February, 'Complaining of headache. Disc raised. To contact Stepping Hill. 2 in Brain'; 17 December 1997, 'Complaining of headache. Comes goes dull. Feels nausea odd times legs not steady to tell S/hill when attends'.

In fact, when Miss Ward was actually seen at Stepping Hill on 14 January 1998, on her annual review by Dr Craven, he recorded an absence of any neurological problems such as headache, weakness or unsteadiness. The falsification of Miss Ward's medical record was both brazen and remarkably incompetent. In its final form, there were five entries for 17 February 1998, of which at least three are patently false, and two entries exist for days when there is no documentary evidence to show that Shipman ever saw her.

The prosecution called Dr Andrew King, a consultant neuro-surgeon, to comment on Miss Ward's medical history, and he concluded that the death certificate and medical record as created by Shipman were entirely at odds with medical notes from both the Breast Clinic and Dermatology Clinic at Stepping Hill, which stated that there was no evidence of either local or distal reoccurrence of either of these two malignant tumours.

He was a most impressive witness and, with an air of genuine incredulity, pointed out that it was simply not possible for any

medical practitioner to state such a diagnosis in the death certificate without any supporting evidence, namely ante-mortem
scans of vital organs, and in the absence of this evidence, it
would be mandatory to perform a post-mortem. He went on
to explain that a patient in the condition asserted in the death
certificate would have been in a poorly condition for some time
prior to her death, and her close friends had seen no such
evidence.

Dr Grenville made his final entrance to the witness box. He
had been calm, reassuring, and dependable throughout. He was
possibly at his most assertive in Miss Ward's case. He doubted
the veracity of the medical records. If they were truthful, he
would be extremely surprised by Miss Ward's sudden death; he
would expect a long and progressive illness. A woman killed by
a brain tumour would not have been carrying a big black bin
liner of washing to the launderette and shopping for holiday
outfits in Hyde on the morning of her death, as her friends had
described. He did not believe her death to be due to a secondary
brain tumour and could think of no mechanism by which a
secondary brain tumour would produce a sudden but peaceful
death in such a person.

This was the last of the fifteen murder counts and we regarded
it as the most powerful of the cremation cases, containing as it
did a sudden death very shortly after Shipman had access to
Miss Ward alone, an implausible cause of death, a false account
on the cremation certificate, multiple alterations to the medical
records, compelling evidence of Miss Ward's fitness on the day
of her death, lies by Shipman in the immediate aftermath, and
the most powerful medical evidence ridiculing the asserted cause
of death.

It was no accident that this was the final count to be placed
before the jury.

## Prosecution Expert Evidence

There remained two further and necessary phases of the prosecution case. The first was to inform the jury of the possible use and misuse of morphine and diamorphine. Peter Wright QC had taken silk during our preparation for this trial and I was anxious that he was able to deploy his skills as an advocate. I had every confidence in his ability and, in the years that followed, Peter demonstrated that he was in the very front rank of criminal advocates.

I asked him to take four critical witnesses, Professor McQuay, Julie Evans, Dr Karch Steven and Dr Hans Sachs. If indeed the defence were to make any progress in the trial, it could only be in discrediting the pharmacology relied upon by the prosecution, as they purported to do by serving a volume of expert evidence pretrial. The second remaining phase of the prosecution case was Volume Eight, the evidence proving that Shipman had stored a considerable volume of morphine, notwithstanding the fact that he was prohibited by law from doing so.

Professor Henry McQuay, Nuffield Professor of Clinical Anaesthetics at the University of Oxford and an honorary consultant at the pain relief unit, explained to the jury in the clearest possible manner how morphine worked as a painkiller. He explained how diamorphine converted into morphine within a minute of ingestion. Diamorphine used for cancer sufferers was twice as strong as morphine used for accident victims.

He described how molecules made their way to special receptors of the brain. If there was no pain to combat, the brain would slow the breathing instead. In the case of a healthy individual, a morphine injection would slow the breathing within two minutes, and within five minutes breathing would be very slow indeed, two to three breaths per minute. Lips and fingers may turn blue. A fatal dose of morphine or diamorphine would bring death within approximately five minutes; if the brain cannot get any oxygen because breathing has stopped, then you die. The time frame was to prove important in the cross-examination of Shipman in relation to Ivy Lomas's death.

Julie Evans, the forensic toxicologist at the Home Office forensic science laboratory at Euxton, near Chorley, explained how she had taken tissue samples from the nine exhumed victims from deep inside the thigh muscle, and where possible within the liver. She gave individual readings for each victim, stressing that each victim had fatal levels of morphine in their bodies.

She was cross-examined by Nicola Davies and agreed that she was breaking new ground in her analysis and that her work could only be compared to anecdotal studies. She could not say how the drug had been ingested and could not say that her findings reflected the level of the drug at the time of death. She would not, however, be shaken from her finding that all nine women had fatal levels of morphine within their bodies when they were exhumed. She amusingly retorted that if the explanation was that Mrs Grundy had taken kaolin and morphine, she would have had to drink one and a half litres of the medicine to reach that level of toxicity.

Dr Karch Steven, an American from Stamford University, with numerous qualifications and a post with the World Health Organization, dealt with head hair. He explained how tests on the hair of the nine exhumed women demonstrated that they were not regular users of morphine. These were sophisticated and comparatively new tests, but demonstrated conclusively in his opinion that none of the women had used morphine prior to their death. He described them as morphine naïve. As Shipman's defence developed, this evidence was effectively conclusive of guilt.

Dr Hans Sachs from the University of Munster was also an expert in hair analysis and was in complete agreement with his American colleague, dispelling any lurking doubt about the validity of a new scientific test.

## Volume Eight

We moved to Volume Eight and to an especially harrowing part of the trial. We had been observing members and friends of the fifteen families of the deceased on a daily basis. We had been anticipating this evidence and had read their statements time and again prior to the trial. The witnesses themselves had very considerable support from one another and from the police, the Crown Prosecution Service and Victim Support. There was a pattern to all their evidence and little element of surprise.

The witnesses we were about to hear each had a different tale to tell. We had read their statements and judged them to be relevant and probative, but they had not been analysed and contrasted one with another in the same way as the earlier evidence.

We were to hear of twenty-eight patients, most of whom had died, from whom Shipman had taken morphine or diamorphine. These witnesses must have felt themselves to be minor players in this unprecedented saga, but for most of them, the giving of evidence was a massive ordeal. It was to involve speaking publicly of lengthy terminal illness causing unbearable pain, followed by the loss of a loved one whom they believed for some time to have been well cared for by their trusted doctor. They too had been duped.

Nothing in Volume Eight was to suggest that Shipman murdered these patients or hastened their death. The purpose was simply to demonstrate Shipman's stockpiling of the drug. When interviewed by the police, Shipman insisted that he did not keep stocks of morphine either at home or in his surgery and had not done so since his conviction for pethidine-related offences in 1976. It was therefore vital to establish not only that Shipman had access to drugs, but that he stockpiled them.

Widow followed widow recounting their late husband's slow and painful death, coupled with the dreadful realisation that the drug intended to relieve their husband's pain had been used to kill perfectly healthy fellow human beings. Each spoke of Shipman's visit to the home upon being informed of their loss, of his apparently genuine sympathy, of their thanks for all his care over many months, and finally Shipman's removal of the unused morphine with the words, 'You'll have no more use for this. I will dispose of it.'

The evidence disclosed over-prescription, prescription after death, using morphine prescribed for one patient to treat another patient, and most dramatically of all, the case of Lillian Ibbotson, who was prescribed diamorphine in 1993. She was hitherto unaware of that fact. The only pain of which she had complained to Shipman was tennis elbow and that had certainly not called for such drastic treatment.

Examining these witnesses was no easy task. More than one of them was visibly shaking in the witness box and almost all were very upset. Shipman could have admitted this evidence and allowed it to be read, but that was not his style. By way of contrast on Shipman's instructions, junior counsel, Ian Winter, cross-examined by suggesting that the witness was too upset at the time of Shipman's visit to have an accurate or reliable memory of events. A typical response was that it was a day they would never forget. Possibly the saddest tale was that of a daughter whose father endured a painful death from lung cancer. He had never been treated with nor received diamorphine, even though Shipman had cashed prescriptions in her father's name at the chemist.

Immediately after these witnesses, we called evidence of actual physical stockpiling. When Shipman's house was searched in August 1998, an orange Zantac box was seized and the assumption was made that it contained Zantac, an anti-ulcer drug. It was only six weeks before the trial that the drugs were tested and proved to be fifty-four slow-release morphine tablets and four ampoules of diamorphine. This was certainly regarded as an error by Bernard Postles and doubtless the officer responsible heard from him. It may also have encouraged Shipman to assert time and again whilst he was being interviewed that he had no access to morphine, believing that none had been found.

## Police Interviews

The prosecution case concluded with the police interviews. Shipman was arrogant and conceited throughout, regarding the whole episode as an affront to his dignity. He sought to belittle the interviewing officers, both criticising their form of questions and mocking their apparent lack of medical knowledge; Shipman did all he could to disadvantage his interrogators by referring to various drugs by their trade names or generic names. The manner of his denials, as opposed to the content, is likely to have had the greater impact upon the jury. As to detail, however, Shipman hardly helped himself.

In relation to Mrs Grundy, he insisted that he had taken her blood and sent it for analysis; whereas at trial he sought refuge in the excuse that he had mislaid the samples, after the prosecution had proved that no sample was ever received at the laboratory. In relation to the several cases of post-death alteration of medical records, he had not yet conceived the explanation advanced at trial: that the deceased had each shortly before their deaths made a sudden disclosure of complaints existing for some time, but never previously disclosed to Shipman, thus requiring him to make backdated entries in their records.

In relation to his visits to the many homes of the deceased, he had insisted that each visit was in response to a phone call from them to his surgery, notwithstanding that telephone billing conclusively disproved his assertion. Perhaps most significantly, the only deceased he had accused of having a drug habit was Mrs Grundy. By the conclusion of the case, it became clear that he was asserting that every deceased buried was addicted to morphine.

Throughout the first interview on 7 September, Shipman remained composed and in control. During that interview, the officers allowed Shipman a comparatively free run, rarely contradicting him and permitting him to commit himself to a version of facts that was demonstrably false. On 5 October, however, when confronted by telephone billing and late alteration of medical records, he fell to his knees in tears, but most certainly made no semblance of any confession.

The prosecution case concluded with evidence of the search of Shipman's home and the finding of the morphine and diamorphine in the Zantac box. There was no suggestion put to any officer that any planting of evidence or any other form of impropriety had taken place.

Our case had lasted for six weeks; one hundred and twenty witnesses had entered the witness box, and the evidence of many more had been read as agreed evidence. We were pleased with the way the case had progressed. Our experts had not been damaged, nor indeed put under any pressure, and the many friends and relatives of the deceased had been nervous but obviously truthful and genuine witnesses. Their ability to recollect accurately events immediately after the death of their relative was challenged time and again, but such events were very clearly etched in their minds in permanent form.

## The Defence Case

Shipman entered the witness box on 25 November 1999. He did so in the absence of any opening speech by Nicola Davies. This was perhaps an indication that the defence had less confidence than we had anticipated in the several experts whose evidence had been served prior to trial. A rousing opening speech, alerting the jury that the defence intended to show that each and every death was consistent with death by natural causes, was certainly within the scope of our contemplation.

For the moment and for many days to come, our attention was focused on one man. The early part of his evidence was uncontroversial and made easy listening. Nicola was understandably more at ease leading Shipman through his training and the details of his career than she had been challenging relatives on matters of detail. This was very much her field of expertise. She had represented many members of the medical profession and had taken them skilfully through their proofs of evidence in criminal courts, civil courts and before tribunals. It was obvious that this proof of evidence had been prepared with consummate attention to detail.

After a little nervousness, Shipman began to enjoy himself. He was assuming the role of an expert explaining to the jury the workings of a GP's surgery, training courses for his staff, and discussions with his practice manager. None of this had the slightest bearing on guilt or innocence, but for all in court it was a period of relaxation lasting for over a day. Eventually we reached Mrs Grundy.

*Kathleen Grundy.* For some time Shipman asserted that he had suspected Mrs Grundy of abusing drugs and was concerned about her general health. She visited the surgery on 23 June and looked in poor health, so he decided to visit her the next morning to take some blood for tests. He visited at 8.30 a.m. and she looked old and moved slowly. He took the sample and left, but was so busy he forgot to send the sample for testing and later threw it away. Soon after midday, he was called to Mrs Grundy's home and she was dead. He judged the time of death to be about 10.00 a.m. and was satisfied that the morphine in her body was self-administered. 'Abuse of drugs in the elderly is becoming recognised,' he stated, with the air and confidence of an expert witness.

As to the will, Mrs Grundy had borrowed his typewriter and prepared the will. She brought it into the surgery and he had assumed that the document was a will with some £200 or so bequeathed to his surgery appeal, giving him reason not to sign it. He asked two patients to witness the will and then handed it back to Mrs Grundy, which explained his print upon it.

*Bianka Pomfret* requested a home visit on 10 December and on his arrival, she described three earlier occasions when she had chest pains. He concluded that she had angina and offered her glyceryl trinitrate, but she refused, saying she already had too many tablets. He advised her to make an appointment for an ECG and left.

He went back to the surgery and made some backdated entries in her medical record spread over nine months to give a true impression of her medical condition, including some assumed blood pressure readings and comments to give the impression of contemporaneity. He was summoned to the house later in the day and paramedics were in attendance. He thought Mrs Pomfret had suffered a coronary thrombosis and offered the family a post-mortem, which they refused.

*Winifred Mellor* called at the surgery about 4.00 p.m. on the day of her death and described chest pain over a period of several months. He said she must have an ECG and she was to ring him at 5.30 p.m. When she failed to do so, he visited her at home and found her dead. He carried out a full examination to establish death.

*Joan Melia* collected a prescription from the surgery on 11 June, having complained of a cough. She was coughing green sputum and was generally unwell. He told her she should rest and contact him if she had any pain, and if so he would visit the following day. He did so and advised her to take the antibiotic and plenty of liquid and keep warm. He was called later that evening by Mr Steele and he examined her pulse and eyes and she was clearly dead. He did not think it appropriate to send her to hospital.

*Ivy Lomas* travelled to the surgery by bus for a 4.00 p.m. appointment. She entered his room and said she had chest pains for four hours that day; she looked sweaty and had an irregular pulse. He thought she might be having a coronary thrombosis and took her to the treatment room for an ECG. As she got onto the bed, she collapsed and became unconscious. He tried several methods of resuscitation, including cardiac massage and mouth-to-mouth resuscitation, but she did not respond and had died.

He told Mrs Chapman that he had a problem with the ECG machine and would see the next patient; he did not tell her that Mrs Lomas had died, as that would take her off her reception duties. He saw three patients and then told Mrs Chapman of the death and asked her to contact Mr Lomas.

*Marie Quinn* had telephoned the surgery saying that she seemed to be having a stroke and was paralysed down one side of her body. He told her he would come, and she should leave the door on the latch. When he arrived, he found her on the floor, breathing her last, and it was too late to admit her to hospital.

*Irene Turner* rang the surgery and asked for a visit. When he arrived, she said she had been vomiting for five or six days and may have vomited her diabetes tablets. He concluded that she was dehydrated and that her diabetes was out of control and that she must go to hospital, but she would not agree; she said she had been worse in the past and had recovered. She agreed to go to hospital if a urine test contained both blood and protein.

He took a urine sample and left, telling her to get ready to go to hospital and that he would ask her neighbour Mrs Ward to come in and help her, which he did. He went to his surgery, did the test, which was positive, and within ten minutes returned to the house where he found Mrs Turner unconscious. He felt for a pulse, examined her eyes, and was sure she was dead.

*Jean Lilley* had requested a visit and he found her not breathing well, with pains in her chest and producing phlegm. After a thorough examination, he concluded that she should go to hospital, but she refused, asking to be given an antibiotic. He told her to phone her husband, and if she then agreed to go to hospital, he would return and arrange it. He left and some twenty minutes later, he was paged by his surgery and told that Mrs Lilley had collapsed. He returned and found the paramedics in attendance with Mrs Lilley on the bed, obviously dead; he did not examine her, as the paramedics had already done so. The following day he asked Mr Lilley if he wanted a post-mortem, but Mr Lilley did not think it necessary.

*Muriel Grimshaw* was visited by him at home on 2 July, because the previous day she had asked for a repeat prescription. He found her well, but her back was a little troublesome. He visited again on 14 July and she said her back was giving her no trouble. He recorded that visit. The following day he was called to her house as her body had been found. Rigor mortis had set in and, from a discussion with her daughter, he estimated the time of death. He believed her death was due to a stroke associated with hypertension. He offered her daughter a post-mortem, but she declined.

*Maria West* was visited by him on 6 March to see how her back pain was progressing. She said the pain had diminished, but she now had another problem with altered vision and weakness in the arm and leg. He turned away to reach for his stethoscope and spoke to her, but there was no response. She was slumped in her chair; he examined her and she was dead. He telephoned Mr West and explained the circumstances of the death. He mentioned a post-mortem, but Mr West did not want one.

*Lizzie Adams* was visited by him at home as a result of a phone call by her to the surgery. When he arrived, she was obviously poorly and came slowly to the door to let him in. She was breathless, unwell and had a cough. Her heart was racing, she was clammy, and looked pale. On listening to her chest, he heard fine crackles, and her lips were slightly blue. He thought she had bronchopneumonia in both lungs. He said she should be in hospital, but she said she had been equally ill on previous occasions and had stayed at home.

He said he would telephone her daughter and as he went to do so, Mr Catlow arrived, and he told him that Mrs Adams should be in hospital and that he was about to phone her daughter. Mr Catlow went into the living room and after a few seconds called him in saying that Mrs Adams was not at all well. Shipman examined her fully and concluded that she had died. He called Mrs Thorley and explained the circumstances and asked her if she wanted a post-mortem, but she did not.

*Kathleen Wagstaff* was visited at her home as a result of a phone call to the surgery. She said she had chest pains and did not feel well. She let him in and went slowly upstairs to her flat. He sat her in a chair. She looked grey and cyanosed, her pulse was fast, and he thought she may be having a coronary thrombosis. He said she ought to be in hospital and that he would write up the notes and ring for an ambulance. He then realised that her mouth was open and that she had died. He attempted resuscitation and cardiac massage, but to no avail.

*Norah Nuttall* visited the surgery on the morning of her death, and he diagnosed her as suffering from bronchitis and gave her some cough medicine. He decided to visit her in the afternoon to see how she was getting on in her new home. She said she was glad to see him, as she was worse; she was breathless, felt ill, and her legs had swelled up. He examined her and her pulse was thready, her ankles were swollen and she had fluid in the lungs. He decided to give her an injection of a diuretic and went to his car to collect it.

As he was doing so, Mrs Nuttall's son arrived and Shipman told him his mother was seriously ill; he was fetching a drug from his car and then would call an ambulance. He collected the drug and followed Mr Nuttall into the house. He then realised that Mrs Nuttall had stopped breathing. He felt her pulse, listened to her heart and chest, looked at her pupils and realised that she was dead. He did not advise a post-mortem and Mr Nuttall did not want one. Resuscitation would not have succeeded.

*Pamela Hillier* was visited at home on the afternoon of her death, having requested a home visit. He found her blood pressure worryingly high. She said there had been two other occasions when Gillian Morgan, the surgery nurse, had taken her blood pressure and it had been high, namely on 6 January and 5 February. He asked if she had other symptoms and she admitted that she felt tired and her injured leg felt weak. He told her to take another tablet and lie down for a couple of hours and he would see her later in the week. He returned to the surgery and entered all this information on her record. He was called to the house later, but Mrs Hillier had died and the paramedics were in attendance. A post-mortem was not necessary as he knew the cause of death was a stroke.

*Maureen Ward* saw him twice on the day before her death. She had told him she had been having some funny do's with headaches and blurred vision. These had settled and she had not gone to the optician. About a week earlier, she had found herself on the floor and had wet herself. He thought this was an epileptic fit and could be a sign of a brain tumour. He had been unaware of these earlier events and entered them on her record. He made strenuous attempts to get an appointment for her at Stepping Hill, but had been unable to get through and so wrote her a letter of referral, which she could take with her. He went round with this letter and to advise her to attend the next clinic, but found her already dead. The warden had found Miss Ward in a collapsed state.

★　★　★

I have summarised some two and a half days of evidence given by Shipman. It was given without interruption, either from myself or from the judge. It consisted of multiple lies designed to explain away not only fifteen murders, but to neutralise the many mistakes he had made. The only diversion during his evidence in chief occurred initially outside court in a radio programme.

During an afternoon show at about 5.00 p.m., when the jury might have been travelling home or at home, a DJ on Red Rose Radio, a local station, announced, 'Did you see the Harold Shipman trial? We have to be delicate because it's ongoing. I'm supposed to be delicate, but I really don't care. We all know Shipman is as guilty as sin. Why don't we save the taxpayer a lot of money and end the trial now?' To make matters even worse, the travel presenter was shouting in the background, 'Guilty! Guilty!'

This was a blatant contempt of court and my immediate apprehension was that it might result in the discharge of the jury and a consequent retrial, with so many distressed witnesses having to undergo their ordeal a second time. When the judge brought the jury into court and asked if anyone of them had listened to a radio programme the previous evening on Red Rose Radio in which the trial was mentioned, there was genuine anxiety on the prosecution benches. Fortunately, no juror had heard the outburst and the trial continued. In due course, the culprits were required to attend in the absence of the jury. Thayne Forbes gave them a stern lecture and they seemed suitably chastened. Other judges may well have taken more punitive action.

## Cross-Examination

Nicola Davies's final question of Shipman was, 'Did you murder Maureen Ward?' to which his answer was, 'No.' Being the last count in the indictment, Nicola sat down and I simultaneously stood up to cross-examine and began by saying, 'The evidence is that on the first of August 1998 . . . ,' but before I could finish the sentence, Shipman had turned to the judge and declared himself unwell and was immediately granted an adjournment.

We speculated that this may be a ploy to avoid cross-examination in its entirety, which had much to commend it. Remarkably, nobody in the prosecution team had ever encountered such a tactic, indeed I have never heard of such a course being taken. The judge could take a number of measures to defeat the scheme, including discharging the jury, but with Shipman's medical expertise, it would not have been beyond him to fake a stroke or some other disabling infirmity. We were proved wrong, however, and after a twenty-minute break, Shipman was ready to face the questioning.

One theory doing the rounds was that Shipman realised I was about to question him on Volume Eight, whereas he was prepared to answer questions on Mrs Grundy and the will. I was even complimented by a member of the press for wrong-footing Shipman by starting with Volume Eight. In fact, this was no brilliant tactic; I was merely taking the evidence chronologically. First he acquired morphine and then he administered it.

This was the beginning of a seven-day period of intense questioning.

I had no idea that this was to be my final act of cross-examining, but I could have wished for no more than this opportunity. The relatives were lovely people, who deserved to see Shipman comprehensively brought to justice. The team behind me had given everything in terms of hard work and devotion to duty. We knew we were prosecuting the nation's most prolific serial killer of all time and we were aware of Dr Bodkin Adams' acquittal at the Old Bailey in 1957. In his case, some one hundred and sixty patients died in suspicious circumstances, many of them having bequeathed substantial sums of money to the doctor.

However strong our case was, and it certainly was strong, there was no room for complacency or half measures.

The cross-examination was an opportunity to bring all the evidence together. How coincidental that so many victims should actually die in his presence: Mrs Lomas, Mrs Quinn, Mrs Wagstaff, Mrs Adams, Mrs Nuttall and Mrs West, whilst Mrs Grundy, Mrs Pomfret and Mrs Hillier were found dead shortly after he left. How strange that so many of the deceased were found sitting comfortably in a chair or on a sofa; how often were medical records altered either immediately before or shortly after death. How often did Shipman pretend he had called an ambulance or a hospital, when no such call had been made? Shipman's most pressing problem was Volume Eight. What happened to all the morphine that he had taken so much trouble to stockpile?

Assessing one's own performance in court is never easy. In one respect, I failed. I really believed there was a chance that during cross-examination Shipman would surrender and change his plea to guilty. Prescribing morphine for tennis elbow, Mrs Lomas left dead whilst he saw other patients, alteration of medical records between his visit and the body being found; all represented moments when Shipman must have considered throwing in the towel. Boxing expressions were frequently in use in the prosecution conference room, possibly because Peter Wright's nickname in those days was 'Biffer'.

Shipman spent seven days on the ropes, but lasted the duration avoiding any knockout. He deployed a standard defensive technique, namely, 'There is no sensible answer to that question.' Shipman grew more and more arrogant as his case weakened, and his arguments grew even more ludicrous and implausible.

The closest Shipman came to being knocked out was during a consideration of Ivy Lomas's case. He accepted that she had travelled to his surgery by public transport and walked along a corridor to his room. The transcript then reads:

Q: When you first saw Ivy Lomas in your consulting room, were there any apparent effects of diamorphine poisoning?

A: She didn't appear to have any effects of opiate poisoning.

Q: Was she able to walk along the corridor to your examination room?

A: Yes, she was.

Q: You remember Professor McQuay's evidence, don't you, that the effects of a fatal dose of diamorphine would be seen within a five-minute window?

A: I remember him saying that.

Q: Well, if this lady died at ten minutes past four, she must have been administered or administered to herself diamorphine between four o'clock and ten minutes past four?

A: You can put the evidence that way, I would agree.

Q: You were with Ivy Lomas throughout all that time, were you not?

A: I don't disagree with that statement.

Q: You were continuously with her, were you not? We can see when you were first with her from the computer screen, 'Seen in GPs surgery, Dr H F Shipman, 3.57'.

A: I'm not disagreeing with that.

Q: And you say to us here and now that you were continuously in her presence up to the moment she collapsed and died.

A: Allowing for the time taken for resuscitation, yes.

Q: How then did Ivy Lomas get that diamorphine into her system?

A: I have no knowledge.

Q: Dr Shipman, there is simply no sensible explanation, is there?

A: Was that a statement or was it a question?

Q: You know very well it was a question, formulated as a question, requiring an answer. Dr Shipman, there is no sensible explanation, is there?

A very long pause followed, and a scribbled note was placed before me by Peter Wright. It read, 'Ask Shipman if he would like to phone a friend.' I resisted the temptation and simply allowed the pause to continue for a considerable time. Eventually he replied:

A: I have no knowledge.
Q: There is simply no sensible answer, is there?
A: I do not know of any explanation.

At that moment I concluded that any remote chance of an acquittal had been comprehensively eliminated.

In retrospect, I may have cross-examined Shipman for longer than necessary, but with fifteen separate and distinct murders, we were covering more than two murders a day, plus the twenty-eight incidents in Volume Eight and the forged will. It had become certain that convictions must follow and our uppermost thought at this stage was to ensure that every count was proved. It would have been distressing in the extreme for one or more families to be deprived of the verdict they understandably craved.

The cremation counts were necessarily less certain of proof than the burial counts, and of those we were unable to show a close temporal association between Shipman's contact with the victim and the victim's death, except in the case of Joan Melia. The temptation was to concentrate rather more on the apparently less certain counts. The cremation cases, however, were hand-picked and when the jury were in retirement, Peter Wright commented that if anything the cremation cases were more compelling than the burial cases.

The defence called a single expert, who spoke of the finger-prints on the forged will, accepting as he did so that Shipman's print was on it. No toxicologist was called, no pathologist was called, no professor of clinical cardiology or consultant respiratory physician, no professor of chemistry and no professor from Heidelberg University to deal with head hair. Nine of the ten experts, whose evidence had been served, failed to enter the witness box. Had any of them done so, their professional reputations as expert witnesses would have been irreparably damaged. Shipman had seen to that. He had accepted that all burial victims must have died from morphine poisoning, rendering virtually all the expert evidence valueless.

The evidence concluded on 13 December 1999 and the judge decided that speeches and the summing up should take place in the next millennium. That was a most satisfactory arrangement. The detail of sixteen counts needed careful analysis and I looked forward to a closing speech with more than sufficient time to craft it. There is nothing more comforting than having a speech prepared and 'in the can' and my wife and I were able to celebrate New Year in the Lakes with my task effectively complete. We had no idea what awaited us in the year 2000.

## Closing Speeches and Summing Up

The gap in proceedings had been substantial when we reconvened in early January and I was anxious to reassert the prosecution's initiative. I reminded the jury that not once in all these cases did he call an ambulance, not once did he admit any patient to hospital, and not once did he permit a post-mortem. I highlighted his abuse of trust of his patients:

> They trusted him to care for them, their relatives trusted him to tell the truth about the circumstances in which his patients died, and the community trusted him to complete records with honesty and integrity. We submit that he breached that trust. He did not care for those fifteen patients, he killed them. He did not with truth relay the circumstances of death to grieving relatives, he duped them to save his own skin, and falsified records to cover his tracks. He took advantage of their grief and lesser knowledge of medicine. As they grieved, this determined man deployed any and every device to ensure that no post-mortem took place. He would overbear, belittle, bamboozle

and disadvantage relatives, until they accepted the doctor's word that they should not 'put their mother through it'. The reason why no post-mortem was called, was because the poisoner fears pathology, ambulances and hospitals.

I concluded my closing speech by reminding the jury of a small piece of evidence given much earlier in the trial by the practice nurse, Nurse Gilchrist. In the early days of the police inquiry, when Shipman was still practising, he turned to her and said, 'I read thrillers and I would have me guilty on the evidence.' The evidence then was nothing compared to the evidence now.

Nicola Davies had a far more difficult task, but approached it fearlessly and with apparent confidence. She stressed that no genuine motive had been advanced and that the 'power complex' was an amateur psychological theory. The stockpiling of drugs was a red herring. He was doing no more than anticipating the pain of patients and the medicine to deal with it. He was not cold and unsympathetic in the aftermath of death, but was bringing a calm and professional attitude to the deaths. He was a dedicated doctor, who often went calling on patients when they had not summoned him, but not for any sinister purpose.

Keeping accurate records was not his forte; he was more interested in patients than paperwork. The toxicology evidence was not safe because of the decomposition of the bodies, and because the prosecution expert Julie Evans admitted she had broken new ground in carrying out some of the tests. 'The scientific evidence in this case is inherently unreliable and these are uncharted scientific waters. The prosecution case stands or falls on the toxicology evidence.'

The judge's summing up lasted for two weeks. It was flawless, detailed and absolutely fair. One member of my chambers asserted it was too long, but I absolutely disagree. Volume Eight, Mrs Grundy, the forgery and the law occupied the first week. Thereafter he was dealing with well over two murders a day.

This was a case packed with critical detail, which required the most careful analysis. The jury retired to consider their verdicts on 24 January 2000.

Spending time during a lengthy jury retirement is never easy for advocates. My practice was to work on future cases whenever possible, but that was not always easy, not least because of constant interruptions. One such was a request by the jury for a flip chart to display the name of the deceased whose case they were considering. Apart from that, the jury went about their work without sending out any further requests, unusual in a case of this length.

Many cups of coffee are consumed and much speculation takes place. Peter Wright made an interesting observation, when he said that the only chance Shipman would have had, was if the death penalty had still remained. I responded by conceding it was the best chance that he might have had, whilst asserting that I believed he would have faced the death penalty. I have long been an opponent of the death penalty, on the simple and pragmatic ground that it would result in a significant number of guilty defendants being acquitted.

It may well be that Peter's observation was prompted by our consideration of Dr Bodkin Adams' acquittal in 1957, some eight years before the abolition of the death penalty for murder in 1965. Whilst preparing for this trial, I had read or rather reread Patrick Devlin's book, *Easing the Passing*. Patrick Devlin as Mr Justice Devlin was the trial judge and later became Lord Devlin. Whilst the prosecution in that trial did not have available either the toxicology or the pathology of the present day, the case against Bodkin Adams was substantial. Critics of our trial process would do well to contrast the trials of Bodkin Adams and Harold Shipman and to observe the progress that has been made.

During the jury retirement, I received news that whatever verdict was returned, it was the intention of the Secretary of State for Health, Alan Milburn MP, to announce the setting up of an inquiry under the National Health Service Act, to be chaired by Lord Laming. This would be held in private. This was disastrous news for the whole of our team. We had assured the hundred or so families not included in the trial process that a public inquiry was inevitable, having regard to the many deaths involved. I had never contemplated the possibility that anything other than a judge-led public inquiry would be ordered. I was both furious and apprehensive.

Detective Superintendent Bernard Postles had months earlier warned me that he could not guarantee my safety in the presence of the hundred disappointed families. The number had since grown and I appeared now to have misled them with a false promise; I asked that my views be communicated to the Department of Health. The following day, with the jury still in retirement, my chambers informed me that Lord Irvine, the Lord Chancellor, wished to see me as a matter of urgency. I assumed it concerned the Laming Inquiry and set off for London, leaving Peter Wright in charge.

When I arrived at the House of Lords on Wednesday 26 January, the Lord Chancellor had in mind a very different proposition. He offered me an appointment to the High Court Bench, giving me until Friday at noon to make my decision. My wife Toni had travelled to London with me and I delayed telling her of the offer until we were across a dinner table in a small bistro in Knightsbridge. I wanted to assess the situation myself and reach a provisional decision.

I had never considered myself a candidate for the High Court. I had not been in a civil court for a very long time and I was enjoying life in silk more than I had ever hoped for. On the other hand, I had the highest regard for High Court judges. As circuit leader, I had met many of them socially and was immensely flattered by the invitation to join them. I was conscious too of the pleasure it would give my father if I was appointed. In a state of indecision, I sat down with Toni for dinner. I delayed telling her until our main courses had arrived. Thereafter not a mouthful of food passed her lips. We agonised for some time before reaching the decision that neither of us has ever regretted.

I returned to Preston and was unable to disclose the reason for my London summons, but somehow bluffed my way along. It took until the following July for the Laming problem to be resolved. The Divisional Court upon an application by the Tameside Family Support Group set aside the Secretary of State's decision as being unreasonable and remitted the matter to him for redetermination.

With no alternative option, he set up 'The Shipman Inquiry' to be chaired by Dame Janet Smith DBE, an Appeal Court judge. The report is compelling reading and covers every aspect of Shipman's criminality. The circumstances of every suspicious death are examined in meticulous detail, culminating in the estimate of Shipman's total murder count at 215.

## The Verdicts

It was late in the afternoon of Monday 31 January when we received word that the jury had reached verdicts. The drama of such occasions is intense. Usually I have anticipated the verdict correctly, but by no means always. Experience has taught me that when the foreman has no document in hand, verdicts are almost always the same throughout the indictment. In this case, the foreman stood empty-handed and consistently repeated the word 'guilty' sixteen times.

Immediately thereafter, it was my task to inform the court of Shipman's previous convictions, not because it would affect sentence in this particular case, but merely to follow well-established procedure in all criminal trials. In any event, it was of some importance that the public knew what had transpired over twenty years earlier.

On 13 February 1976, Shipman had pleaded guilty at Halifax

magistrates' court to eight specimen charges: three offences of obtaining pethidine by deception, three offences of unlawful possession of pethidine, and three offences of forging a prescription. He asked for seventy-four further offences to be taken into consideration, most of which involved obtaining pethidine by deception.

As these convictions were read out, there was an undisguised gasp of shock from every quarter of the court. For those of us who had known of the convictions throughout, simply hearing them, or in my case reading them, was in itself a shocking experience. Few if any of the relatives were aware of any previous conviction, and hearing of them and the nature of them must have been a body blow.

They were soon to be distracted, however, as Mr Justice Forbes proceeded to pass sentence:

> You have finally been brought to justice by the verdict of this jury. I have no doubt whatsoever that these are true verdicts. The time has now come for me to pass sentence upon you for these wicked, wicked crimes. Each of your victims was your patient. You murdered each and every one of your victims by a calculated and cold-bloodied perversion of your medical skills for your own evil and wicked purposes. You took advantage of and grossly abused their trust. You were, after all, each victim's doctor. I have little doubt that each of your victims smiled and thanked you as she submitted to your deadly ministrations.
>
> None realised that yours was not a healing touch, none knew in truth you had brought her death, death disguised as the caring attention of a good doctor. The sheer wickedness of what you have done defies description. It is shocking and beyond belief. You have not shown the slightest remorse or contrition for your evil deeds and you have subjected the family and friends of your victims to having to relive the tragedy and grief you visited upon them.

The judge then proceeded to pass sentences of imprisonment for life on each of the fifteen counts of murder and four years imprisonment for the forgery. He continued:

> In the ordinary way, I would not do this in open court, but in your case, I am satisfied that justice demands that I make my views known at the conclusion of this trial. I have formed the conclusion that the crimes you stand convicted of are so heinous that in your case life must mean life. My recommendation will be that you spend the remainder of your days in prison.

Shipman having been taken to the cells, there followed a most moving and personal address directed towards the families and friends of the deceased. Thayne Forbes removed his wig and spoke to them not in his capacity as judge, but as a fellow human being: 'I would like you to know how much I admire the courage and quiet dignity you have shown. Your evidence was at times intensely moving and touched the hearts of all who heard it. Your contribution to the course of justice in this terrible and tragic case will stand as a moving memorial and tribute to your loved ones.'

The judge then thanked the police, commending particularly Detective Superintendent Bernard Postles and Detective Chief Inspector Mike Williams, and thanked both legal teams before turning to the jury, saying this: 'On a personal note, I would like you to know that I count myself privileged to have had you as my jury in this dramatic and significant trial.'

As the judge finished speaking, applause came from the back of the court. The court rose with many in tears, and even more still wondering how these events could ever have taken place.

I have found the decision of the General Medical Counsel in 1976 acutely disturbing. Had they erased Shipman's name from the medical register, these tragedies would have been avoided. Quite remarkably, the case never reached the Disciplinary

Committee. It came before the Penal Cases Committee who concluded, having received evidence from two psychiatrists who had treated Shipman, that no inquiry should be held by the Disciplinary Committee. Shipman was sent a letter informing him that if he was further convicted, he would then be referred to the Disciplinary Committee.

The great majority of Shipman's convictions involved an element of dishonesty. All of his convictions involved misuse of a drug and there were in all eighty-two offences. For my part, I find it shameful that a man's name should remain on a register of individuals authorised to administer medicine to the public, and thus to be trusted by the public, having breached the criminal law on so many occasions, and at a time when he was in practice as a GP.

The Home Office could also have prevented these many tragedies. Following Shipman's conviction for drugs offences under the Misuse of Drugs Act 1971, the Home Secretary had power under that Act to make a direction prohibiting Shipman from having in his possession, prescribing, administering or otherwise dealing with such controlled drugs as were specified in the direction. Regrettably, the Home Office officials dealing with the case appear to have been influenced by the decision of the GMC and thus failed to give any such direction.

It is manifest that procedures in place to prevent cremations being used to conceal homicide were woefully inadequate. Before a cremation can be authorised, a second doctor must confirm the cause of death and the cremation documentation must be checked by a third doctor employed at the crematorium. These procedures were wholly ineffective in preventing Shipman effecting the cremation of the vast majority of his 215 victims.

In March 1998, Detective Inspector David Smith conducted a police investigation into the number of deaths amongst Shipman's patients. Dr Reynolds, a partner in the nearby medical practice, had expressed concerns to the coroner who initiated the investigation. Having regard to the volume of evidence available in this trial and the number of murders already carried out prior to that investigation, the conclusion that the resources deployed were wholly inadequate is hard to avoid when learning that the investigation concluded that there was no evidence to substantiate the concerns expressed by Dr Reynolds.

Dame Janet Smith in her report made numerous well-considered recommendations, not all of which have been adopted. It is a recurring thought that had not Shipman forged Mrs Grundy's will so incompetently, he may well have continued murdering his patients indefinitely. No system should have permitted such events.

By way of postscript, Shipman committed suicide in prison in January 2004. This was no act of remorse on his part. Death before sixty guaranteed his wife Primrose a lump sum of £100,000 and an annuity of £10,000 per annum. Had he died having attained sixty, she would have received only £5,000 per annum. Failure to include a suicide clause in his policy of insurance left his insurers as vulnerable as Shipman's many other victims.

# HIGH COURT JUDGE

# Chapter 9

## The Trial of the Leeds United Footballers

IN JANUARY 2000, Leeds United were a Premiership Football Club with European ambitions. Two of their leading players were England international Jonathan Woodgate, aged nineteen, and future England international Lee Bowyer, aged twenty-three. On 12 January 2000, both footballers, in separate groups, went into Leeds centre for a night out.

Woodgate had invited three friends, Clifford, Caveney and Hewison, from his home town, Middlesbrough, to join him. Bowyer was celebrating his twenty-third birthday, albeit nine days after the event, together with three other Leeds United footballers, namely Bridges, Kewell and Hackworth.

The early part of the evening was spent in various establishments consuming a large volume of alcohol. Both groups arrived independently at the Majestyk club, where they met up. At the same time, a group of five Asian students were in the club. One of Woodgate's group, James Hewison, nicknamed 'Gorilla', was required to leave the club for drunkenness, and shortly afterwards, both groups left the club and saw Hewison outside.

One of the Asian students was seen by a club doorman to be initially taunting the ejected Hewison and then punching him in the face. This prompted a chase of the Asian students through the streets for several hundred yards, resulting in Sarfraz Najeib, aged nineteen, being knocked to the ground, sustaining a broken leg, cheekbone, nose and facial injuries caused by a bite. He was rendered unconscious in the attack, remembered nothing of the assault, and spent seven days in Leeds General Infirmary. Woodgate phoned his friend and teammate, Michael Duberry, who came by car and drove Woodgate and others from the scene.

In March 2001, Woodgate, Bowyer, Clifford, Caveney, Hackworth and Duberry were in the dock at Leeds Crown Court standing trial before Mr Justice Poole. All but Duberry were accused of both affray and inflicting grievous bodily harm with intent. All but Bowyer and Hackworth were also charged with conspiracy to pervert the course of justice by fabricating an alleged cover-up. Save for the fact that those charged with the conspiracy were found not guilty, and Hackworth was discharged on the judge's direction on the other charges he faced through lack of evidence, the trial came to a premature and unsatisfactory conclusion.

Whilst the jury were in retirement, the *Sunday Mirror* published an interview with Sarfraz Najeib's father, in which he asserted, contrary to Mr Justice Poole's ruling, that the attack on his son was racially motivated. The description of the attack contained facts not given in evidence. Having ascertained that at least one member of the jury had read the article, the judge felt obliged to discharge the jury and to order a retrial involving Woodgate, Bowyer, Clifford and Caveney, all charged with both affray and inflicting grievous bodily harm with intent. The *Sunday Mirror* was prosecuted for contempt of court and ordered to pay £130,000 in fines and costs.

Shortly after the jury discharge, I was asked by Lord Justice Kennedy to preside over the retrial. Ordinarily cases of causing grievous bodily harm with intent would be tried by circuit judges, rather than High Court judges. This case, however, had already attracted a vast amount of media attention and public anger.

In the words of Paul Cheston, the former court reporter of the *London Evening Standard*, in Sir Desmond de Silva QC's admirable memoir, *Madam, Where Are Your Mangoes?*

Premiership wages had skyrocketed and an outcry grew over spoilt, overpaid young players and their drunken antics. The headlines were full of reports of drink-fuelled violence by the idols of the football pitch who, it was widely said, had too much money too young. By the time a group of Leeds United players were arrested in January 2000, after a young Asian student was chased through the city centre streets, caught and given a sickening kicking and beating, public anger was demanding that something be done.

It came as no surprise that Desmond de Silva selected this case for his memoir: he defended Lee Bowyer. David Fish QC defended Woodgate; Nigel Sangster QC defended Clifford; and Raymond Walker QC defended Caveney. The case was prosecuted by Nicholas Campbell QC.

I can recollect no case in which the Bar as a whole conducted the trial process to better effect. The hallmarks of a sound prosecutor are clarity and fairness, and Nicholas Campbell displayed these throughout. In his closing address to the jury, he acknowledged 'how a few moments of misjudgement would be especially catastrophic for two precociously talented young sportsmen.'

Nigel Sangster's task was worse than hopeless on behalf of Clifford, the alleged biter. The prosecution had taken casts of his teeth and were able to match the casts to photographs of the bitemarks in a compelling way. Clifford's teeth were by no means regular, and every imperfection could be made out in the bitemark. No conviction has ever been more certain.

Before the trial commenced, I was met with two applications, both conducted by eminent counsel specifically briefed for the sole purpose of each application. Ben Emmerson QC was briefed by Bowyer's solicitor to argue that the mountain of prejudicial press reports rendered a fair trial for the defendants impossible, notwithstanding Desmond de Silva's presence together with his learned junior. Clare Montgomery QC was briefed to submit that the prosecution's decision to call Duberry as a prosecution witness, having in the first trial unsuccessfully alleged that he had conspired to pervert the course of justice, was irrational and an abuse of the process of the court.

Here were two young stars of the criminal Bar, fluent both on paper and on their feet, and most certainly learned in the law. I could not resist the temptation of contrasting their precocious talents with the seasoned polish of David Fish and Desmond de Silva, neither of whom had been seen in a law library for several decades, whilst both with great charm and easy manner had won the attention and more often than not the votes of numerous appreciative jurors.

Ben Emmerson came loaded with newsprint lambasting Woodgate and Bowyer. They had been described as racists, bullies, drunkards, and overpaid thugs. No jury, it was submitted, could possibly give them a fair hearing. I was not unfamiliar with this line of argument. The press were less than kind to Dr Shipman and more than critical when describing James Bulger's killers, and in both those cases, I opposed similar applications on behalf of the prosecution. Bowyer's eventual acquittal demonstrated the competence of juries to decide cases on the evidence they see and hear in court.

This was an argument that Desmond de Silva could have advanced in his sleep. Many advocates of his standing and seniority would have taken umbrage at his solicitor's decision to instruct the bright, young, well-informed Emmerson QC, carrying with it the subtext that de Silva was not up to the task. Some would have returned the brief, but not so Desmond. He appeared to take pride in the battalion he commanded.

Several days into the trial, with Ben Emmerson long departed, Desmond de Silva asked for the jury to retire whilst he made a legal submission concerning the conduct of an identification parade. The jury having left court, I could not resist asking 'whether Mr Emmerson would be returning to court to argue the point?'

De Silva responded, 'Your Lordship will be amazed to know that I have been entrusted with this weighty point.'

Clare Montgomery's point was more unusual. The prosecution in the first trial had alleged that Duberry had agreed with others to fabricate a cover-up by way of alibi, and thus was a liar. They now sought to call him as a prosecution witness and in the same proceedings were now putting him forward as a witness of truth, intending to give evidence against a former co-conspirator, namely Woodgate. It was, she submitted, a situation in which the judge should intervene to prevent such double-dealing. Duberry was a defendant in the first trial and was now a most reluctant prosecution witness. I ruled against her.

The prosecution had acted in good faith. At the outset of the first trial, they believed that Duberry had agreed with others to tell a series of lies to extricate his friends. In the witness box at the first trial, however, Duberry had departed from any agreed script and asserted that Woodgate had confessed to him that on the night of the attack he had been in a fight with Asian lads. 'My best mate Woody begged me not to go into the box,' he said. Prior to the second trial, the prosecution believed that Duberry could give truthful and relevant evidence. Indeed, he had done so at the first trial on oath.

The trial lasted for ten weeks. Much of the evidence focused on the chase through the streets and a great deal of it was confusing and contradictory. Some witnesses were Leeds United supporters. One purported to recognise Woodgate as a participant in the chase by the manner and style of his running; he had seen him numerous times at Elland Road and his gait was most distinctive. I had spent many a day in court in my youth, usually defending Glaswegian youths for pursuing and assaulting local lads on Blackpool promenade. I was very much at home in this trial, and most appreciative of the quality of advocacy during it.

A moment of high drama arose when the prosecution called Duberry to give evidence. He was a central defender in the Leeds United team. So too was Woodgate. They played alongside one another, were great friends, and had been central to the success of Leeds United. Clare Montgomery in the absence of the jury had indicated Duberry's reluctance to give evidence. However, Duberry gave his evidence as the prosecution had anticipated. Woodgate had confessed his involvement to him and had asked him not to give evidence at the first trial.

David Fish cross-examined him firmly and fairly, but there was no shaking Duberry. In his closing address to the jury, David Fish said, 'Rarely, if ever, can a prosecution team have called, knowingly called, such an accomplished and persistent liar.' When first interviewed, Duberry had told detectives that he had not been aware of any violence in Leeds city centre that night.

An even greater problem for the Woodgate team was the evidence of Andrew Clarke, a window cleaner, who stated that he saw Woodgate lash out at an Asian youth and that he tried to kick a group of Asians. When challenged by David Fish that he had not mentioned any attempt to kick Asians in his statement to the police, Mr Clarke said, 'My first concern was for my family, not football. Football doesn't mean anything to me anymore.' He thought Leeds supporters would attack him after seeing his photograph in the press.

In an immaculate closing speech, David Fish stressed that there was no forensic evidence linking Woodgate to the attack and although he had lied to the police investigating the assault, he had done so out of loyalty to his friends. 'No blood was found on him or his clothing, no injuries.'

Lee Bowyer's principal difficulty was blood from the victim found on his Prada jacket. Two possible innocent explanations were advanced for this. CCTV evidence showed Bowyer embracing someone said to have been involved in the attack. Forensic scientist Mark Webster also told the jury that Bowyer could have slipped and fallen into a pool of Sarfraz's blood on the ground.

A further difficulty arose from the fact that when he was arrested, Bowyer was asked to hand over the clothes and shoes that he was wearing on the night of the attack. The shoes he submitted bore no bloodstains and the prosecution claimed they were different to the ones he could be seen wearing on CCTV footage at the entrance to the club, which looked as if they had buckles. There were white patches to be seen between the trouser legs and the shoes. These were the buckles, said the Crown. Bowyer had handed in the wrong shoes, fearing that the shoes he was actually wearing would provide damning forensic evidence. Bowyer's case was that the white patches were his white ankles and not buckles.

It was a critical matter for the jury to determine, namely white ankles or buckles. This involved prolonged study of CCTV evidence, which on any view lacked definition and clarity.

At the first trial, there had been a moment of humour when Desmond de Silva had asked Bowyer to put the trousers on that he had worn that night. He assured him, 'Don't worry, the jury won't see you.'

Bowyer replied sheepishly, 'I am not wearing any under-pants.'

De Silva spluttered, 'What . . . you don't wear underpants either?'

In the retrial, Bowyer changed outside court, walked up and down in front of the jury and then changed back. From my perspective, the demonstration was inconclusive, which was sufficient for defence purposes, of course, if the jury reached a similar conclusion.

One matter attracted considerable debate, both in the press and on social media, namely was this a racially motivated attack. The prosecution made it clear from the outset that they did not allege it was so motivated. I unhesitatingly agree with that decision. Whether I agreed or not was in fact irrelevant, since the prosecution were not alleging racial motivation. There was no evidence to support such an allegation. Indeed, there was positive evidence to the contrary, namely the taunting and attack upon Hewison outside the club by an Asian youth.

Whilst the *Sunday Mirror* article alleged that the word 'Paki' was shouted towards the Asian group, there was no such evidence given in court. The clear evidence was that the initial aggression came from the Asian students mocking the ejected and drunken Hewison. David Poole expressed himself most clearly in declaring that any attack upon any member of the Asian group was not racially motivated.

In a trial lasting for ten weeks, a judge has every opportunity to assess the performance of the jury. This jury demonstrated intense application and took five days to reach their verdicts. The evidence was both detailed and contradictory. Bowyer was acquitted of both counts and Clifford convicted of both counts, whilst Woodgate and Caveney were acquitted of inflicting grievous bodily harm with intent, but convicted of affray. I sentenced Clifford to six years' imprisonment and Woodgate and Caveney to 100 hours of community service. A spokesman for the family of Sarfraz Najeib said the verdicts were a 'tremendous disappointment'.

For my part, the verdicts came as no surprise and were easily justified on the evidence. An affray is 'intentionally using or threatening unlawful violence such as would cause a reasonable person to fear for his safety'. In the context of this case, a person using violence, having regard to the actual violence inflicted, would inevitably be convicted of inflicting grievous bodily harm. Those involved in the chase and threatening violence, but not inflicting violence, committed the offence of affray.

More than one newspaper chose to criticise me for failing to jail Woodgate. It is important to note that the maximum sentence for affray is three years' imprisonment, whilst the maximum sentence for an assault occasioning actual bodily harm is five years' imprisonment. It follows that an affray is a less serious offence than an assault occasioning actual bodily harm. Sentencing guidelines for affray were not effective until August 2008. Applying those today to Woodgate's conduct and accepting, as a sentencer must, that he chased but did not assault or cause injury, the appropriate starting point based on a first-time offender pleading not guilty would be a high-level community order.

I had in mind at the time the case in 1995 of the footballer Eric Cantona, who immediately after being sent off, and having been abused by a member of the crowd, left the pitch, entered the stand and kicked and punched his abuser several times. He was sentenced to two weeks' imprisonment, but on appeal had his prison sentence quashed and was ordered to do 120 hours of community service. Whilst the facts are plainly different, the case had two connections to the present.

Firstly, Eric Cantona had earlier played for Leeds United and secondly, when his prison sentence was quashed, he was represented by David Poole QC, as he then was. It was significant that Woodgate was in full-time employment with no previous convictions and faced further disciplinary action from his club. He was suspended from international football during the trial process and faced a substantial bill for representation over two lengthy trials. I had observed his demeanour over ten weeks, and I was satisfied that he was shaken and visibly distressed by the prolonged court process. I remain satisfied that a sentence of imprisonment would not have been appropriate.

My abiding recollection of the case is the very high standard of advocacy of all involved and the success that both Woodgate and Bowyer have made in their playing careers and coaching careers thereafter. As I write, Woodgate is manager at Middlesbrough, whilst Bowyer is manager of Charlton Athletic.

# Chapter 10

## The Murder of Jill Dando

IN JULY 2002, numerous cardboard boxes appeared in my room at the Royal Courts of Justice. They bore the name Barry Michael George. I recognised the name instantly and realised that I must be part of the constitution assigned to hear the appeal of the convicted murderer of Jill Dando. I was to sit with the Lord Chief Justice, Lord Woolf, and Mr Justice Curtis. In April 2001, Barry George had been convicted by a majority of 10 to 1. After an appeal lasting several days, we concluded: 'Looking at the evidence as a whole, we have no doubt as to the correctness of the conviction.'

In his outstanding book *Memoirs of a Radical Lawyer*, Michael Mansfield, who conducted both the first trial and appeal on behalf of Barry George, wrote, 'When the jury returned the guilty verdict, I could hardly contain my feelings of pain, distress and anger. How could this be?'

In November 2007, the new Lord Chief Justice, Lord Phillips, Lord Justice Leveson and Mr Justice Simon heard a reference from the Criminal Cases Review Commission and having received fresh evidence, not before the jury and likewise not before our constitution, they quashed the conviction and ordered a retrial. At that retrial, he was found not guilty and discharged. His counsel at the retrial was Bill Clegg QC. In his very readable book *Under the Wig*, he wrote, 'To this day I have no better idea than anyone else who killed Miss Dando, but I am certain that it wasn't Barry George.'

When two pre-eminent Queen's Counsel express themselves so forcefully and ten jurors and three judges sitting in the Court of Appeal (Criminal Division) have expressed themselves as having no doubt as to the correctness of the conviction, it is important to consider the chain of events and if possible to learn from them.

At about 11.30 a.m. on 26 April 1999, Jill Dando was shot in the head outside her front door at 29 Gowan Avenue, Fulham. Nobody witnessed the shooting. It was a single shot to the head behind the top of the left ear. An impression of the muzzle was discernible, indicating that it had been pressed firmly against the left side of her head when fired, and no silencer was used. A fired bullet and casing were recovered from the vicinity of the doorstep.

Two days after the murder, police received information directing their attention to Barry George, but it was almost one year later that he was first spoken to by police officers on 11 April 2000; he was then arrested on 25 May 2000 and charged on 29 May 2000. It is fair to say that the police received over 1,100 messages in the two weeks immediately following the murder, but the message relating to Barry George was given a low priority until the following February.

In submitting that the trial should be stayed on the grounds of delay, Michael Mansfield submitted 'that it should have been glaringly obvious that witness statements should have been taken from a number of witnesses.' The alibi depended on the accuracy of timings and it was submitted that Mr George had been disadvantaged by the unreasonable delay. This submission failed at trial and we agreed with the judge's decision on appeal. It seemed to the judge, Mr Justice Gage, reasonable in the context of this massive investigation that at the time, the information should not have received a higher priority.

There were four strands to the prosecution case, namely, eye-witness evidence, repeated lies told by Barry George, an attempt by him to create a false alibi, and a single particle of firearms residue found in the inside pocket of his overcoat after his arrest.

The witness who made a positive identification of Barry George from a video identification procedure stated that she saw the man identified at 6.57 a.m. on the morning of the shooting almost directly opposite Jill Dando's house, looking at houses on the opposite side of the road. She had him in her view for about one minute and wondered what he was doing. When she drew level with him, he looked at the ground and then started to clean the windscreen with his hand, with his left arm against his face. He had stopped when she turned and looked back. The car was maroon and was double-parked outside No. 28 Gowan Avenue, almost directly opposite No. 29.

Her description of the man prior to the identification was a good one and the prosecution submitted that this identification was unassailable. She had a close view of the man. Her evidence was clear and compelling, and her description tallied with others who knew him. The defence contended she was mistaken. No maroon car has ever been traced and a witness in Gowan Avenue at 7.15 a.m. saw no car double-parked.

The jury heard evidence from four other witnesses that had seen a man similar in appearance to Barry George close to the scene of the murder, who were able to give detailed descriptions similar to those of Barry George, but who were unable to make positive and unequivocal identifications at the video procedure. An overriding problem at the video procedure was that two men, No. 2 (Barry George) and No. 8 (a volunteer), were very similar in appearance, as Michael Mansfield readily conceded.

Further problems for the prosecution arose from the fact that two of these four witnesses were transported to their homes in the same police vehicle as the witness who had made a positive identification of Barry George at position No. 2, combined with the fact that one of these four witnesses had an affair with one of the officers in the case.

The most important problem was that the identification procedures took place in October 2000, some eighteen months after
the observations. It may be significant that one of these four
witnesses stated that 'one arm was concealed as if in his pocket'.
These observations of a man bearing a description strikingly
similar to Barry George in Gowan Avenue, alone and on foot,
were at 9.30 a.m., 9.50 a.m., 10.10 a.m., and 11.35 a.m. approximately. The observation at 10.10 a.m. was by a postman
delivering letters to the deceased's home, when he saw a man
in the road looking directly at 29 Gowan Avenue.

Having reviewed the identification evidence, we concluded
that there was sufficient evidence from which the jury could
conclude that each witness saw the same man and that the man
was Barry George. We accepted the Crown's submission that
there was an underlying unity of description, not only in the
descriptions, but in the circumstances of what each witness saw
the man doing. There was a general consistency in the identification evidence. The Crown submitted that it was
inconceivable that there could have been two such men of similar
appearance behaving in a similar manner in Gowan Avenue, in
a period of time so proximate to the murder of Miss Dando.

Apart from the identifying witnesses, we concluded: 'There
was a considerable volume of other circumstantial evidence,
independent of the identifying witnesses, which suggests there
was no error made and coincidence is not the explanation for
similarity in what the identifying witnesses stated they saw.' We
listed the other circumstantial evidence as: The Murder Weapon,
The Firearms Discharge Residue, The Fibre, Links with Gowan
Avenue, Fascination with Celebrities, Fascination with Firearms,
Flawed Alibi, and Lies.

The agreed expert evidence was that the weapon was either
a deactivated or reactivated 9mm handgun, or a converted 9mm
handgun, originally capable of firing blanks only, or a handgun
that had a smooth barrel, originally over 24 inches in length,

which may or may not have been shortened. The police had found amongst Barry George's documents a note written by him containing details of three handguns, including a Colt Bruni handgun. They also discovered a photograph of him holding a Colt Bruni handgun whilst wearing a gas mask. Barry George's finger was on the trigger.

When questioned about this photograph, he denied that it was of him and denied also that it was taken inside his flat. Both denials were manifestly false. The police also found within his possession an advertisement for 'deactivated weapons', which demonstrated the ready availability of such weapons and Barry George's interest in them. A shoulder holster was also found in the flat.

When interviewed by the police, Barry George denied that he had ever owned a gun and said he had no access to them. Two witnesses were called to give evidence to the contrary. David Dobbin spoke of an occasion in 1985 when Barry George came to the door of his house and discharged a pistol at the door. It was a blank gun and he saw the cartridge ejected. Susan Coombe had twice seen Barry George with handguns and also gave evidence that the photograph of him holding a gun whilst wearing a gas mask was taken in his flat. On the second occasion she saw him with a handgun, he showed it to her and then put it under the bed. Further, Barry George had been in the Territorial Army between 1981 and 1983 and went to the Kensington Pistol Club, his last attendance being in September 1982.

Evidence of familiarity with handguns was significant. The agreed evidence of Dr West, an eminent pathologist, was that the killer was used to and experienced in handling handguns. The deceased had been shot at very close quarters, with the foresight of the gun in contact with the left side of her head.

Barry George's flat was searched on 17 April 2000. A coat was hanging on the kitchen door. It was taken to the Forensic

Science Laboratory. Within the inside pocket of the coat was a small particle, 11.5 microns in size, which on analysis was found to be Firearms Discharge Residue ('FDR'). Two particles with matching chemical constituents had been found in the victim's hair and on her raincoat; the constituent chemical compounds were barium, lead and antimony. There are five principal manufacturers of cartridges and the particles recovered from the victim and from Barry George's inside coat pocket were chemically indistinguishable. Other chemicals are used, including silicon and aluminium; however, the two particles from the victim's head were identical in manufacture with the particle in the coat pocket.

Mr Keeley, a senior forensic officer specialising in FDR, gave evidence that the micron particle recovered from the coat was consistent with having come from the same cartridge used in the killing. The finding of only one particle was not significant. Residue would more often than not be found on the firer of the gun, but would not be found on ordinary members of the public, unless they had been associated with firearms. Dr Renshaw, equally well qualified, agreed with Mr Keeley's findings.

Dr John Lloyd, a forensic scientist of thirty years' experience, gave evidence for the defence. He said:

> There could scarcely be less residue at all. The presence of a single particle does raise serious doubts as to where it may have come from. It might have been something which is just a casual contamination. Some laboratories have in fact not reported findings as significant when so little residue is found. It should be said that in this case, this is the first occasion when it has been suggested that the single particle could be the relic of an event which has occurred a year ago. It is quite a unique suggestion. The claims that it is so related are based on scientifically unsupported assumptions. The evidence is dependent on flawed police procedures. It is my view that this evidence is not reliable as evidence of the defendant's involvement in the shooting.

There was accordingly a significant difference between the views of the two prosecution scientists and the defence scientist. A large part of the trial was given over to the issue of possible contamination. Mr Keeley considered it most unlikely that the particle might have entered the coat pocket when the defendant visited a military clothing shop on 9 April 1999, some seventeen days before the shooting. Dr Lloyd disagreed, saying that nothing could be ruled out. There was lengthy debate as to whether contamination from the search might have taken place, and whether gloves worn by officers should have been forensic gloves, rather than rubber gloves.

The main thrust of the defendant's argument on contamination was that the photographic sessions had corrupted the integrity of the coat, the police procedures were flawed, and precautions should have been taken at the studio to demonstrate that no contamination had occurred. The prosecution called substantial evidence designed to show that no contamination could have occurred during the session. We were satisfied that there was no reasonable possibility of contamination from the police or forensic scientists.

Michael Mansfield submitted that the judge should have excluded the evidence relating to the FDR on the grounds that its admission had adversely affected the fairness of the trial. We could see no sound basis for the judge to have excluded the FDR evidence from the jury's consideration. Resolving a conflict between experts is a matter for a jury and not for the judge. On the evidence before this jury, it was clearly open to them to conclude that the particle in Barry George's inside coat pocket and the particles recovered from Miss Dando had a common origin.

A fibre was recovered on the deceased's raincoat that was microscopically indistinguishable from the trousers worn by the appellant. It was, however, a common fibre and too short for a test to extract dye. The defence expert described the finding as insignificant. We concluded that it was not more than weak support for a connection between Barry George and Miss Dando, but that it was still a minor part of the whole picture.

The flawed alibi involved Barry George signing an alibi statement prior to the trial in which he asserted that at the time of the murder he was at the offices of Hammersmith and Fulham Action for Disability (HAFAD). He asserted that he left home between 10.30 and 10.45 a.m., that the journey took about half an hour, and he left at approximately 1.00 p.m. Therefore he was at HAFAD for between one and three-quarter hours and two hours, according to his alibi statement. He asserted that he then went to the offices of Traffic Cars at approximately 1.15 p.m. The prosecution called four witnesses, who stated that Barry George stayed only for a short time, because he had made no appointment.

Barry George, in his signed alibi statement, asserted that he made a telephone call from HAFAD on his mobile phone. The prosecution proved that such a call was not in fact made from HAFAD. The route that Barry George asserted he took from his home to the HAFAD offices made no sense, was circuitous, and appeared designed to avoid his being in Gowan Avenue. We concluded that the evidence relied on by the Crown, including CCTV evidence, effectively destroyed Barry George's alibi and further amply demonstrated that he had told significant lies when interviewed by the police.

On 28 April, two days later, Barry George again visited HAFAD, wearing different clothes to those seen by witnesses on the day of the murder in Gowan Avenue. There was no sensible purpose for this visit. Barry George sought to explain it by saying that he was concerned that his friends said he bore a striking resemblance to a published E-FIT picture and he wished to assure them that he was not the murderer. In fact, the E-FIT was not published until 30 May.

Barry George told the police when they interviewed him that

he did not know where Gowan Avenue was. In fact, he had a card in his flat from a doctor's surgery in Gowan Avenue and a photograph of a woman walking past the same surgery. He had told an acquaintance that he had a special friend who lived in Gowan Avenue and it was a lady friend. In fact, the circuitous route to HAFAD told to the police took him along Gowan Avenue.

Barry George told the police when they interviewed him that he had not heard of Jill Dando. The prosecution called two witnesses to establish that Barry George knew Jill Dando. One worked in a jeweller's shop in Carnaby Street. He had told her that he had met a number of celebrities through his cousin Freddie Mercury. These included Princess Diana and the lady from *Crimewatch*. When asked if that was Jill Dando, he said, 'Yes.' The police recovered a volume of material from the appellant's flat, including newspapers with photographs of Jill Dando that went back as far as 1990.

There were four copies of the same BBC internal magazine, *Ariel*, dated 27 April 1999, with a full-page photograph of the deceased on the cover and inside was the story of the murder. Barry George also had in his flat a number of pictures of celebrity female newscasters, several taken by him from the television. He had shown extraordinary interest in the aftermath of the murder, stating that he looked like the killer. He told the postman that he had seen the killer.

Finally, the prosecution established that Barry George was fascinated with firearms. He had in his possession a document setting out the recent legislation in respect of deactivating firearms. He was photographed holding a Bruni pistol and in a different photograph holding a Kalashnikov rifle. When asked about this photograph by the police, he denied that he was the person holding the gun. He had a list of guns in his own handwriting, a gunsmith's card and various entries in *Exchange and Mart* relating to deactivated firearms, private investigators and

ID cards. Having initially denied ever owning a firearm, he eventually admitted having owned two.

Barry George was asked by the police in interview if he had ever been a member of a gun club. He replied that he had been many years earlier, but had not been accepted as a full member. He was asked what names he had used during his lifetime. He replied, 'Barry Michael George, Steven Francis Majors, Thomas Palmer, Barry Bulsara, Barry Michael George again.' He had missed out Paul Gadd, and also an earlier claim that he was the cousin of Jeff Lynne of the Electric Light Orchestra. He was asked if he was Freddie Mercury's cousin and said he was not, but admitted telling a number of people that he was.

Michael Mansfield sought to counter the prosecution case with an alternative scenario. In short, it was submitted that Miss Dando's killing was in retribution for the NATO attack upon the headquarters of Serbian television, owned by Slobodan Milosevic, with a cruise missile that killed seventeen people only three days before Miss Dando's murder. The link to Miss Dando was said to be twofold. Firstly, she had made an appeal on television for Kosovan refugees, who were the victims of the genocide carried out by the Milosevic regime, and secondly, the chief executive of BBC News, Tony Hall, had received a death threat the day after Miss Dando's murder.

In support of this scenario, Michael relied on the fact that the discharged round had been manually crimped, which was commonplace amongst the armies of the former Soviet bloc, including the Balkans, Yugoslavia, and Serbia in particular. There was nothing discovered amongst Barry George's many documents to suggest that he had any knowledge of or experience for carrying out this adaptation. It was contended that with her image on the front cover of the *Radio Times*, Jill Dando was the public face of the BBC and an obvious target for a Serbian hit squad, who had only two weeks earlier shot dead the owner of a newspaper in Serbia that had criticised Milosevic.

This alternative scenario did not trouble the court. The jury by their verdict had rejected it and there was simply no evidence to substantiate the theory, nor has any ever been forthcoming, notwithstanding the most thorough ongoing investigation. The jury were faced with two scenarios and unquestionably there was significantly more evidence against Barry George than there was against any alternative Serbian hitman.

Bill Clegg QC, in *Under the Wig*, wrote: 'My tactics for the retrial were different to those employed by Michael Mansfield seven years earlier. I wanted to put all the onus on the prosecution to prove my client had been responsible for Miss Dando's death. I refused to put up any distracting alternative scenarios suggesting who might have been responsible and would drive home my message that "It wasn't Barry". Ruling your client out as the killer is usually a far better course of action than trying to solve the crime yourself.'

At the end of the first appeal, Lord Woolf, Mr Justice Curtis and I stated our conclusion that we had no doubt as to the correctness of the conviction. That judgment was delivered on 29 July 2002.

## The Retrial

Five years later, on 5 November 2007, the case was back before the court, now presided over by Lord Phillips of Worth Matravers, the Lord Chief Justice, upon a reference by the Criminal Cases Review Commission on the ground: 'New evidence calls into question the firearms discharge evidence at trial and the significance attached to that evidence.'

The single ground of appeal advanced before the court was that the evidence in relation to the discovery of the particle of FDR in the pocket of the appellant's overcoat, which was relied on by the prosecution at the trial as of great significance, was, in reality, of no probative value.

It transpired that in January 2006, the Forensic Science Service introduced new guidelines in relation to conclusions to be drawn from single particles. It concluded by stating that 'in most cases it is unlikely that any evidential weight can be attached to the finding'.

In September 2006, two experts reappraised the evidence in relation to FDR that was given at trial. They concluded that the FDR findings should be reported as inconclusive with regard to the issue of whether or not Mr George shot Miss Dando. The evidence provided no assistance to anyone asked to judge whether Mr George was the man who shot Miss Dando, or whether Mr George had nothing to do with the incident. It appears that every bus, train and Underground station will contain particles of FDR, in the same way that almost every used banknote will have traces of cocaine.

Unsurprisingly the court allowed the appeal, but considered there was a sufficiency of other evidence to justify a retrial. In the absence of any reference to the finding of the single particle of FDR, it came as no surprise that a second jury could not be sure of Barry George's guilt and accordingly, after eight years in custody, he was found not guilty and released. As Bill Clegg observed at the conclusion of his chapter on the case, 'He received no compensation, because he was unable to prove beyond reasonable doubt that he was innocent, which is the high test before compensation is awarded.'

What went wrong? Should Barry George have been traced sooner? The defence complained that the police received information between 26 April 1999, the day of the murder, and 14 June 1999, which should have caused the investigating team to appreciate by that date that Barry George was a person whom they needed to interview as a matter of urgency. Steps taken to trace and identify him between February and May 2000 should have been made, it was said, between April and June 1999.

Delay can be highly prejudicial in a defence of alibi. An

accused person will have increased difficulty in recounting movements over twelve months after the event. Delay can also adversely
prejudice both prosecution and defence where visual identification is in issue. Remembering with accuracy a face more than
twelve months after a short period of observation is beyond
many potential witnesses.

In their defence, the police pointed to the 1,109 messages
received between the murder on 26 April and 12 May. They
were overwhelmed by the volume of information flooding in.
However, there were multiple calls naming Barry George, or
his alias Barry Bulsara (one of the many used by him). Barry
George had a significant criminal record. According to David
James Smith, author of *All About Jill: The Life and Death of Jill
Dando*, Barry George had been accused of other sexual offences,
back in the 1980s, when he had also been found late at night
lurking in bushes near Kensington Palace (then the home of
Princess Diana), dressed in military clothing and carrying rope
and a knife.

As David James Smith observes and a profiler so advised, the
police should have been very aware that the assailant might have
been a stalker. He refers to the murders of John Lennon, Gianni
Versace and Rebecca Schaeffer, all shot dead outside their homes
by dysfunctional obsessives.

As a court, we accepted that there had been an element of
delay, but not sufficiently serious to justify the exceptional course
of staying the proceedings. There is, of course, a solution to
being overwhelmed by an abundance of information and that
is the deployment of additional personnel; this was the highest
profile murder necessitating efficient and timely investigation.
The public's confidence in the criminal justice process was at
stake and ultimately the process failed.

An element of the community must share responsibility for
the delay occasioned by the volume of information showered
upon the police. Much of it was genuine and well intentioned;

a small proportion, however, in this case and in other high-profile cases, was malicious, obstructive, deviant or simply false. Those who supply false information commit the offence of wasting police time, or attempting to pervert the course of justice, but more often than not are dismissed as crackpots fixated with the case and with celebrity. Proceeding against them would afford them the publicity they crave and waste even more police time.

As David James Smith observed in an article for the *Sunday Times*, 'A number of strange people tried to insinuate themselves into the inquiry after her death, suggesting they were either the killer or had assisted the killer.' Every such disclosure necessitated investigation.

A further aspect of this process demands consideration. The evidence of the prosecution scientists in relation to FDR at the trial in 2001 was comprehensively undermined by the same two scientists in the second appeal in 2007. It is not suggested that they were other than honest and genuine in the evidence they gave on each occasion. Discussions had taken place prior to the first trial in November 2001 between Mr Keeley and Dr Evett of the Forensic Science Service (FSS), in which Mr Keeley had expressed the opinion that the finding of a single particle was neutral. It was no more likely to have come from the gun that killed Miss Dando than from some extraneous source.

When Dr Evett came to read the summing up, he observed 'that it was unbalanced in the way that it presented the FDR evidence to the jury in that, while it paid much attention to the fact that it was unlikely that the single particle would have come from an extraneous source, it paid little attention to the fact that it was equally unlikely that the particle had come from the gun that killed Jill Dando.' However, whilst noting his disquiet, Dr Evett took no action, feeling that the jury should have gained the right impression, assisted in no small measure by the evidence of the forensic scientist Dr John Lloyd.

Significantly, Dr Evett's disquiet was not brought to our attention at the first appeal in 2002 and never saw the light of day until 2006, when the FSS introduced its guidelines on conclusions to be drawn from single particles. Had Dr Evett's disquiet been fully aired and canvassed amongst senior members of the FSS, and contact made with Barry George's solicitors in 2002, it is at least arguable that Barry George would have avoided some five years in custody.

It is to be noted that the FSS became extinct in March 2012. It had previously provided forensic science services to the police forces and government agencies of England and Wales as well as other countries. Monthly losses of up to £2 million were cited as justification for the closure of the service. Forensic work is now contracted out to the private sector or carried out at in-house police labs, but in 2015 the National Audit Office warned that standards were slipping, because police were increasingly relying on unregulated experts to examine samples from suspects and crime scenes.

I was astonished and alarmed at the decision to close the Forensic Science Service. I observed at close quarters the work of the service and have no doubt that the closure will not only have damaged public confidence in the criminal justice system, it will seriously impact criminal justice. Smaller police forces will be unable to equip themselves with all the necessary specialisms in forensic science and the independence of private firms used by police will be open to adverse comment by defence advocates. In-house work is not independent and will carry less weight with juries.

The FSS provided a nationwide shared service and best practice in a comprehensive field of specialisms. It attracted scientists of the highest calibre and integrity. I cannot say the same of all private firms; few if any operate nationwide covering every specialism. I anxiously await the reintroduction of a Forensic Science Service announced by the BBC in March

2016, accompanied by the observation that digital analysis of computers and smartphones was being conducted in an 'ad hoc manner', which did not provide value for money.

Finally, I pose a question for the reader's consideration: should Barry George have received compensation for the time he spent in custody?

# Chapter 11

## The Appeal of Jeremy Bamber

IN OCTOBER 2002 I sat with Lord Justice Kay and Mr Justice Wright, hearing the appeal of Jeremy Nevill Bamber. This was in several respects the most shocking case to come my way, either at the Bar or on the Bench. The case involved the planned killing by shooting of five members of the same family, allegedly by the sixth member. The defence involved blaming the appellant's deceased sister for the murders of her parents and twin sons, aged six, and claiming that thereafter his sister had taken her own life by shooting herself twice in the throat. The asserted motive was self-enrichment by the inheritance of his parents' substantial estate.

On 28 October 1986, Bamber was convicted of five counts of murder by a majority of 10–2 following a nineteen-day trial at Chelmsford. He was refused leave to appeal after a full hearing presided over by the then Lord Chief Justice, Lord Lane. The case had now been referred by the Criminal Cases Review Commission, solely because of fresh scientific evidence.

The killings occurred in the early hours of 7 August 1985. The police were alerted by a phone call at 3.26 a.m. made by Bamber.

He told them: 'You've got to help me. My father has rang me and said, "Please come over. Your sister has gone crazy and has got the gun." Then the line went dead.'

Bamber continued saying that his sister had a history of psychiatric illness and that guns were kept at his father's farmhouse. A police car was despatched to the farm and Bamber was asked to meet the police there. En route to the farm, police officers overtook Bamber, who was driving uncharacteristically slowly. At the farmhouse, the police feared there may be a hostage situation and decided to wait outside until daylight. Bamber was asked if it was likely that his sister had gone berserk with a gun and he replied, 'I don't really know. She is a nutter. She's been having treatment.'

At about 7.45 a.m., armed officers entered the premises and found all five occupants dead from gunshot wounds. Mr Bamber lay dead in the kitchen, his wife was dead on the floor in her bedroom, the twin boys were dead in their beds in another room, and Bamber's sister lay on the same floor as her mother. Across her chest and pointing up at her neck, through which the shots that had killed her had been fired, was the rifle used to kill all five members of the family. The rifle bore no silencer; beside her body lay a Bible.

Later examination established that Mr Bamber, aged sixty-one, had been shot four times whilst upstairs, but that he had been able to make his way downstairs, where a violent struggle took place in the kitchen and he was struck a number of times with the rifle. He was found dead in the kitchen. He had numerous injuries consistent with a violent struggle, including a severely fractured jaw, broken teeth in that area, black eyes, a broken nose, bruising to the cheeks, right forearm, left wrist and forearm. Significantly, his injuries meant that he would not have been able to engage in purposeful talk.

In Sheila Caffell's case, there was no mark or injury such as might have been suffered during a fight or scuffle; her fingernails were well manicured and not broken, and there were no marks or indentations on any of her fingers. She had received two contact or near contact bullet wounds to her throat and the higher of the two wounds would have killed her almost instantaneously. The lack of heavy bloodstaining to Sheila Caffell's nightdress suggested that she had not been shot where she lay.

In all, some twenty-five cartridge cases were recovered from the scene and the firearms expert gave evidence as to which of these could be associated with each particular victim. In order to discharge this number of cartridges, some eighteen cartridges must have been placed within the magazine, necessitating two reloads that involved the physical handling of eighteen cartridges. Sheila Caffell's hands and forehead were swabbed and extremely low traces of lead were detected when the swabs were examined, but such levels were consistent with the everyday handling of things around the house.

These results were compared to hand swabs taken from volunteers at the laboratory, who were required to load the magazine with eighteen rounds of ammunition. Significantly higher traces of lead were found than those recorded on the hands of Mrs Caffell. The forensic scientist gave evidence that if Sheila Caffell had loaded eighteen cartridges into a magazine, he would have expected the hand swabs to have revealed appreciably higher deposits of lead.

Mrs Caffell's nightdress was bloodstained. When tested, the blood was consistent with being her own blood. The garment was also examined for the presence of any firearms discharge residue or oil from the rifle. No such traces were found. The scientist gave evidence that there would be a strong chance of finding such residues or markings on the clothing of an individual who had fired a rifle twenty-five times.

The Bible found by Sheila Caffell's body was not hers, but belonged to her mother. It was examined for fingerprints and many belonged to June Bamber, but no print identifiable as Sheila Caffell's was found.

June Bamber's sister had given evidence that she had never known Sheila Caffell use a gun and in her opinion, she would not know how to use one. June Bamber's niece had given evidence that she had never seen Sheila Caffell with a gun and that she would not know one end of the barrel of a gun from another.

Other witnesses called during the trial said they had never seen her with a gun, save for an occasion when she had been photographed carrying one as part of a modelling assignment.

At the trial, the jury were given an opportunity to load cartridges into the magazine, which had a capacity of ten. They found it progressively harder to load as the number of cartridges increased; loading the tenth was exceptionally hard. Assuming a full capacity at the commencement of the shooting, the discharge of the rifle twenty-five times would require it to be reloaded a minimum of two more times. With an empty magazine at commencement, three loadings would be necessary. The prosecution questioned the ability of Sheila Caffell to perform such task.

The stock of the rifle was damaged, with a piece of wood missing. A broken fragment of wood recovered from the kitchen floor was that missing piece, confirming that the rifle had been used in the struggle in the kitchen. There was blood smearing on the barrel and splashes of blood on the left side of the weapon, consistent with it having been used to strike a bleeding person. There were no traces of blood within the barrel itself.

The weapon was examined for fingerprints. A print from the appellant's right forefinger was found on the breech end of the barrel, above the stock and pointing across the gun, and Sheila Caffell's right ring fingerprint was found on the right side of the butt pointing downwards. There were three further finger marks on the rifle, each of insufficient detail for identification purposes.

Three days after the murders, the sound moderator or silencer was found by relatives at the back of the gun cupboard in the downstairs office. David Boutflour found the moderator and the finding was witnessed by his father, his sister and the farm secretary. They immediately observed that the surface of the silencer had been damaged; there was red paint and blood upon it. The moderator was packaged and collected by the police.

Red paint was recovered by scientists from the knurled end

of the moderator and found to match recent damage to the underside of a mantel shelf in the kitchen. Each was found to contain some fifteen layers of paint and varnish. Casts were taken from the marks and impressions on the underside of the shelf and these were consistent with having been caused by the moderator, and there had been more than one contact between the moderator and the shelf.

Traces of blood were found in three places on the outside of the moderator and confirmed to be of human origin, but there were insufficient quantities to permit grouping analysis. Inside the moderator, at the end from which the bullet would exit, there was a considerable amount of blood, sufficient for a number of grouping tests. The forensic scientist, Mr Hayward, testified that the blood could have come from Sheila Caffell, but not from any of the other individuals involved. There was a possibility it was a mixture of blood from Nevill and June Bamber, but that possibility was a 'remote' one.

He concluded that since (a) the blood inside the moderator belonged to the same group as Sheila Caffell and (b) there was no blood within the barrel of the gun, that Sheila Caffell had been shot whilst the moderator was fitted to the rifle.

Mr Fletcher, the firearms expert, reached a similar conclusion, namely that the moderator had been fitted to the gun when Sheila Caffell had been shot. He attributed the presence of blood within the moderator to the phenomenon of 'back-splatter'. This occurs when the expansion of gases created by a bullet being discharged creates back pressure, which in turn propels blood from the wound back towards the weapon. This effect is seen only when the muzzle of the weapon is in contact with, or very close range to the victim.

Exercises and tests were carried out within the forensic science laboratory, which established that it would have been physically impossible for a woman of Sheila Caffell's height and reach to have operated the trigger and shot herself with the moderator attached to the rifle. She could not have positioned the weapon so as to have shot herself in the throat. She could only have committed suicide if the moderator had been removed.

The sole basis or referral to the court related to fresh evidence in the form of DNA testing of the moderator. The Criminal Cases Review Commission expressed itself thus:

> In the Commission's view, the new DNA evidence undermines a key aspect of the Crown's case as presented to the jury and to which the trial judge gave considerable emphasis in his summing up. The new evidence is admissible, is capable of belief and affords a possible ground for allowing the appeal. There is a reasonable explanation for the failure to adduce this evidence at trial, in that the DNA techniques used were not available at the time.

The Commission recorded the information available to it as:

> The silencer had been submitted by the Commission to the Forensic Science Service for examination in order to establish whether there was more than one person's DNA inside it. On 6 March 2000 the Commission was informed that the tests had identified the DNA of at least two people inside the silencer and that there was both male and female DNA present. The female DNA was stronger than the male DNA and was present through the inside of the silencer. They were not able to say that the DNA readings were derived from blood and they were not able to identify from whom the DNA had originated. All blood exhibits from which sample references could be taken for June Bamber and Sheila Caffell were destroyed in 1996.
>
> A sample of DNA was subsequently obtained from Sheila Caffell's natural mother and tests carried out, which indicated that the DNA in the silencer could not have come from Sheila Caffell.

The Commission concluded:

> Whilst it may be arguable that the recent DNA tests do not establish that the source of the female DNA was blood, the Commission believes, as a matter of probability, that it is from blood because it was found deep within the silencer by the scientists, and the Commission does not believe that any possible contamination from them is likely to have been found that far down inside. Also given that it is an accepted fact that blood was in the silencer in 1985, the Commission considers it is much more likely that the DNA is from blood found in the silencer at the time.
>
> Considering the length of time that has passed and the fact that much of the blood was swabbed out for blood grouping, the Commission does not consider that the negative KM result strengthens the possibility that the DNA does not originate from blood. In any event the Commission considers that the absence of Sheila Caffell's DNA is significant. The Commission considers that the fresh evidence relating to the silencer severely undermines the Crown's case against Mr Bamber as it was presented to the jury.

Ground 15 of the Appellant's Grounds of Appeal read:

> Fresh DNA evidence not available at trial and now available supports the contention that blood in the silencer said to be that of Sheila Caffell was in fact a mixture of the blood of Nevill and June Bamber. The appellant has been denied the opportunity of strengthening this ground by the deliberate destruction of exhibits by the police in February 1996 in breach of their own guidelines as to the destruction of such exhibits.

It may be considered irrelevant to enquire into the origin of human blood within the moderator, since the undoubted presence of blood within the device established that the device was attached to the rifle at the time of the shootings; therefore with the moderator attached, Sheila Caffell could not, by reason of the length of the weapon, have shot herself. However, Mr Turner on behalf of the appellant, advanced the following scenario: Sheila Caffell shot her sons, her mother and her father with the moderator attached. She then removed the moderator and stored it in the cupboard, before returning upstairs and shooting herself twice in the throat, only the second shot proving instantly fatal.

We considered the ground of appeal at length and heard four expert witnesses on this topic, two on each side. A rehearsal of their evidence is unnecessary. Subsequent to the reference of the case to the court, further DNA testing took place on other parts of the moderator. All seven results indicated that DNA from more than one person was present. Components matching Sheila Caffell's profile were detected in five of those seven results. What was not clear was whether Sheila Caffell's DNA derived from blood or whether it was within the moderator. However, we reached the conclusion that having regard to the most recent tests, Sheila Caffell's DNA may have been within the moderator.

There was nothing to establish whether the DNA derived from blood. The moderator had been examined by expert after expert from its recovery to the most recent tests. In September 1986, Dr Lincoln, the defence expert, swabbed the upper baffle plates and found no trace of any blood. In March 1999, Mr Ismail and Mr Webster examined the moderator and a number of discrete tests for blood were performed, but no blood was detected. We found it impossible to conclude that any particular finding of DNA necessarily came from blood.

Accordingly, we rejected the Commission's proposition that the source of the female DNA was from blood because it was deep inside the silencer. The silencer/moderator had been dismantled, examined and swabbed numerous times before these tests with no finding of blood.

We necessarily considered how DNA might have entered the moderator other than by blood. We considered the full history of the moderator. The Commission asserted that no contamination from the scientist was 'likely to have been that far down inside'. That conclusion ignores the examination by Dr Lincoln in 1986, when all the baffles were removed. It also ignores the use of the moderator at trial, where no sorts of precaution were taken.

Both Mr Hayward and Mr Fletcher had handled the moderator in the witness box, a place where other exhibits were produced without any preventive measures being taken to avoid contact. The judge specifically told the jury that they could 'empty the baffles out later'. They were provided with plastic gloves, and thus the real possibility existed that bloodstained items were handled by the jury with no precautions being taken to ensure that if they then went on to handle the baffles, there was not contamination.

We had no hesitation in concluding that the results of the test giving rise to this reference were completely meaningless. We found no basis for suggesting that Mr Hayward was wrong in his conclusion that part of the flake of blood that was tested from within the moderator was the blood of Sheila Caffell, with the remote possibility that there was a mixture of blood from June Bamber and Nevill Bamber.

We found support for this conclusion from the hitherto undisclosed report of the defence expert Dr Lincoln, dated 19 September 1986, in which he recorded: 'Mr Hayward states that he could detect visible staining on the "upper baffle plates" and that he swabbed these plates so that the blood was taken onto cotton material which could subsequently be used in grouping tests. On this material Mr Hayward successfully determined the ABO and EAP groups and showed the blood to be groups A, EAP BA.'

It has never been contended that Mr Hayward was in error

in his conclusions. At trial, they were never challenged and the disclosure of Dr Lincoln's report now supported them. It was apparent to us that in making their decision to refer this case, the Commission failed to have regard to the full history of the treatment of the moderator and further failed to have full regard to all the evidence in the case.

On 7 September 1986, one calendar month after the murders, Julie Mugford went to the police. She was twenty-one years old and had been Bamber's girlfriend for some three years. On the day after the murders, she made a statement to the police in which she said nothing adverse to him, telling them only that he phoned her about 3.30 a.m. saying there was something wrong at home. On 7 September, however, she told the police that she had omitted a number of matters from her earlier statement.

She told them that soon after their meeting, it became obvious that he disliked his family and wished he could get rid of them. At the trial, she said that he did not get on with his sister, Sheila Caffell, and wanted to get rid of them all; he said his father was getting old, his mother was mad, Sheila was mad as well, and the twins were emotionally disturbed and unbalanced. He told Julie Mugford he had seen copies of his parents' wills.

Miss Mugford's evidence was that Bamber repeatedly spoke of killing his family and the conversations became more frequent between October and December 1984. His initial plan was to burn the farmhouse down with his family inside, but he then appeared to realise that he would destroy the valuables within the property. Later he decided to shoot his family, saying that he could gain entry by a window with a defective lock. He told Miss Mugford that Sheila would be a convenient scapegoat, because of her admission to hospital during Easter 1985. He said it would seem that Sheila had done it and then killed herself.

Miss Mugford spent the weekend before the shooting with Bamber at his home. She saw his mother's bike there and other witnesses saw it there after the killings. He rang her about 9.50 p.m. on the evening of the murders, saying he was 'pissed off', had been thinking about the crime all day, and that it was going to be tonight or never. He rang her again at her lodgings in London between 3.00 and 3.30 a.m., saying, 'Everything is going well. Something is wrong at the farm. I haven't had any sleep all night. Bye, honey, and I love you lots.'

Bamber rang Miss Mugford later in the morning, saying that Sheila had gone mad and that she should not go to work, as a police car would come to pick her up. Later that evening, she asked him if he had done it and he said that he got a friend of his, Matthew MacDonald, to do it, that is to kill his family. Bamber had paid MacDonald £2,000 for the killings.

When Miss Mugford told the police this, they arrested both Bamber and MacDonald. Inquiries revealed that MacDonald could not have been at the farm that night and he was called by the prosecution to give evidence that he had nothing to do with the shootings. Miss Mugford told the police and the jury at trial that she did not want to believe what Bamber had told her, but she became scared and he threatened her that if anything happened to him, she would be implicated.

In the month between the murders and her going to the police, Bamber took her out for frequent meals and bought expensive clothes for himself and for her. They went to the family funerals together, after one of which they drank champagne and cocktails. Miss Mugford began to feel increasingly guilty and he told her he was doing everybody a favour and there was nothing to feel guilty about. On 3 September, she heard Bamber talking on the phone to an ex-girlfriend and him asking her out. She slapped him and he twisted her arm behind her back. Four days later, she went to the police.

When giving the police this information, Julie Mugford told them that at Easter 1985 she had helped Bamber steal about

£970 from a caravan site owned by his family. She also admitted using a cheque book that had been falsely reported as stolen and obtaining some £700 of property. The money had since been repaid and she had been cautioned for the offence.

This was not the only evidence of Bamber's dislike of his family. Julie Mugford's mother gave evidence that Bamber had often told her that he hated his adoptive mother and he described her as quite mad. Bamber had told a farmworker that he was not going to share his money with his sister and gave the impression he did not get on well with Sheila Caffell. Bamber had told a student friend that his parents kept him short of money and that his mother was a religious freak. He said, 'I fucking hate my parents.' He had also told his uncle, 'I could kill anybody . . . I could easily kill my parents.'

Bamber raised fourteen other grounds of appeal, not one of which was remotely arguable. Relating them here would add nothing of interest. The prosecution sought to call additional evidence, but we refused permission on the grounds that it could have been made available at trial if the prosecution had sought to explore the matter. We had no regard to this material when considering the merit of the appeal. The evidence was significant, however, and if accepted, could have led to a finding of guilt quite apart from the many other matters relied upon.

Martin Ismail was a senior scientific officer and major crime service manager with the Forensic Science Service. From the bloodstaining, he concluded that following the second and fatal shot, Sheila Caffell was lying almost flat on her back with her head propped against a bedside cabinet. For her then to slide to be found in the position depicted in the photographs would have required the downward force to be greater than the friction of her body against the floor. In his opinion this simply was not possible, as there would be only the weight of the head providing the downward force.

He concluded that an additional force would have been necessary. It could not have come from Sheila Caffell, since the second shot would have been instantly fatal, and thus she must have been moved by someone else, for example by her legs being pulled. He also considered that the weight and the friction between her skin and the nightdress was likely to have been less than the weight and friction between the nightdress and the carpet. Therefore, he would expect movement of the body within the nightdress, rather than the body and the clothing sliding together across the carpet.

The photographs demonstrated this effect at the back of the nightdress, with the back of the nightdress staying rucked up in its original position. However, the front of the nightdress had not demonstrated this effect. Accordingly, Mr Ismail concluded that the nightdress had been pulled down after Sheila Caffell slid into her final position. Since on the evidence, she was dead by this stage, Mr Ismail concluded that someone else had arranged her nightdress.

My abiding memory of this case is twofold. Firstly, as we recorded in our judgment: 'We do not doubt the safety of the verdicts and the more we examined the detail of the case, the more likely we thought it to be that the jury were right.' At no stage of the case did any member of the court entertain the slightest doubt as to the guilt of the appellant.

Indeed, the proposition that Sheila Caffell shot her parents and twin sons with the moderator attached, battled uninjured and unmarked with her father, reloaded the magazine three times, removed and stored the moderator before shooting herself twice in the throat, was in itself ludicrous. That was regardless of the compelling testimony of Julie Mugford and the plainest of motives for these killings, fittingly described by the trial judge, Mr Justice Drake, as an 'exceptionally monstrous crime'.

Secondly, I remember Lord Justice Kay with both great admiration and affection. He was one month older than me and a good friend. Although having chambers in different cities, we were regular opponents. John was a handful as an adversary. He combined a most powerful intellect with robust and forceful advocacy. Our simultaneous appointments to the High Court and Court of Appeal accurately reflected our respective talents. Four years later, John died, aged sixty.

In the Court of Appeal, John was fashioning an outstanding reputation both as a judge and an administrator. He was at various times chairman of the Criminal Committee of the Judicial Studies Board, the National Criminal Justice Board, the Criminal Justice Council, and the Criminal Justice Consultative Council. In only four years in the Court of Appeal, he had established a reputation that led many, including myself, to have considered him an outstanding candidate as a future Lord Chief Justice.

# Chapter 12

## The Tragedy of the Morecambe
## Bay Cockle Pickers

O N 5 FEBRUARY 2004, at least twenty-one Chinese migrant labourers were drowned by an incoming tide, after picking cockles on the sands of Morecambe Bay. Fifteen members of the group survived. The workers were all undocumented immigrants, mainly from the Fujian province of China, and all apparently untrained and inexperienced. They were trapped by the tide more than one and a half miles from shore.

Commencing in September 2005 at Preston Crown Court, I tried a Chinese gangmaster, Lin Liang Ren, charged with the manslaughter of twenty-one cockle pickers in Morecambe Bay, with facilitating illegal immigration, and three offences of conspiring to pervert the course of justice. His girlfriend, Zhao Xiao Qing, was charged with the immigration offence and the three offences of conspiracy to pervert the course of justice. His cousin, Lin Mu Yong, was charged with the immigration offence. A father and son, David Eden senior and junior, fish merchants, were charged with the immigration offence.

Lin Liang Ren, his girlfriend, and his cousin were convicted on all counts. The Edens were acquitted. Lin Liang Ren was sentenced to a total of fourteen years' imprisonment, Zhao Xiao Qing to four years and nine months, and Lin Mu Yong to four years and nine months.

The trial began in unique fashion with a journey aboard a hovercraft in Morecambe Bay, in order to allow the jury to view the location of the tragedy.

The day was a most balmy, still, sunny day and a total contrast to the February night when the disaster occurred. The defendants waived their right to attend the view and thus the jury, counsel, the court associate and I boarded the vessel, all wearing wellington boots or similar footwear. From the shore, a large expanse of sand appears to be flat, but that is an illusion. We were able to observe that Morecambe Bay is riddled with deep channels, some thirty or forty feet deep, making a speedy escape in the dark virtually impossible either in a vehicle or on foot. The hovercraft travelled away from shore for between one and a half and two miles, before stopping and parking with its engines shut down.

It was mid-morning and on board there was an artificial silence. Jurors and counsel were in close proximity and both realised, and had been told, that intercommunication was not permitted. There was not the slightest breeze and only an occasional seagull or a nervous cough disturbed the tranquillity. Within minutes, however, we heard a sound; it began as a gentle whistle, increasing in volume as the skipper announced that the tide was approaching.

We were to be told later that on a windy night with a high tide, the speed of advance is that of a galloping horse, approximately thirty miles per hour. On this perfect autumnal morning, the tide passed our hovercraft certainly at the speed of a cantering horse, possibly twenty miles per hour. No human being could have outrun that tide. We watched as it filled the channels and gullies and pondered the thought of being on those sands at night in a howling wind, as the water rose. I permitted myself a glance at the jurors: the impact was profound.

Back in the courtroom, we soon learned that Lin Liang Ren was to contend that he was not responsible for the presence of the workers on the sands that night. He was not the boss; he owed none of the deceased a duty of care and was thus not guilty of manslaughter. The principal issue in the trial was simply this: was Lin Liang Ren in control of, and responsible for, the Chinese cockle pickers who died?

The count of facilitating immigration offences alleged that the several defendants made it easier for the immigrants to breach immigration law by housing, feeding, equipping, transporting, clothing, paying, obtaining permits for, and buying and selling of cockles for them. It was alleged that Lin Liang Ren provided accommodation for the labourers, equipped them, paid them, obtained cockling permits for them and, most significantly of all, sold their cockles.

In Miss Zhao's case, it was alleged that she acted as Lin Liang Ren's translator, that she played a significant role in fabricating bogus cockling permit application forms, and played a part in acquiring vehicles and house-hunting for accommodation. In Lin Mu Yong's case, it was alleged that he was a subordinate boss, accommodating, feeding, equipping, playing a part in obtaining permits, and providing his own permit. The case against the Edens was that they facilitated by buying and agreeing to buy cockles, knowing that the labourers were illegal immigrants.

The three conspiracies alleged against Lin Liang Ren and Miss Zhao were that they deliberately removed Lin Liang Ren from the shore in the immediate aftermath of the tragedy, in order to interfere with the police investigation; that at Lancaster police station they both told a series of lies in interview and statements that four travelled to Morecambe and that Miss Zhao was in the car; and finally, both agreed together to instruct and encourage others to give false information to the police.

## The Prosecution Evidence

The evidence commenced with a description of Morecambe Bay given by the bay's leading authority, Cedric Robinson MBE, the Queen's Guide to the Sands. Mr Robinson had spent his life on the sands and became the guide in 1963. The first official guide was appointed in 1548, when the sands were a major transport route, but in recent times, a crossing of the sands has become a popular charity function and walks took place fortnightly through the summer led by Mr Robinson, with groups of up to five hundred taking part. The walks are from either Hest Bank or Arnside over to Flookburgh Point or Kents Bank.

Nobody alive has spent more time on those sands than Cedric Robinson and he explained how the tide comes up the river then the lyring, and then the water comes in all directions, cutting off all possible routes of escape. The Kent Channel and the Kear Channel have changed position, rendering the bay the more dangerous; but whatever danger there may be by day, the bay was more perilous still in darkness, at high tide, and with a strong north-westerly wind or a lot of rainwater. He stated that it was foolhardy of the authorities to open the cockling beds to all and sundry, in his words, 'madness'.

Mr Robinson believed it was a disaster waiting to happen, and before the cockle beds had been opened, he thought those cockles at Warton would never be gathered, because they were in such a dangerous place; far out with hollows, a river on one side, and quickly surrounded by water. There were beds in safer places.

Over the years, he told the court, many people have died in Morecambe Bay. Even experienced people get into difficulties; it can be a trap for people who do not know what they are doing. Mr Robinson went on to describe an occasion when he led a party cockling in the dark; they were thankful to complete the journey, and were received by Mrs Robinson with great relief. He said you cannot play with the tides: five or ten minutes can make all the difference, and any delay can be disastrous.

Whilst cockling was an ancient practice, he went on, with skills passed from father to son, all that has changed; the beds have been poached, both cockles and immature cockles being removed. As to permits, he said no knowledge of cockling or the sands was required. Mr Robinson complained that his advice had not been sought by the authorities before the beds had been opened and the result was bedlam. There was an invasion with quad bikes, litter, damage to the beds and no control.

John Bromley-Davenport QC began his cross-examination on behalf of Lin Liang Ren with what appeared to be an extraordinary question. He said, 'It was pretty obvious, just looking at the situation, to anyone with any nous whatsoever that these Chinese people were illegal immigrants. That was obvious, was it not?'

Mr Robinson answered, 'Yes.'

I asked him why.

'Well, they seem to be in such large numbers, and there did not seem to be much organisation about them. They just seemed to be in gangs, with no knowledge whatsoever. They kept together, they kept themselves to themselves, they didn't seem to mix with the local fishermen, and naturally, if they could not speak English that was much harder for them.'

The question was extraordinary, because it was Lin Liang Ren's case that between late July and mid-August he was boss of a group of workers, before selling his equipment and van to Lin Li Shui. Lin Liang Ren's evidence was that he did not know that his workers were illegal immigrants.

Cedric Robinson was a most impressive witness and established beyond question that Morecambe Bay on a windy February night was a most dangerous place to be, if positioned almost two miles from the shore. The prosecution now went further by calling evidence of earlier incidents in which cocklers had found themselves in difficulties. Not only was Morecambe Bay a dangerous place, the practice of cockling was in itself hazardous.

On three occasions in August 2003, cocklers were in difficulties on the River Dee. On 28 October 2003, eighteen cocklers waded ashore at Southport with the assistance of the police helicopter. On 15 December 2003, at Aldingham, a helicopter was used to lead Chinese cocklers to safety. On 5 January 2004, at Morecambe Bay, a white van got stuck in the sands and was completely abandoned. Cockling had continued after the tragedy and cocklers continued to find themselves in difficulty.

Three weeks later, on 26 February 2004, forty cocklers were in difficulty in Morecambe Bay, but came ashore unaided. On 18 April, four cocklers were cut off by the tide at Hest Bank; the coastguard was deployed, they were recovered and landed ashore. On 28 April, ten persons were reported cut off at Morecambe; the coastguard was deployed and in fact nine persons were rescued by hovercraft. On 3 August 2004, seven cocklers were trapped by fog on the Wirral and subsequently guided ashore. On 13 September, fifteen to twenty people were reported out on the sands at Morecambe, but they managed to make it ashore in safety.

The prosecution relied on this evidence to demonstrate the dangers inherent in cockling away from the shore, necessitating great care on the part of organisers. The defence relied on it to show that the present tragedy was less exceptional than it may have appeared.

The prosecution next called Trevor Fleming, a local cockler. He was some forty years of age and had cockled in Morecambe Bay for twenty years. He worked in a small team of five and they went out about 3.00 p.m., four hours after high water; they could not go out earlier because of high rainfall, which made it impossible to cross the gulley. They were using a quad bike and he described the conditions as very wet, very cold and overcast. They were some two miles from the shore between the Kear and Kent channels and it had taken 20 to 30 minutes to get there, not in a straight line.

He first noticed some Chinese cocklers between 5.00 and 6.00 p.m., when he saw them going out quite late in the shift.

A van drove them out together with a pick-up truck, which was dropping the workers off. Some were walking out and both vehicles were full of people; he said that about thirty to thirty-two workers were dropped off near him. The two vehicles then returned to the shore and were ferrying backwards and forwards. About 5.30 to 5.45 p.m., Mr Fleming's team decided to come in; there was slight rainfall, the wind was picking up, and the tide was going to be coming in a lot quicker than normal. As they came in, the Chinese party were still working or even going out on foot.

He was very much concerned: it would take the Chinese walking out another 35 to 40 minutes to reach the cockling beds, and then they would have to walk back, which would leave literally no time on his calculations for any cockle gathering.

Mr Fleming approached a Chinese worker, but he either did not understand or refused to speak English, and so Mr Fleming tapped his watch, to draw attention to the time. He had calculated that there was only one and a half hour's safe time until the tide turned. Other members of the party also tapped their watches, trying to explain to the Chinese that they were cutting it fine to be walking out on the sands.

Cross-examined, he said he had been on the bay since he was a young lad, taught by his father and uncle. He said you get to respect the area you work in and you learn that from an early age. People who do not know what they are doing should not go out in the bay; you need guidance and instruction over a long period of time. Anybody going out on the sands is risking their life.

He disapproved of the decision to open up Warton sands to a large number of people. He warned the Fisheries Authority before the tragedy happened that it was only a matter of time; it was basically a free-for-all. No authority seemed to be taking any steps to remedy the situation, no guidance was given, and nothing was done to prevent them coming out. Even after the tragedy the same situation prevailed until March 2015, when the beds were closed after having been fished out, decimated.

In the weeks prior to 5 February, there was an incident offshore from Newbiggin when fifty-five or so Chinese workers were cut off by the tide. It was a close shave; the coastguard and different people came in to help them. He had seen the Chinese have problems with their vehicles: they had broken down before they got out there. One broke down five or six times before it reached the cockle beds, whilst carrying Chinese workers.

On 5 February, Mr Fleming would have left the sands by 7.00 p.m. at the latest; he would not have stayed out later because of the wind and excess rainfall. He was then asked if he was so concerned about the Chinese going out at that time, why did he not do something about it? Why did you not inform the coastguard, as you had done the previous August? Why not call them out this night?

Mr Fleming replied most movingly, his voice breaking, 'That is a question I have asked myself every night since the tragedy, and it caused me a lot of distress. How can I police the people who go out on the bay when the authorities, the police and the coastguard did not know they were working in and around that area? I tried to warn the people who were there. Maybe I could have rung the coastguard.'

It was difficult not to sympathise with Mr Fleming. He was clearly most distressed by his failure and yet it was easy to see where this was leading. The Chinese cocklers were deeply resented by the English cocklers. Evidence would later be adduced that petrol had been poured on cockles harvested by the Chinese; the Chinese cocklers worked far faster than the English, and were saturating the market. The point would surely be made that the English, Mr Fleming included, were more than content to see the Chinese perish. The battleground was now firmly established.

The defence case was that Lin Liang Ren was not the boss, and the real culprits were the English cocklers who let them go to their death, the local authority who did nothing to control the sands and granted permits to the untrained and incompetent, the police who did nothing to prevent breaches of immigration law, and the coastguards who failed to guard the coast. The prosecution for their part made two simple points: Lin Liang Ren was the boss and he was grossly negligent in causing his gang to go far out on the sands at that time and in those conditions.

A number of English cocklers who were out that evening gave evidence. Each spoke of the necessary knowledge of the sands and tides, the irresponsibility of those who issued permits to persons with complete ignorance of Morecambe Bay, the damage to the fishing industry, and the major safety issues. We learned that Chinese fishermen first arrived in the bay in the early summer of 2003. They were different; other gangs who came from all over the UK were better provided for. The Chinese did not have any waterproofs or boots when they first arrived, but the group on 5 February seemed better equipped.

As to conflict between the groups, there did not seem to be any more conflict between the British and the Chinese than between the Scottish and the Welsh, or the Scousers. A retired fisherman, Mr Manning, spoke for all. He was a man who had learned from his own father, and six generations or more of his family had fished. He was annoyed at the invasion of the beds, both on grounds of conservation, and on the grounds of safety.

He said, 'One was always taught to look at the tide table before you go out, to know what time the tide would be coming up in any particular channel you were working, and experience would tell you that. Look at the book of the next tide that is coming. Three hours before that is the cut-off to be safe.'

High water that night was 11.20 p.m. and thus cut-off time

in good conditions would be 8.20 p.m., 'but,' said Mr Manning, 'making allowance for the wind and rain that night, I would have been off by 7.30 p.m.'

Andrew Towers managed the Morecambe Lodge caravan park, which overlooks the bay. In late November 2003, he was advised that Warton Bank cockle beds were to open on 1 December. It was full on, he said, from the first day. About 200 on the beach, increasing through December. He saw no Chinese cocklers initially, but saw two Chinese gentlemen in a red Toyota, very smartly dressed. He saw the same car on several subsequent occasions and the two men ordered coffee at the snack bar. In due course, Lin Liang Ren agreed that he had visited the site in early December.

The Chinese began cockling on 26 January. Andrew Towers saw them as they brought cockles from the beds and they were building up piles of cockles. He then saw some British cocklers set fire to the pile of cockles. The young men who set fire to the cockles ran off and were chased; he thought one was caught. The following day, only thirty Chinese came and again there was an attempt to set fire to the cockles.

The Chinese cockled successfully on the 29th and 30th, but on the 31st, the Chinese Land Rover got stuck in the sand and they could not cockle. He did not see any Chinese cocklers again until 5 February, when he saw about twenty walking out at about 2.45 p.m. The first thing that happened out of the ordinary was when the fire brigade and ambulances came.

Cross-examined, he said he knew nothing about the cockle beds being opened until they were. It was a horror story from what he heard across the bay. The foreshore was very crowded, bedlam; no order was being kept. There were not enough Fisheries men to check the permits and there were no warning notices in Mandarin. Some of the groups other than the Chinese were feckless; those who set fire to the cockles were aged around eighteen to twenty, and up to 300 people were on the beach at any one time. The problem did not improve after 5 February; it went on for nearly a year until PC Johnson was assigned as a beach officer.

## The Tragedy

Before the evidence moved to the unfolding tragedy, the jury were given four critical times to note:

> The call to Miss Zhao for dry clothes was at 20.15 and 52 seconds.
> The first call to the police was at 20.47 and 16 seconds.
> Lin Li Shui's last response by phone was 21.11 and 36 seconds.
> Lin Liang Ren's call for help was 21.16 and 4 seconds.

The times were of critical importance. The prosecution pointed to the fact that Lin Liang Ren did not call the workers back in after 8.00 p.m., when he crashed the vehicle, and he did not call them back when he called for dry clothes at 8.15 p.m. He delayed calling for assistance for a further one hour and one minute, by which time Lin Li Shui was no longer responding, and it was clearly too late. The defence for their part asserted that it was not Lin Liang Ren's responsibility to call for help as he was not in charge, and the response of the police, they claimed, was lamentably slow.

The jury then heard from Andrew Bowker, the person making the initial call to the police. He had seen a vehicle going in a straight line very quickly towards Grange, with people walking in front of the headlights. He was with Susan Moore, who also gave evidence and they were on the promenade in Morecambe having been in a nearby gym. They made subsequent calls at 9.00 p.m. to the police, at 9.48 p.m. to the coastguard, and again to the police at 9.54 p.m. Susan Moore drew a plan at the time depicting the location of the vehicle and it was a considerable distance from Warton sands and the location of the Chinese.

When cross-examined, Andrew Bowker said that when he made the second phone call to the police at 9.00 p.m., he was told that the police were on a shift change or break, and it would probably be half an hour before anybody could get there. Shortly after that, Andrew Butler came out of the gym and spoke to them. Another witness, Andrew Bowker, was extremely angry at the police response and later lodged a formal complaint.

Andrew Butler had seen lights out at sea before going into the gym. When he came out, Andrew Bowker and Susan Moore pointed out a car driving rapidly on the beach, and the fact that its lights were dimming. They told him they had seen a car flying out and they had phoned the police, but they could not attend.

Andrew Butler immediately phoned the secretary of the life-boat station. The call was at 9.10 p.m. and the assembly signal was given within seconds and pagers activated. Within minutes, a hovercraft, a lifeboat, and a helicopter had all been called into action: the hovercraft was launched at 9.30 p.m., the lifeboat at 9.42 p.m., and the helicopter was en route at 9.42 p.m.

Soon after they were launched, the conditions worsened. The wind was about the maximum limit; the waves were about two metres, and the hovercraft could have rolled over. The hovercraft came level with Morecambe Golf Club, but was beaten back and they decided to head to the shoreline and put down on the shore at Morecambe Lodge.

At 10.00 p.m. the coastguard, using the thermal imaging system, located a person stranded on a rocky area called Priest Skear. Directions were immediately passed directly to the RNLI inshore rescue boat, which attended the scene and effected the rescue; the hovercraft then assisted by meeting the lifeboat and collecting the casualty. Having done so and having returned him to the shore, the hovercraft went out again, but they were beaten back by the waves.

A Sea King helicopter searched the bay and eventually

recovered a total of twelve bodies, either on sand or soft mud. The crew were assisted by a number of local fishermen who turned out. The work took all night until 7.00 a.m., and they worked the next day for a total of twenty-two hours.

All communications to and from the coastguard station are tape-recorded. At 9.18 p.m., a coastguard speaking to the RAF observed: 'We have some idiots down here, basically. We have some Chinese you know, here. They are actually just going out when they want to. And there has been this thing that we have been watching for. Oh God.'

At 9.22 p.m., in a further conversation with the RAF, he said: 'Yes, they could be cut off by the mud banks. The cockle beds have opened up, and there are loads of people turning up to go cockling – you know, foreigners.'

At 9.23 p.m., the coastguard contacted the police force incident manager, asking for the police helicopter to come to Morecambe. The coastguard said: 'We have twenty-three people cut off at Hest Bank, Morecambe, to do with these cocklers.'

The force incident manager replied: 'Oh Christ, I bet they are bloody illegal immigrants as well.'

The coastguard said: 'Probably.'

Sometime later at 10.43 p.m., in a phone call to the RAF, the coastguard said: 'We have come up with another theory. We believe they may be illegal immigrants. Some of them might have got ashore and just ran. That is the police theory at the moment, as we could be searching for nothing at the moment, but we just don't know. The cockle bed has been, to put it mildly, a pain in the butt for the last few months, and they drive, I think, 600 permits to go cockling on the sandbank. And these Chinese, we think they do not have permits, so if they are coming ashore, they are probably running, and the police are saying they are probably illegal immigrants.'

## The Prosecution Witness

We moved to a new phase of the case with the calling of Janie Bannister, the girlfriend and partner of the defendant Lin Mu Yong, whom she called Yammi. At the time of the tragedy, she was twenty-four weeks' pregnant with his child. She was, in legal terminology, an accomplice, in that she was very much involved in the cockling operation.

She went to estate agents in relation to three different properties occupied by the workers, she bought food and delivered it to workers, she was involved in purchasing vehicles, and actually went cockling, loading cockles onto quad bikes. She regarded herself and Yammi, and Lin Liang Ren and Miss Zhao, whom she called Lin and Eva, as a foursome. Janie Bannister played a significant role in the operation, because she was English and could negotiate with estate agents and motor dealers in her own tongue.

She told of her meeting with Yammi in Liverpool, where they both worked in the same chip shop; he spoke no English and she spoke no Chinese. Lin Liang Ren lived one floor above, and at some stage moved in with them. Soon after, large numbers of Chinese moved into their flat with fifteen or twenty sleeping on the living-room floor. In June or July 2003, Miss Bannister became aware that Yammi was involved in cockling and later he told her that he had 120 cocklers working for him.

Lin also became involved in cockling. Yammi was the first, and then Lin must have thought he would make some money because he was also a chippy. He worked independently of Yammi as his own Chinese boss, with his own group of men. She told of Lin importing 110 sets of waterproof clothing for the cocklers; there was confirmation of this, because Lin had failed to pay the customs duty and delivery charges owing to the carriers TNT.

She said that Lin started cockling around a month after Yammi, about July 2003. She had been with Lin to pick up vans on more than one occasion, and he had a Fiat Punto, an LGV, and a transit van. She said Lin also spent a lot of money in casinos. The night before the tragedy, she went with the three defendants, Yammi, Lin and Eva, to a casino in Liverpool, where Lin had a £600 bet at blackjack – a losing bet. Janie Bannister observed that was the same amount that her wedding dress was due to cost.

On the night of the tragedy, she had been in Liverpool and was travelling to Morecambe with the defendants Yammi and Eva. During the journey, Yammi received a phone call from Lin Liang Ren saying that 'the boys are stuck out'. Eva told Janie Bannister to phone the police and to report the matter to them. In fact, Miss Bannister phoned the coastguard. As frantic messages were received in the car by Lin Mu Yong, Miss Bannister relayed the information to the coastguard. 'It was,' she said, 'just madness. You cannot imagine what it was like, and whatever information they were telling me, I was telling the coastguard.'

They arrived at the beach and she saw a large heavy goods vehicle, a refrigerated lorry and a police car. There were police helicopters, hovercrafts and flares. She ran to the police to talk to them and said that she was the one who had been ringing the coastguard. She then saw Lin in a transit van with some Chinese in the back, driving away from the scene. When Lin saw Yammi's Toyota car, he stopped the transit van and got into the Toyota, immediately lying down so nobody could see him. Eva said, 'Lin is going to have to go,' and that she was going to leave with him.

Miss Bannister told her, 'No, you have to stay here and help get them back.' She said it was mayhem at that time. There was an ambulance there and one of the Chinese was being carried into the ambulance. As all this was going on, Yammi drove the Toyota away with Lin and Eva in it, leaving Miss Bannister behind on the shore with Eva's mobile phone. Three times she rang Yammi, urging them to come back, and after ten or fifteen minutes they came back without Lin.

As they arrived, another Chinese worker was being put into an ambulance and she saw several Chinese behind the car, five or six of them, and they were wet and shaking and worried that they were going to be arrested. They tried to hide in a farmyard and Miss Bannister spoke to them in what she termed really bad Chinese, saying she was Lin Mu Yong's wife. It was, she said 'pitch black, dead windy and rainy'. She told them to come out of the farmyard, but the police intervened and ordered her and Eva into a police car and they were told they would be taken to Lancaster Police Station.

During the journey, Miss Bannister said that Eva tried to give her Lin's wallet and she refused to accept it. She asked what had happened to its contents and Miss Zhao said she had chucked it. As they drove off the beach, they came to a fork in the road where Lin's car had been stopped by a police car. They pulled up and a police officer asked if they could identify Lin as one of the cocklers. Eva said, 'No,' but Miss Bannister said, 'Yes, it is.' Lin was then put in the police car and the three of them were taken to Lancaster. Yammi was taken there independently in his own car.

At Lancaster, Miss Bannister was persuaded to say that Lin Liang Ren was with them on the journey from Liverpool that night and thus not in charge of the ill-fated cockling expedition. She made a statement to that effect, but in evidence said that she did so under considerable pressure from those she was with.

Cross-examination of Miss Bannister would be of critical importance to all defendants. I was impressed with her evidence-in-chief. She had candidly admitted her own part in the management of the two cockling gangs and she had identified Lin Liang Ren to the police on the shore during the tragedy. She had however lied in the police station, asserting that Lin Liang Ren had been with them in Liverpool in the hours leading up to the tragedy. The jury would in the summing up be directed that they must approach the evidence of Miss Bannister with caution, as she was plainly an accomplice in the cockling operation and had an interest of her own to serve by giving evidence for the prosecution.

She said that Lin was like a big brother to her. He was generous, he looked after her when she had an argument with Yammi, but he told her a lot of lies, and there were a lot of things that she did not know. She described Yammi as a prime example of someone who lies when it suits them to do so. She said that Chinese people were very hard-working and keen to earn money to send home to their families, but one of their failings was the casino. She liked going cockling, but thought they went much too far out, about two miles, going way out into the distance.

She agreed that she had signed for cars, but said she was not the owner; she merely signed receipts because she was an English speaker and could understand the documentation. All the cars she signed for were owned by Lin or Yammi. They bought old cars and bangers on many occasions; they were always breaking down on motorways, and they were not concerned about documentation. She said they often got stuck on the beach.

John Bromley-Davenport now came to a critical point in the defence case, when he suggested that it was wrong to talk about Chinese bosses, 'because everybody worked together, and there was really no organisation as such, it was a co-operative.' Janie Bannister did not agree. She said, 'There were cocklers, there were Chinese bosses, there were English bosses. There was a hierarchy.'

She agreed that the Chinese shared bank accounts, that people would get phones in one another's name and that they used each other's identities at casinos. People also signed up for tenancies in one another's name, just as they did with vehicles. They were terrified of being sent back to China. She remained adamant that there were Chinese workers and Chinese bosses and that Lin and Yammi were the bosses.

She was pressed about her evidence that Lin was sitting in a red Mitsubishi when she identified Lin to the police. She said that she never saw a blue Peugeot. The evidence from the police officer, a superintendent, was that Lin Liang Ren was in fact in a blue Peugeot when she identified him, but this was hardly a massive point for the defence, as Lin Liang Ren was in a car, close to the shore at a time and place indicated by Miss Bannister. Clearly, she had seen Lin Liang Ren and assumed that he was in the car he drove at that time, a red Mitsubishi.

More than once it was put to her that Lin never told her to say that he had come to Morecambe in Yammi's car with her, Yammi and Eva. She replied, 'He did.' The question was repeated and again she insisted that he did: whilst detained by the police, Lin had on two occasions told her to say that he had accompanied her to Liverpool in Yammi's car.

She was cross-examined by Simon Russell-Flint QC on behalf of Miss Zhao, and she began by saying that she did not know Eva very well, but regarded her as a friend. Eva was a student at John Moore's University and Lin's girlfriend. She had asked her to be a bridesmaid at her wedding to Yammi, in part at least because Yammi was Lin's cousin.

Janie Bannister agreed that she had been acting as interpreter for the making of arrangements to go cockling and had arranged wages and prices, and said this under cross-examination: 'I may have given the impression that I was an English boss, but I was a Chinese/English wife, not a boss.'

She agreed that she had been to the offices of the Environment Agency and had obtained a leaflet explaining how to apply for a cockling permit, but she did not submit any application for a permit or write out any documentation; although she might have handled the permits. She admitted that she had been out cockling and had counted bags, and written down numbers of bags picked against names. She had also signed forms when vehicles were purchased and knew the forms were for the DVLA.

She agreed that at 3.30 a.m., she had shouted at the cocklers, 'Come on. Come on. Let's get up. Come on, get on!' She had been to purchase waterproofs at B&Q and signed for the deliveries, and after cockling, she had held the money and distributed the money amongst the cocklers in the amounts that they had earned. She also confirmed that she visited casinos, but said that she and Eva only went to keep an eye on Lin and Yammi, and on occasions they took the chips off them and cashed them. She was adamant, however, that she was not a boss. Everything she did was for Yammi and Lin.

On the night of the tragedy, Miss Bannister said that she first saw Lin getting out of the van and into Yammi's Toyota Space Cruiser; he was head down on the seat crying and Eva said that Lin was going to get into trouble. Yammi, Eva and Lin then drove off down a country track away from the shore and Janie said she rang Yammi's phone and spoke to Eva, trying to get them to come back, but they returned without Lin. She and Eva were then put in a police car, and Eva tried to give her Lin's wallet, showing her it was empty, but Janie refused to accept it.

Stephen Grime QC cross-examined Janie Bannister on behalf of Lin Mu Yong and established that the relationship between his client and the witness ended upon their arrest.

She said, 'As soon as I was arrested, I took my engagement ring off. He hurt me. I don't hate him. I wanted them, that is Yammi, Lin and Eva to tell the truth, to make it better for them. I gave them a chance, and I told them because I bought equipment for them, that I could get into trouble for it because they are illegal immigrants. I have a baby. I could not live in that lifestyle. I could have had my baby in prison because of him, and that is what I thought when I was arrested.'

She first met Yammi, she said, when they worked in the same chip shop in Liverpool. He was a hard worker with gambling debts; he was trying to pay off those debts and he was also sending money home to China. She described the functions of a Chinese boss as she understood them: to supply workers, pay workers, and take workers out. English bosses used to contact the Chinese to tell them when the parties should go out cockling, and when they got to the beach, the English bosses would be there. The English bosses generally had quad bikes or tractors and helped to take the Chinese to where the cockling was going to take place. When the time came to come back, the English would say: 'Right, off the beach.'

She named the Chinese bosses as: Lin, Al Qing, Yammi, Sung, and Ping. The proposition was put to her that Yammi's men worked with Yammi, and not for him, and she replied that they worked in the same conditions. When the suggestion was made that they earned the same money, she replied, 'I don't know. I don't think so.' When it was suggested that Yammi was a modest gambler, she replied, 'I would not say he was a modest gambler, obviously.'

She said that the Chinese worked hard and played hard. They gambled, they sent money home, they kept erratic hours, and they picked far more cockles than any other cockle pickers on the beach.

Janie Bannister was in the witness box for a considerable time and my assessment of her evidence was that she was truthful, brave, and also ashamed of the role she had played in helping in the running of the two gangs. On any view, she was guilty of facilitating the commission of immigration offences, indeed she appeared to have played a rather more substantial role than Miss Zhao.

Nevertheless, the decision to use Miss Bannister as a prosecution witness and not a defendant was plainly a good one. She had identified Lin on the shore, cooperated thereafter, and more than anyone was familiar with the workings of the cockling gangs. She had done her three former friends no favour.

## The Survivors

The stage of the trial had been reached for the survivors of the tragedy to be called. It was first necessary to explain to the jury how the authorities had dealt with them between the event and the trial. They were all illegal immigrants and a Detective Sergeant was called to explain how a number of Chinese survivors gave initial statements, some did not, and afterwards they all disappeared into the Chinese community. Generally, they failed to abide by the Immigration Service conditions of residence and/or reporting and thus the police were faced with the prospect of losing their witnesses. They all feared being returned to China.

Accordingly, an advertisement was placed in the Chinese newspaper and a letter sent by Detective Superintendent Gradwell to the Home Office, asking how best they could be dealt with by the Immigration Service. The Home Office replied granting immigration status to all the survivors, including the four not yet traced, and required all of them, as well as those who had already applied, to go through the asylum process again; thus granting them permission to stay temporarily in the United Kingdom.

Zhang Ping was the first of the survivors to give evidence. She was a young woman in her early twenties. She said that she came by air to Manchester in 2003 with her own passport, and after entering the country, a group leader took her passport and she had not seen it since. She went to Liverpool to a flat above a shop, where she shared a bedroom with five or six others and slept on a mattress. She started as a cockler on the day of her arrival and everyone in the house also raked cockles.

She went cockling at Southport, Barrow, Scotland, and Morecambe; sometimes they raked once a day, other times twice, depending on the tides. They worked both day and night, and she could not swim. She said that the boss of the people raking cockles was Lin; he provided the rakes, boots, and overalls and paid them £5 per bag of cockles. She would usually fill two, three or four bags and Lin paid her the wages. A foreman, Lin Shui, kept count of the bags and raked with them, but the defendant Lin was higher than the foreman Lin Shui. Lin's girlfriend travelled with him to the cockling, but she never picked cockles.

She was shown a cockling permit with her photo upon it, but said that the particulars upon it, the name, address, and phone number were all false. She said that Lin Shui, the foreman, used to keep the cards until they went out to sea. On their return, Lin Shui collected the cards back.

On 5 February, more than twenty Chinese cocklers assembled at Morecambe. Zhang Ping was driven out on to the sands and worked for over an hour. It was very dark, the wind was raging, and she was only able to pick one bag before feeling unwell. She walked back to the shore, taking about half an hour, but other Chinese workers continued cockling. She tried to cross two trenches or ditches, and the water was knee deep.

Back on the shore, Lin was sitting in his car. After a while, he drove the car onto the sands to collect bags of cockles, while Zhang Ping remained on the shore. Lin returned, but had been unable to collect the bags as they were already too deep in water, so he went out a second time and he came back wet. He removed his wet clothes and put on a padded jacket, and later his girlfriend brought him some dry clothes.

Soon after he returned, Zhang Ping heard him say, 'The tide is rising,' and then she heard him make a series of frantic phone calls in his native dialect.

She then saw people swimming ashore. The wind was raging

and she was petrified. She took shelter in the cab of a refrigerated vehicle parked on the shore. Soon afterwards, one of the
workers appeared naked, having swum ashore; he was shivering,
very cold, and they wrapped him up. Soon the police arrived
and she and other survivors were taken to the police station.

At the police station, she saw Lin and his girlfriend. Lin told
her that if she was questioned, she should say that she had not
been cockling and she should not give her true address. She
should also say that she did not know who the boss was.

Next, Wei Si Mao gave evidence. He had entered the country
in 2003 on a false passport, arriving in London and then travelling to Liverpool. He was a friend of Lin Li Shui, who told
him there was work to be had there. He went to 55 Priory
Road, a house occupied by Chinese workers, where every
bedroom housed seven or eight people; they all slept on the
floor, without any mattress, on a quilt cover. Two days after
arriving, he first went cockling, first to Southport, then Barrow,
and finally Morecambe.

On 5 February, everyone in 55 Priory Road went cockling,
except one, who was employed to do the catering. He said that
Lin Li Shui was in charge of the work and kept the record of
how many bags each worker picked. Lin Liang Ren was the
boss; he did not live at 55 Priory Road, but would visit the
house to make payment for the cockles picked. It was Lin Liang
Ren who told the workers where to go and when to go.

They travelled from Liverpool to Morecambe in four vehicles,
mini vans, and there were about thirty workers in all. He had
a cockling permit with his photograph on it and the correct
date of birth; the name on it, however, was not his, the address
was incorrect, the mobile phone number was not his, and the
National Insurance number was false. He had obtained his own
photograph at the railway station and handed it to Lin Liang
Ren, who had later handed him the completed permit.

At the outset of the cockling, Mr Wei's role was to sit in one of the vans on the shore and to record the bags collected. Lin Liang Ren drove the workers out to rake cockles. Later on, Lin Liang Ren drove a jeep out to collect the bags, but because the water was deep, the jeep became trapped, and he jumped into the sea and got very wet and cold. He had phoned Lin Li Shui, who in turn phoned Mr Wei instructing him to recover the bags of cockles in the stranded jeep. Mr Wei drove out in a pick-up, but could not fill up the back of the vehicle because it was too low and could not be driven through deep channels.

He made three journeys out to the stranded jeep to collect bags, taking with him a number of other workers to assist in the collection. On the third trip, with eight passengers, some in the cab, some on the back, he realised the tide was very high and that it was no longer possible to drive back. 'We all became quite worried, and we felt quite chaotic in our head. We could not think straight.'

Mr Wei decided to leave the pick-up. The water had risen to the door; it would not open, so he wound down the window, climbed out and jumped into the sea. The water level was very high and everyone from the pick-up was in the water. He took off his jacket and trousers and then swam up the channel towards a pile of rocks on the beach. It took him about ten minutes, and he could not stand up. Four of the others also escaped, but his friend Tian Long swam in the wrong direction and drowned.

Once on the shore, he found some dry clothes in one of the vehicles and shortly afterwards the police took him to the police station, where he saw Lin Liang Ren and Miss Zhao. Lin told all the survivors to say that he was not the boss. He told them to blame Tian Long and Lin Li Shui for the deaths, because by then, they all knew that those two had died. As a result, Mr Wei did not give a truthful account to the police and did not tell them that Lin Liang Ren was the boss; he was shown a photo of Lin Liang Ren by the police and did not pick him out.

Three days later, he made a statement to the police that contained a number of lies. He explained this in evidence by saying that he had been pressurised into giving a false account. He was worried about the consequence of telling the truth.

Lin Mei Fu then gave evidence. He had flown to London from China on 13 December 2003. He had his own passport, but after being admitted, someone took it off him. He was met by Lin Shui and followed him to Liverpool, where he also went to stay at 55 Priory Road and slept on the floor with seven or eight others in the same bedroom. He said that Lin Li Shui was some kind of foreman and everybody living at No. 55 worked as a cockler. Two days after arriving, Lin Li Shui gave him some waterproof clothes and a rake and showed him what to do. He told them when to go to work and they all followed; they were paid £5 per bag.

He worked for one week and was paid over £100, but he was never paid the rest of the money; he was owed over £500 or £600. His photograph was on a permit, but not his own name. He didn't know whether Lin Li Shui was employed by other people. He said, 'I'm only a peasant worker. I do not ask questions about who is in charge. I only do my work and earn my money.'

On the day of the tragedy, he was driven to Morecambe in a van with over ten people in the vehicle. He walked out to the cockling beds in the late afternoon. It was not completely light and they could see a little, but it was very windy. He worked with a friend, Lin Guo, and together they collected ten bags. A pick-up came to collect the bags and he travelled to shore in that vehicle. Nobody had instructed him to stop work, but he felt very, very tired and thought that if he carried on, he would die.

Having reached the shore, they were then told to go out again to collect some bags from a jeep that had become stuck in the sands. They drove out, but suddenly the water level was very high, so all eight or nine of them jumped into the water. The pick-up could not get through the channel. They were all very scared and confused; no one knew which direction to go, and it was pitch black. The witness had a particular problem: he could not swim. He took off his waterproofs when his friend Lin Guo told him to, as they had become very heavy, and he walked towards the shore. He drank a lot of seawater; the water level was now up to his chin, to his lower lip.

Eventually he, Lin Guo, and five or six others reached the shore, but not everyone escaped. He went to the van in which he had travelled from Liverpool. Within minutes the police arrived and took him to the police station.

Lin Ah Hua was smuggled into the country in late 2003, and came to Liverpool from London. He also lived at No. 55 and travelled to Morecambe in the same vehicle as Lin Guo and Lin Mei Fu. In his case also, the only accurate element of his cockling permit was his photograph.

He said it was after 5.00 p.m. when they went out onto the sands; he had no watch and no mobile phone. He worked with a friend, Cao Chao Kun, and between them they filled six or seven bags, then they were collected in a red pick-up driven by Ah Long, quite a tall person. By this time it was dark and he and his friend had decided to stop work as one of their rakes was broken. His friend had a head torch, but he did not.

In all, ten people decided to get on the red pick-up to return to the shore. By now the water level was rising and the vehicle set off in the direction of the shore, but as the level rose, they could not get through and when the vehicle could travel no further, all ten of them jumped off. Six went in one direction, Lin Ah Hua and three others went in the other. The smaller group included the driver Ah Long and his cockling partner and friend, Chao Kun. At one stage Lin Ah Hua removed his waterproof clothing, then he reached a point when he decided to turn back.

That was a life-saving decision. He shouted to his companions, 'Do not walk in that direction,' but three of them carried on walking. He joined the other six, and now the water was too high to walk. They all swam in the same direction, seven of them, but one did not dare to swim. He was later rescued by helicopter from some rocks, but the three original companions all perished.

Back on shore, he went to the vehicle that had brought them from Liverpool. He said he saw Lin Liang Ren, the boss on the shore, who was walking about dressed in shorts. Soon afterwards they were all taken to the police station and he again saw the boss, who said to him, 'The people down there are probably all dead.' He also said, 'Don't tell others I was the boss, otherwise I will be arrested and none of us could leave and get out.'

Lin Guo was the next survivor to give evidence. He was the nephew of Lin Li Shui. He had come by air to this country from China with a genuine passport, which the 'snakehead' (Chinese people smuggler) took once Lin Guo arrived in London. He had paid the snakehead gang to help get him to London and he had left China for two reasons: he had two sons, which was contrary to the one child policy, and he wanted to make some money. He came from the same village as Lin Liang Ren and said that Lin Liang Ren's parents were quite rich, very rich. When in China, Lin Guo had been employed driving motor vehicles.

When he began cockling, it was for another boss before being transferred to Lin Liang Ren, when his original boss stopped cockling; a number of others had transferred at the same time. Lin Guo said that Lin Liang Ren was the boss: he supplied the waterproof clothes, a jacket and trousers, and tools for raking cockles; he also paid the wages and supplied the food. At No. 55 Lin Guo had a bed, but most of them slept on the floor, seven to nine in a bedroom.

Nobody gave Lin Guo any instruction in the way to collect cockles and nobody asked him if he could swim. The cockling permit given to him had his photograph attached, but a different name and all the other particulars were false. His uncle was the foreman and used to give the permits out on the beach, and collected them afterwards. Initially at Morecambe Bay their group consisted of between ten and twenty; later there were more, and on the night of the tragedy, there were thirty to forty. They were to be paid £5 per bag by Lin Liang Ren and in a day they collected between 100 and 200 bags. A jeep was used to take the bags to the shore, and the English bosses sent a big vehicle to carry them away.

The day of the tragedy was the fifteenth day of the Chinese New Year. That is another festival, and quite a number of Chinese gathered in the house, that is, No. 55. In fact, everyone in the house, roughly forty, travelled to Morecambe in two vehicles and Lin Liang Ren drove one of the vehicles. Lin Guo went out on the sands with Lin Mei Fu, and they collected fifteen bags, by when it had become dark. The bags were collected in a red vehicle driven by Lin Li Shui and they then walked to the shore.

At the shore they boarded the red pick-up, now being driven by Wei Si Mao; they were required to pick up bags of collected cockles, but he felt very tired by this time. There were nine passengers, a driver and the collected cockle bags. Once they got to the river, the water became quite high and once the vehicle got into the channel, it could go no further. He was wearing night clothes under a leather jacket, with waterproofs on top. He jumped into the channel fully clothed and saw that the water stretched for 300 to 400 metres, so he took off his clothes and swam across the channel. The water was above head height. Six workers swam to the shore and three drowned, but he himself reached some rocks and was rescued by a helicopter. When he arrived at the shore, the police were already there and he was taken to Lancaster police station.

The remaining survivors gave very similar evidence. They all stated that Lin Liang Ren was the boss and the majority spoke of him telling them at the police station to say that he was not. Each had the same terrifying tale to tell of their escape, when they literally swam for their lives. Each confirmed that their cockling permits contained their photograph and a collection of false information. All the survivors were illegal immigrants, as indeed were the deceased; they had all paid a lot of money to come to the United Kingdom and many of them had huge debts in China.

The police had assisted the survivors by making appointments for them to attend the Immigration Service offices. The survivors were told that once they had been processed, they would be able to remain until the end of the trial and they would be allowed to work. In cross-examination, Mr Bromley-Davenport sought to undermine the credibility of each survivor by asserting that their evidence was influenced by a desire to keep on the right side of the police and the authorities, in an endeavour to avoid being returned to China.

Possibly the most significant evidence given thereafter was that the market rate for a bag of cockles on the shore was £12.50, meaning that if Lin Liang Ren was the boss, he was profiting by £7.50 a bag, resulting in a daily profit of £750 to £1,500. With double-tiding, the profit would be double. Evidence was called relating to the renting of premises, the purchasing of cars, cockling equipment, overalls, bank accounts, credit cards and dealings with fish merchants.

At the end of the prosecution case, it was clear that the single issue on the critical manslaughter charges was whether the Crown had proved that, on the day of the tragedy, Lin Liang Ren was the boss.

## The Defendant

Lin Liang Ren gave evidence. He was now twenty-nine years of age, and he had been twenty-seven at the time of the tragedy. He had no criminal convictions in any country. He was born in the Fujian Province of China, on the south coast, a few minutes from the sea, but he had no experience of fishing in China. He had an accountancy certificate from polytechnic school and a national bookkeeping qualification, and he had worked in China for a mining company and a building firm. His father worked for a national transport system and they were as a family 'at the edge of middle income'.

In 2000, his father suggested he came to the United Kingdom to help his future and he arrived with a valid passport in September 2000. He went to Liverpool to study English at a community college. It cost £2,700 a year and he worked part-time in the evenings in a restaurant, before going to work in a takeaway. Later he went to live with his older cousin, Lin Mu Yong.

In July 2003 he heard about cockling and was curious. He went to Aldingham with a group of friends and eventually agreed to work for a man by the name of Wayne Miller. He cockled in Aldingham for three weeks raking cockles, and at this time, he decided to purchase some vehicles, a transit van and a Fiat. Wayne Miller would provide buckets and sieves and rakes, but Miller said they had to provide a vehicle and accommodation for the workers, together with waders and waterproofs. He recruited a small group of eight and they were working for Wayne Miller; Lin Liang Ren drove a car and picked cockles.

After a while he decided he could not carry on in the cockling industry, but Lin Guo said he wanted to form his own group. Lin Guo introduced him to Lin Li Shui and he agreed to sell the transit van and the cockling tools to Lin Li Shui for a total price of £2,100. On the night of the tragedy, Lin Li Shui and Tian Long were in charge. Lin Liang Ren, together with Tian Long and Eva, went to the Liverpool city centre about 9.00 a.m. to sort out telephones. Tian Long and Lin Liang Ren then drove to Lancaster to look at properties to house workers, before going to the beach about 3.00 p.m.

He and Tian Long sat and talked before workers arrived about 3.30 to 4.00 p.m., when the tide was receding. Tian Long asked Lin Liang Ren to drive the workers out to the sea, but there was a problem with the exhaust of the vehicle and Wei Si Mao took the workers out in another vehicle, making two trips, whilst Lin Liang Ren tried to repair the exhaust. Lin Li Shui had told the workers before they left the shore to finish by 8.00 p.m. He normally told the workers when to finish work and had never previously made a mistake.

Lin Liang Ren then drove the red pick-up with Tian Long with him to collect the full cockle bags. About twenty bags was a full complement, and having picked them up, he set off for the shore, but made a mistake in the dark and drove into a channel where there was a rock and the vehicle became stuck. He told Tian Long that he could deduct the cost of the vehicle from his wages. They got out of the vehicle and the water was up to their waists; they could not free the vehicle and they walked back together to the shore.

Once on the shore, Lin Liang Ren telephoned Lin Mu Yong, telling him that his clothing was wet and he needed some dry clothes. He would telephone Eva and ask her to bring his clothes and then he would go back to Liverpool with them. Soon afterwards he saw a Toyota arrive carrying Lin Mu Yong, Janie and Eva. He collected some clothes and asked Lin Mu Yong and Eva to look for any survivors who had escaped. Lin Liang Ren then drove off in his own vehicle to look for survivors, but it was difficult because there were so many police around.

He decided to go to the Packet Boat public house, where he ordered a cup of tea. He took issue with the landlord, who had given evidence that he had asked if there was accommodation available. He said he did not. He then left and shortly after was arrested and taken to Lancaster police station. There he threw the contents of his wallet in a bin and decided to give a false name, not because he feared being accused of manslaughter, because at that time he did not know whether the missing persons were saved or not. It was his natural and impulsive response to being arrested. Eventually, and on legal advice, he disclosed his true identity. He was not in charge that night; Lin Li Shui and Tian Long were.

When cross-examined by Tim Holroyde, Lin Liang Ren agreed that as soon as he was asked a question at the police station, he told a lie. He admitted that every official was told a lie about his name and what he did that day. He reasserted that he did not fear being charged with manslaughter, because he thought everyone might still be alive.

It was put to him that he knew full well that tragedy had befallen several of his countrymen, because of phone calls with those out on the beach where water had interrupted transmission of those calls, and as survivors were brought into the police station, the talk must have been about the loss of life. Ren stood his ground, asserting that he did not know that anybody had died that night.

It was also put to him that he was falsely stating that Lin Li Shui and Tian Long were in charge because they were dead and in no position to dispute the fact. He replied that he told the police that they were in charge at a time when he did not know they had died. It was put to him that from his own experience he knew the tide was very high and it was impossible to cross the channel, and it was obvious that people were likely to die.

A: All we could do was call the police.

Q: What chance did they have?

A: They did what Lin Li Shui instructed them to do. He did not always wait until the tide came up.

Q: What hope was there for the people two miles out to survive?

A: I did what I was asked to do. I drove the first group of workers out to the cockle beds. Wei Si Meo drove two further vehicle loads out.

He was then asked why he got into Yammi's car and was hiding and crying and lying down in the car. He replied that everyone was very sad and worried. It was put to him that he must have learned that colleagues had died whilst at the police station, as each survivor told their terrifying tales. He said he did not know what they had talked about. He denied instructing survivors not to say that he was the boss.

He also denied using the command phone that night. He only used it, he said, to call for some dry clothes. It was in a bag with other phones and he reached in the bag and used it by chance.

Q: Do you mean you won the lucky dip?

A: Yes, I won the lucky dip.

He agreed that Lin Li Shui had phoned him from the cockle beds, saying that the water was coming up and they were surrounded by water, and that his phone ceased to operate.

Q: What had happened to stop Lin Li Shui's phone operating?

A: Lin Li Shui said his phone was wet. He said they were surrounded by water, but no one said they were threatened by death.

He was asked if he was a worker and not a boss, why did he have a room to himself, when other workers were seven or more to a room.

233

A: I always wanted my own bedroom.

He was asked why he was able to drive himself to the sea, whilst other workers were all driven in a minibus.

A: I do not know the business of others.

He was asked whether he employed illegal immigrants during the period when he admitted that he was a boss.

A: I only did for three weeks. I do not know whether they were legal or illegal. I never asked them.

He agreed that he provided accommodation and food. He provided the waterproof clothing and took them to work, brought them back and paid them. In those three weeks, he said, there were no problems. In those weeks he made £2,800. He wanted to carry on the business, but everyone else left and went to work for Lin Li Shui. He also went to work for him as a driver and was paid the same amount as for working in a takeaway. He could not explain why his name did not appear in any wages book.

He continued throughout a lengthy cross-examination to assert that on the night of the tragedy, Lin Li Shui and Tian Long were in charge, and therefore he was not guilty of manslaughter.


## The Verdicts

No other defendant gave evidence. Whether that was attributable to the fact that Tim Holroyde's very thorough examination of Ren caused them to appreciate their vulnerability, or whether loyalty to Ren was the decisive factor, only they can know.

John Bromley-Davenport made a spirited closing speech in which he submitted that it was a tragic accident with many causes, including the Government's failure to control immigration. The authorities knew full well what the Chinese were up to and did nothing to stop them. The permit scheme was a meaningless farce: no applicant was ever asked a basic question concerning safety, there was no input from Health and Safety, and no effort was made to warn the gangs on the sands.

The English gangs had wickedly destroyed Chinese cockles by pouring petrol on them and driven them into going out later and further from shore. When observing the Chinese going out, no effective warning was given to them by the English cocklers returning, nor did they inform the coastguard or police of the obvious danger. They left them to their fate. When Mr Bowker raised the alarm, the response of the police was lamentably slow. Even if Lin Lian Ren was in charge, it was reasonable for him to delegate the timing to Lin Li Shui; control of the tiding necessarily fell to someone on the sands.

Turning to Lin Liang Ren, counsel faced greater difficulty. There was compelling evidence that his client was the boss, and it followed that if he was the boss, he had the responsibility for the workers' safety. The contrast in style and content between John Bromley-Davenport and Tim Holroyde was vivid. John, educated at Eton and RADA, was loud, dramatic, spontaneous and amusing. Tim was measured, prepared, accurate and incisive.

The guilty verdicts were predictable and accurate. Convictions for facilitating immigration and perverting the course of justice were inevitable in the cases of Zhao Xiao Qing and Lin Mu Yong. They were heavily involved in the day-to-day running of the cockling gang and were well aware of the immigration status of the cocklers.

The Edens were not so informed. Lord Carlisle QC represented the father-and-son fish merchants, who had purchased cockles from their co-defendants. He successfully submitted that his clients were entitled to assume that when permits were issued to cocklers, those issuing the permits had made elementary enquiries as to their immigration status: the permit scheme was advertised on the basis that applications would be checked. There was simply no evidence to support the prosecution allegation that the Edens knew the cocklers were illegal immigrants, and thus they could not be found guilty of facilitating illegal immigration. I agreed with the jury's not guilty verdicts.

This was an appalling and wholly avoidable tragedy. The criticism of the permit scheme, coastguards, Health and Safety and the police was all well founded. The conduct of Lin Liang Ren, however, involving a total and callous disregard for his wickedly exploited workers merited a very long prison sentence. Fourteen years represented the longest sentence passed for gross negligence manslaughter by some distance. I was amazed that this gang of exclusively and obviously illegal immigrants could move into a residential street in a Lancashire town, attracting no adverse intervention from any authority.

So far as I know, no form of inquiry into the multiple failures in this case has ever taken place. The response of the police, namely, 'Sorry, we cannot attend at present. A changeover is taking place. Nobody can attend for half an hour,' was a disgrace. This was a critical emergency meriting instant action.

The case provoked two incidental thoughts. Firstly, it became apparent from the evidence that the Chinese cocklers were far more productive than their English counterparts, most of whom had far more experience. Although living in the most cramped and crowded conditions and being fed the most modest fare, they farmed cockles with far greater application and intensity than their local rivals. It was primarily for this reason that their cockles were soaked with petrol.

Secondly, and in contrast to the dispiriting facts of the case, Morecambe Bay on a fine day is a place of great beauty. Views across the bay from Morecambe to Grange-over-Sands are as fine as I have seen.

# Chapter 13

## The Shooting of Jean Charles de Menezes

THERE IS NO more inspiring or impressive court than Court I at the Old Bailey, the venue for many high-profile criminal trials. As I entered court on 2 January 2007, I was conscious both of my extreme good fortune to be sitting there and the dreadful catalogue of misfortune that gave rise to the case I was about to try.

The simple and barely credible facts were that on 22 July 2005, a perfectly innocent young man, on his way to work, boarded an underground train where he was seized by one police officer, and shot seven times in the head and once in the shoulder with hollow-tipped bullets at point-blank range by two other police officers. The name of the deceased was Jean Charles de Menezes. His assailants were officers of the Metropolitan Police.

That distressing, indeed shocking, event resulted in criminal proceedings being brought by the Health and Safety Executive against the Metropolitan Police, alleging that by their numerous failures they had failed to provide for the health, safety and welfare of Jean Charles de Menezes, pursuant to the Health and Safety at Work Act 1974.

The indictment set out nineteen different failures by different police officers on 22 July 2005 and, if proved, amounted to a catalogue of mismanagement and incompetence. The alleged failures involved misdirection in briefings, poor incident planning, technical issues relating to communications, unclear operational objectives, inaccurate profiling, ambiguous instructions and individual errors. The allegations were cumulative and required one single verdict.

Jean Charles de Menezes was twenty-seven years old, and he was brought up in the town of Gonzaga, in a remote mountainous region of Brazil. He was a trained electrician and travelled to this country with his cousin, Vivian Figueiredo, arriving in April 2005. They went to stay with another cousin in a flat at 21 Scotia Road, Tulse Hill, in south London. Jean Charles had found electrical work at a house in north London.

He spent the final night of his life in 21 Scotia Road. The nine flats within the building shared a single communal entrance, and Scotia Road is a cul-de-sac, with only one exit for both cars and pedestrians.

The context of this tragedy is important. Fifteen days earlier, on 7 July 2005, three suicide bombings were carried out in London at three Underground stations (Aldgate, Kings Cross and Edgware Road) and a fourth on a bus in Tavistock Square, in Bloomsbury. Fifty-six people were killed and 977 were injured. I was safely in the Royal Courts during the bombing, but my wife was 250 miles away, with all telephone lines blocked and mobile phones not functioning. My stepson, David, used the Underground daily to travel to work. All we knew in the Courts was that several bombs had been detonated with numerous casualties. It was, however, court business as usual, so far as was possible.

I cannot overstate the trauma of these terrorist acts. London remained in a state of panic, shock and distress for many months.

Fourteen days later, on 21 July 2005, there were four attempted suicide bombings in London, three at Underground stations (The Oval, Warren Street and Shepherd's Bush) and the fourth on a bus on Hackney Road. Unsurprisingly, these further attacks, notwithstanding their failure, added to the sense of terror in the capital. Police recovered property abandoned by a Shepherd's

Bush bomber as he made off, which contained a gym member-
ship card in the joint names of Hussain Osman and Abdi Omar.
The card indicated that these two individuals resided in a flat
at 21 Scotia Road. The flat below was occupied by Jean Charles
and his two cousins.

It took some time to discover this gym card, but this was
understandable. Bomb disposal experts had to search rucksacks
containing unexploded bombs and four sites had to be sealed
off and meticulously searched. No complaint has ever been made
related to any delay in finding the gym card. In one of the
pockets of the rucksack was a torn-up wedding photograph of
a man and a woman together with other photographs. The
detective finding the pieces of the photograph pieced them
together, photographed the reconstruction, and was satisfied the
male was Hussain Osman.

Unfortunately and incompetently, this reconstituted photograph was never used for the purposes of identifying persons
leaving 21 Scotia Road, nor were the other photographs in the
rucksack, nor was any attempt made to trace any other photograph of Hussain Osman that might permit a reliable
identification to take place. A driving licence photograph could
have been obtained by use of an out-of-hours hotline from the
DVLA at Swansea, as Michael Mansfield QC established at the
inquest. Osman was well known to the police and to the security services and appropriate enquiries would have swiftly revealed
a number of useful photographs for identification purposes.

As it was, the police chose to rely on the gym card photograph, which was both out of date by up to two years and of
very poor quality, and showed only Osman's head and shoulders.
The police had from 2.15 a.m., when the gym card was found,
until 9.33 a.m. when Jean Charles left No. 21, to seek these
further photographs or identifying features, but failed to do so.

At 4.55 a.m., the officer in charge, Commander McDowell,
set his strategy; namely for the address 21 Scotia Road to be

controlled and contained by surveillance, with specialist armed back-up as soon as possible. In fact, no armed officers ever arrived at Scotia Road, apparently never having been required to do so. It was left to surveillance officers, ill-equipped to stop and question suspected terrorists, to keep observations on the flats. They were *in situ* by 6.30 a.m. The surveillance team were provided with no map, no details of the access or egress from No. 21, and critically no information as to the nearest bus stop.

The surveillance team leader repeatedly sought information from the control room, wanting to know the whereabouts of the nearest bus stop, and asking for the bus service to be suspended or the route diverted, in order to afford more time to arrest the suspect. Information as to the whereabouts of the nearest bus stop was never forthcoming from the control room, who were in the same state of ignorance. The team leader very clearly appreciated the necessity to prevent the suspect from boarding any public transport and the limited window of opportunity for doing so.

Since the front door of the Osman/Omar flat was within the block of flats, the surveillance officers were tasked with the responsibility of observing every departure from the nine-flat block and using copies made from the gym card photograph to attempt to identify Osman. Not all of the team were in possession of a copy of the photograph and they had only a short period of time to study it.

Between 7.45 and 8.30 a.m., five or six occupants of the flats were seen to depart. One of them was Vivian, Jean Charles's cousin. All were easily eliminated and were filmed as they passed the unmarked observation vehicle.

At 9.33 a.m., Jean Charles left the flats, having received a call to go to north London to reset an alarm. The weather was fine and he wore a denim jacket and jeans; he carried nothing in either hand and had no rucksack or other bag. The member of the surveillance team entrusted with the recording camera (code-name Frank) had switched it off in order to conserve both film and camera. When Jean Paul emerged from the flats, Frank was engaged in urinating into a bottle and unable to activate or operate the camera.

Had film been taken and transmitted to the control room, the dissimilarities between Jean Charles and Hussain Osman would have been obvious and the pursuit would have been ended. Whilst Frank had one hand holding the bottle, in the other hand he held an airwave radio transmitting messages, because the main Cougar headset radio system had broken down.

At 7.00 a.m., Commander Cressida Dick, now the Commissioner of the Metropolitan Police Service, then the designated senior officer, came on duty. Unfortunately, she was unaware of Jean Charles's emergence from the flats, only becoming aware when he had boarded the No. 2 bus to Brixton. The explanation for her failure to hear this event as it happened was that she was briefing her loggist, who had arrived late.

Frank's initial conclusion as broadcast to the control room was that Jean Charles was IC1, meaning Identity Code One, which in police code means white European, and thus was not a suspect. As Jean Charles reached the surveillance van, however, Frank broadcast, 'Worth somebody else have a look.' From that moment and with those words, Jean Charles became a suspect.

It took Jean Charles six minutes to walk to the nearest bus stop on Tulse Hill. Although there were approximately twenty surveillance officers on that route and another six close to the bus stop on Tulse Hill, none had more than a fleeting glimpse. None of them purported to identify this person as Hussain Osman, and none sought to eliminate him as a suspect. Four of the six officers on Tulse Hill were armed; another six armed officers were nearby in unmarked police cars.

Notwithstanding the manpower available and the danger to the public of a suicide bomber boarding public transport, there was no order from the control room to prevent the suspected suicide bomber from boarding the bus. The buses in Tavistock Square and on Hackney Road had been selected as suitable targets by suicide bombers. The prosecution placed great reliance on the failure to prevent the boarding of the No. 2 bus.

Jean Charles boarded the No. 2 bus at 9.40 a.m., planning to travel to Brixton, where he would take the Underground to north London. A surveillance officer (codename Ivor) did the same. At this point, Ivor told the control room that the person under observation was not the person they were looking for. The decision was made to stop the bus and search and question him, but that plan was abandoned when the surveillance officer sent a message to the control room saying he thought that this was the suspect they were looking for.

At 9.45 a.m., the bus reached Brixton, where Jean Charles left the bus intending to take the Underground. He swiftly found the station closed and contacted his employer by mobile phone and then reboarded the same bus towards Stockwell Underground Station. Unbeknown to Jean Charles, the officers following him considered that getting off and back on the same bus was a typical anti-surveillance technique. This was the critical moment in the operation. The officers had become convinced that they were trailing a terrorist, one of four men who had attempted to detonate suicide bombs only twenty-four hours earlier.

Another surveillance officer (codename Laurence) had replaced Ivor on the bus. As the bus approached Stockwell Underground Station, Jean Charles went down the bus stairs and left the bus. Laurence instantly reported this to the control room. A conflict of evidence arose between Commander Dick, who contended that she said the suspect must be stopped from getting on the tube 'at all costs', and the surveillance officers, who said they were never asked to stop and search Mr de Menezes outside; something they would have been able to do if asked.

Indeed, armed surveillance officers were on the pavement

between Jean Charles and the entrance to the station. One of them was Ivor, who went in first and positioned himself to the right of the entrance. It takes between two and three minutes to walk from the bus stop to the station, affording ample opportunity to stop Jean Charles had the order ever been given. There were some three surveillance officers and six specialist firearms officers available and situated so as to prevent Jean Charles entering the station.

No order was given until Jean Charles was on the escalator descending within the station. By this stage, his fate was determined. As Michael Mansfield QC put it at the subsequent inquest, he was 'virtually dead'. The reboarding of the bus had convinced the surveillance officers, and through them the control room, that Jean Charles was Hussain Osman.

There was a conflict of evidence as to whether Jean Charles was ever identified to the newly arrived firearms officers, and confusion as to information given to the firearms officers before they shot Jean Charles. Much of the confusion arose from the very limited reception on police radios underground. Ivor had preceded the firearms officers onto the train and into the same carriage as Jean Charles.

Ivor pointed at Jean Charles and said, 'That's him.'

In response, Jean Charles stood up and Ivor grabbed him in a bear hug. Nine shots were fired.

There were approximately nineteen passengers in that carriage. Observing this unspeakable destruction of a fellow human being at such close quarters will have inflicted incalculable trauma and distress to those unfortunate spectators. Neither they nor the firearms officers who shot Jean Charles were called to give evidence. The failures alleged by the prosecution preceded the shooting.

A number of operational failures were alleged. There was an inexplicable four-hour delay in sending specialist firearms teams to Tulse Hill, leaving the surveillance officers unsupported.

Assembling, kitting up, briefing a firearms team, and travelling to a rendezvous point for a further-up briefing all takes time. During this four-hour period, an overnight firearms team was available, kitted up, and in New Scotland Yard, yet never deployed.

Further criticism was made of the fact that the firearms team who were actually deployed, followed the bus in cars that were unable to communicate either with one another or the control room, as the main radio system was playing up. Some communication was intermittent, some inaudible, and some non-existent. It was also alleged that within the control room there was a state of chaos, noise and indiscipline, with Commander Dick as designated senior officer relying on an intermediary to report radio communication from surveillance officers.

It was also asserted that the briefing of the firearms team was over aggressive, in that they were told 'that they would almost certainly have to confront a suicide bomber and shoot him dead'. At the very heart of the case, however, was the failure to intercept Jean Charles, either on Scotia Road, or on Tulse Hill, or at Brixton, or between the bus stop and Stockwell Underground Station.

Clare Montgomery QC appeared for the prosecution and conducted the case with clarity, precision and authority. She had a strong case, but had mastered every detail and added to her escalating reputation. Ronald Thwaites QC was briefed to defend. He has been described by the *Guardian* as 'a performer, a street fighter, a Rottweiler with witnesses, and he talks the jury's language'.* A Health and Safety prosecution was not his natural or regular habitat. On more than one occasion, I chose to intervene.

At one point, Ronald Thwaites cross-examined an immigration official over a counterfeit stamp found in the Brazilian's passport, asking if that meant he was in the country illegally. I

* Marcel Berlins, *Guardian*, 23 January 2002.

intervened: 'He was a member of the public who is entitled to the protection of the Health and Safety legislation, whatever his immigration status, was he not?'

Thwaites's response was: 'I don't think that is relevant.'

I replied: 'I wondered what the inquiry was about.'

Thwaites: 'I'll make it clear in due course.'

He never did so, and of course the immigration status of Jean Charles was of no relevance. In fact, that witness made it clear that Jean Charles had an automatic three-month leave to remain, which had not expired on the day he was shot, and thus he was not an illegal immigrant. The questioning of his status caused visible distress to the Menezes family. This was but one of several exchanges between us emanating from untenable and unworthy defence assertions, or suggestions made, that Jean Charles by his own behaviour had brought about his own death.

Further problems arose when Ronald Thwaites produced a composite picture, prepared by others, one half containing half of the face of Jean Charles, the other half containing half of the face of terrorist Hussain Osman. This was shown to the jury in an attempt to explain why the police shot the wrong man dead. Clare Montgomery instantly objected on the grounds that the image 'had been altered by either stretching or resizing so the face ceases to have its correct proportions'.

Later she called a forensic consultant, who indicated that the composite produced in court by the police lawyers appeared to have been brightened and had lost definition as compared to the original. The brightening appeared to have got rid of the definition of some of the characteristics, including the area around the left nostril and chin. The consultant produced an alternative composite, in which the two faces had different skin tones and their mouths and noses were not aligned.

The relationship between prosecution and defence was strained at its best. At one stage Ronald Thwaites said this: 'The prosecution are attempting to dictate to the police how they should be doing their job. We submit that if this prosecution is successful and the Metropolitan Police Service is convicted, it will have the effect of putting handcuffs on the police and will seriously inhibit their effectiveness in combating serious crime. It will also make police operations more difficult and dangerous in the future.'

This was no case for a street fighter. A chain of events had taken an innocent young man's life in tragic circumstances. Compassion, explanation and some degree of contrition were the order of the day. They were conspicuously absent.

By way of contrast, there was a pleasing, indeed exhilarating phase of the case when Clare Montgomery came to cross-examine Commander Cressida Dick. Counsel had an abundance of ammunition. Commander Dick explained her predicament at each and every stage without equivocation, fully communicating the very real problems she faced and quite admirably explaining to the jury the predicament she found herself in. The questions kept coming, and yet without evasion or any hint of truculence, every question was answered in an honest, undemonstrative and at times in a humble manner.

From Cressida Dick there was no implied criticism of the prosecution for bringing the case, nor resentment at having to face questioning. She readily acknowledged the scale of the tragedy and the necessity to examine the facts in the closest detail. As I watched this cross-examination, I concluded that both combatants had very bright futures.

Notwithstanding Cressida Dick's evidence, there remained cumulatively a number of failures that were factual and beyond explanation. The jury retired for a short time only, before returning with a note. They had reached a verdict but wished to add a rider. I had spent my working life in the criminal courts, but had never been in a case in which a jury had added a rider to their verdict. I had, however, read of many capital murder trials where juries had added a rider asking for leniency. *Archbold*, the practitioner's textbook, was of no assistance.

I asked them to put their proposed rider into writing and they indicated that they found the case proven, but wished to exonerate Cressida Dick from all blame. I readily agreed to the jury's request. I congratulate them on their wisdom. It may well have contributed to Cressida Dick's appointment as Commissioner in April 2017.

The only remaining matter was to pass sentence. The only sentences available were a fine or a discharge. I was conscious that the more I fined the Metropolitan Police, the less funds would be available to employ police officers or to purchase equipment. On the other hand, a low fine ran the risk of trivialising a very grave case. I imposed a fine of £175,000.

My abiding thoughts are with the family of Jean Charles. From their perspective, this sequence of events must have been beyond comprehension and certainly not resolved by a fine of such modest proportions. A further ordeal awaited them at the inquest. The coroner, Sir Michael Wright, declined to permit verdicts of murder or manslaughter, the only verdicts capable of comforting a family so grievously affected.

For my part, I cannot see that any one individual can be shown to have committed such a crime. In the Health and Safety prosecution, the failures of numerous officers, whether identified or not, could be aggregated as a failure of the Metropolitan Police.

# Chapter 14

## The Alleged Murder of Charlene Downes

In 2007, I tried Iyad Albattikhi, a Jordanian aged thirty-four, for the alleged murder of fourteen-year-old Charlene Downes, and Mohammed Raveshi, originally from Iran and aged fifty, for the alleged disposal of her body. The jury were unable to reach a verdict. A retrial was ordered, but the prosecution decided to offer no further evidence. The trial was the saddest and most dispiriting of any that I was involved in, either as counsel or judge.

Charlene went out on a Saturday night in November 2003 into Blackpool. Her mother had given her £5 spending money. There were sightings of her in the town, the last reliable one upon her leaving the Carousel Bar on the North Pier. She failed to return home that night and her mother reported her missing. Charlene has not been seen or heard of since.

Initial police enquiries gave rise to much concern. There were conflicting accounts of Charlene's movements. Her contemporaries were reluctant to talk about what had been going on in the town and there were a number of false sightings of Charlene. One matter, however, became clear. Grooming, corruption and abuse of teenage girls in Blackpool was rife and many of those responsible were Asian.

Of particular interest was an alleyway running behind a number of Asian restaurants, known by many of Charlene's associates as 'Paki Alley'. The police collated evidence establishing that teenage girls visited the alley and received payment for performing sexual acts with those who worked in the several restaurants. They were able to adduce evidence that Charlene was one of those who visited the alley.

Police also collated evidence relating to a takeaway cafe named Funny Boyz, owned jointly by the two defendants. This establishment was visited on a regular basis by teenage girls, including Charlene.

Weeks and months passed with no positive lead, before David Cassidy, a businessman dealing in slot machines, went to the police with apparently critical information. He told police that he had a conversation with Albattikhi's brother, Tariq, and that Tariq said he knew that a young girl had been murdered and that Albattikhi and Raveshi were involved. The murder had taken place at Raveshi's home; she had been killed and chopped up and there had been a lot of blood.

This information was relied upon to make an application to place covert surveillance into both Raveshi's house and his vehicle by the use of hidden recording devices. Such application must be made to the Chief Constable or an authorised deputy, and in reliance upon Cassidy's statement, authorisation was granted. Albattikhi was resident at the time in Raveshi's house. A search warrant was also obtained to search Raveshi's house for scientific evidence, in order to prove the murder of Charlene. Again, I assume that reliance was placed upon Cassidy's statement in order to obtain the warrant.

For twenty-eight days, recordings were made pursuant to the authorisations. Thereafter Detective Sergeant Beasant undertook the task of listening to the recordings and preparing transcripts. This was an immense undertaking and occupied her for some eighteen months. The final transcript appeared to disclose a compelling case against both defendants.

Amongst a number of apparently incriminating passages were the following:

Albattikhi: I killed her. I killed a girl. I was just angry.

Raveshi: There is nothing left of her. She was here. She died, there really is nothing.

Raveshi: Why did you kill her?

Albattikhi: You're being stupid if you thought that, we think we release her.

Raveshi: The big bones went into the machine as well, you know that, don't you?

Raveshi: It was the last deep one and then it was the heart that finally killed her.

Raveshi: Do you remember she was bleeding to death so that she made a fucking mess.

These are a sample of a large number of sentences that appeared to be highly incriminating. With these very much in mind, Tim Holroyde QC, as he then was, opened the case in graphic style:

Charlene was one of a number of young girls who visited an alleyway in the town to have sex with older men who worked in the fast food shops. She was well and happy, but had a 'chaotic' home life. Expelled from school, she spent her time hanging around shops on the Blackpool Promenade. She was last seen on the evening of Saturday, 1 November 2003. After kissing her mother goodbye, she left alone and vanished.

A missing persons inquiry began, but police later launched a murder investigation after receiving information that Charlene had been killed and chopped up. No trace of Charlene's body has ever been found. A witness had heard Albittikhi and others talking about her. These people were talking about sex with white girls, and there was mention of having sex with Charlene. Albittikhi laughed and said she was very small – the plainest possible indication that he was lying to the police when he said he did not know her. He and others present then laughingly said that Charlene had gone into the kebabs.

Charlene was a familiar figure, hanging around fast food shops where she would sometimes get free food. In addition, she was one of a number of adolescent white girls who went out at night to the alleyway behind the restaurants. She and others went there to meet much older men from the restaurants, and it seems perfectly clear that there was at times some sexual activity. Albattikhi took advantage of one of those vulnerable girls, Charlene Downes.

It is the prosecution case that the background to the murder of Charlene Downes and the disposal of her body is some sexual activity between her and one or both of the defendants.

The defence case could not have been more simple. Both defendants denied any knowledge of Charlene, with both asserting that they had never met her. Both asserted that the transcription of the covertly recorded material was wildly inaccurate. Raveshi challenged Cassidy's hearsay evidence, asserting that it was invented in pursuit of a grudge held by Cassidy against him arising out of a business transaction between them.

The prosecution case rested on two pillars. The recorded evidence and Cassidy. The latter was by no means the most impressive witness; he knew Raveshi and they had been involved in some business activity. In any event, his evidence was hearsay and there was no prospect of calling Tariq. It soon became clear that the prosecution case depended entirely on the recordings.

As soon as we began to hear the recordings, the quality was manifestly poor, but the prosecution were able to display the transcripts visually, permitting them to be matched to the tapes. This form of visual display, with the words moving across a screen, allowed the jury to evaluate the transcripts of DS Beasant. Some words were far clearer than others and for my part, I was able with the assistance of the transcript to make out some of the incriminating material. However, when an alternative and innocent form of words was canvassed as matching the recording, it was certainly possible on a number of occasions for the alternative to be the accurate transcription.

The defence were able to submit that in order to obtain a reliable transcript, the transcriber should be wholly independent to avoid what is known as confirmation bias. It was also submitted that by reason of her involvement in the detection and interviewing process, DS Beasant was subject to cognitive priming, that is a predisposition or heightened readiness to perceive or reach a particular conclusion. The recordings were of very poor quality, the covert device was too close to the television, and DS Beasant was not a forensic audiologist.

Nevertheless, parts of the recordings appeared to be audible and some material potentially incriminating. I was of the opinion that there was sufficient for the jury to consider, together with a strong direction that before convicting, they must be sure that they had themselves heard words that proved guilt. It came as no surprise when the jury, after several days in retirement, were unable to reach even a majority verdict. I ordered a retrial and remanded both defendants in custody.

In April 2008, the prosecution decided to offer no evidence. Tim Holroyde was by now on the High Court Bench and the case was in the equally capable hands of David Steer QC. A recording had come to light of David Cassidy conversing with Tariq Albattikhi. Upon receiving Cassidy's statement, the police had wired up Cassidy and asked him to return to Tariq to discuss further the details of the murder. When Cassidy did so, Tariq gave every appearance of not knowing what Cassidy was talking about and eventually accused Cassidy of falsely blaming Raveshi because he hated him.

Whilst differing inferences may be drawn from this exchange, there can be no doubt that this recording should have been disclosed at the first trial. It was plainly capable of undermining Cassidy's evidence. Of even greater significance is the fact that it predated the application to place the covert recording device in Raveshi's house and would have undermined such application. It would also have undermined the application for a warrant to search Raveshi's house.

The non-disclosure of that recording was a grave error, necessitating a rigorous investigation. It rendered a retrial a practical impossibility. Both the authorisation and the search had been achieved by non-disclosure and thus the material obtained was almost certain to be excluded, having been obtained by unlawful means. The decision to offer no evidence at the retrial was inevitable. My sadness derives from several sources.

Sadness that a young life was almost certainly ended so young and in such squalid circumstances.

Sadness that her family appear to cling to the remotest hope that Charlene may still be alive, as defence counsel argued, either having been abducted or having run away as statistics demonstrate, by no means a remote possibility. We had rehearsed the quite shocking number of missing persons.

Sadness at the numerous mistakes made by the police.

Sadness that corruption and exploitation of young persons should have infested, unchecked and unimpeded, the town in which I grew up.

Sadness that the investigative and criminal justice process has failed Charlene.

# Chapter 15

## The Transatlantic Airline Plot

IN 2009, I tried what was known as the 'Transatlantic Airline Plot'. This was a terrorist plot to detonate liquid explosives by suicide bombers on board transatlantic airliners. Seven flights had been targeted, all from Heathrow, to San Francisco, Toronto, Montreal, Chicago, Washington, New York and a second flight to Chicago. The flights all departed between 2.15 p.m. and 4.50 p.m., so that all would be simultaneously airborne, a detail very similar to the 9/11 attacks.

This was a plan to commit mass murder on a grand scale. In sentencing, I described the plot as 'the most grave and wicked conspiracy ever proven within this jurisdiction. The intention was to perpetrate a terrorist outrage which would stand alongside the events of September 11, 2001 in world history.'

This was a retrial. At an earlier trial, three defendants had been convicted of a general conspiracy to murder, but the jury had been unable to agree upon whether a conspiracy to commit murder, specifically on board aircraft, had been formulated. In relation to four other defendants, the jury were unable to agree upon a verdict in relation to either alleged conspiracy.

There had been some adverse criticism of the trial process and the judge's handling of the case. A lengthy break in proceedings had taken place during the jury retirement. Such problems can be unavoidable and such criticism as I read appeared to reflect disappointment at the verdicts, rather than fair comment.

The downloading of the flight details and the form of explosives being manufactured clearly pointed to an airline plot, but one jury having not been convinced, there was plainly a critically important issue to be tried.

This was a case with the highest profile and it had been the subject of discussions between Prime Minister Tony Blair and President George W. Bush. On 10 August 2006, at the height of the holiday season, airports around the world were thrown into chaos when authorities suddenly imposed a ban on liquids being taken on board aircraft. John Reid, the then Home Secretary, made an emergency statement stating that the security services had swooped overnight on a suspected British-based al-Qaeda cell, which had aimed to smuggle bombs disguised as soft drinks on board aircraft.

The trial commenced with arguments in the absence of the jury. Firstly, it was contended that it would be an abuse of process to retry the three defendants already convicted of a general conspiracy to murder, because they were already convicted of that offence and thus could not be tried again for it. The legal term for this is 'autrefois convict' (previously convicted).

I had no difficulty in ruling that the general conspiracy of which the three had been convicted was a different conspiracy from the airline conspiracy, indeed it excluded any plan to blow up aircraft. Since the three defendants had not been convicted of a conspiracy to blow up airliners, they could now, quite properly, be so tried. There was neither unfairness nor procedural impropriety in doing so.

Secondly, the three convicted defendants contended that there could not be a fair trial having regard to the media publicity after the first trial. The verdicts in the first trial had been both broadcast and widely publicised and an avalanche of publicity followed. In my ruling, I summarised the publicity thus:

The offending material can be categorised in the following ways:
(i) the defendants have strong links with several prominent
al-Qaeda terrorists, including Rashid Rauf, 7/7 bombers and
21/7 bombers, of which the jury were not informed; (ii) but
for the premature arrest in Pakistan of Rashid Rauf, for which
the Americans are to blame, more evidence would have become
available to the prosecution; (iii) the activities of the defendants
were being monitored by phone taps and other forms of inter-
ception and a dummy run was anticipated which might be used
to carry out a real attack; (iv) the investigation had prevented
unspeakable carnage and loss of countless lives; (v) the jury were
incompetent, the evidence was very strong and the jury's verdict
was astonishing; (vi) the trial judge mishandled the trial and in
particular permitted a two-week break during the jury retirement,
the jury returning for only five days at the commencement of
their deliberations before then going on holiday.

I had listened to similar submissions in the Leeds United footballers' case, which was also a retrial, and resisted similar
applications in the case of Thompson and Venables and also in
Shipman. I applied the well-established test, namely whether a
fair-minded observer would consider that a jury, properly
directed, could fairly try the defendants who had been convicted
of the general conspiracy. My application of that test and my
conclusion were approved by the Court of Appeal.

The prosecution's primary case was simple. The conspiracy
was a plan to manufacture improvised explosive devices (IEDs),
to use suicide bombers to carry them onto seven commercial
airliners destined for North America, and to detonate those
devices mid-air. Their secondary case was that if some were not
parties to murder by detonating IEDs, there was a general
conspiracy to murder without any specific means being specified.

The defendants chose not to provide meaningful defence
statements. In cross-examination, it became clear that the three

defendants convicted in the earlier trial of the general conspiracy to murder were asserting that there was a conspiracy to cause an explosion at a single iconic location, such as Parliament, the City, an airport terminal or in a cafe. They were planning a political stunt, including small explosions intended only to frighten people at airports.

In summing up, I posed four questions for the jury:

(i) Was there a plot in existence to murder persons unknown?

(ii) If so, was the defendant a participant in the plot, knowing as he did so, that it was a plot to murder?

(iii) Did the plot involve detonation of IEDs upon passenger aircraft?

(iv) If so, was the defendant a participant in the plot, knowing when he did so, that it involved the detonation of IEDs upon passenger aircraft?

If the answer to all four questions was yes, they were guilty of Count 1 (Conspiracy to murder by detonating IEDs upon passenger aircraft), but if they answered yes to questions 1 and 2, but were not sure or answered no in respect of questions 3 and 4, then the verdict would be guilty on Count 1A (Conspiracy to murder persons unknown).

The defendants Abdulla Ahmed Ali, Assa Sarwar, and Tanvir Hussain were convicted on Count 1 (targeting aircraft); Umar Islam was convicted on Count 1A (conspiracy to murder but not involving aircraft); and after a further retrial, three other defendants were also convicted on Count 1A.

Abdulla Ahmed Ali was twenty-eight when convicted. He is a man of very considerable ability. In the witness box he demonstrated exceptional speed of thought, power of expression, and organisational talent. At City University in London, he studied computer systems engineering, and it appears that he was at that time exposed to the extremist preaching of Omar Bakri Mohammed at the Queen's Road Mosque, in Walthamstow.

Post-graduation he volunteered with an Islamic charity in East London.

Much planning had gone into this plot, which was at a well-advanced stage prior to its interruption. In court during the first trial, Ali described seeing images of concentration camps in Bosnia when he was fifteen, and was aware that those in the camp were Muslims. He said in his suicide video that he had aspired to martyrdom since the age of fifteen.

In the aftermath of the 9/11 attacks on America, the refugee crisis had escalated in Afghanistan and in February 2003, Ali and his co-defendant and second-in-command Sarwar went to deliver aid to refugee camps on the Pakistan-Afghanistan border. In all likelihood, this experience had a radicalising effect upon both of them; they were shocked by the conditions there and further angered by the failure of the 2003 mass protest against the Iraq war.

In January 2004, Ali went on a pilgrimage to Mecca and in August of that year went to Pakistan to give assistance to refugees; he was there at the same time as the 7/7 and 21/7 ringleaders. He returned to the UK in January 2005, but returned to Pakistan in June 2005 and in May 2006, ostensibly on family business.

By now the intelligence services had become interested in him and upon his arrival from Pakistan in June 2006, they arranged for his baggage to be searched before it was moved to the arrivals hall. Inside the baggage was a powdered soft drink, Tang, and a large number of batteries. This find triggered a highly intensive surveillance operation and Ali's baggage was returned to him with no indication that it had been searched.

Over 200 officers were recruited from police forces around the country. Undercover officers observed Ali acquiring a second-floor flat in Walthamstow for £138,000, ostensibly purchased by his brother-in-law. Officers installed a covert listening device and camera in the flat, which revealed that the flat was being used as a bomb-making factory and as a film set for Ali and others to record suicide videos promising terrorist attacks against the West.

Ali was observed using public phone boxes, mobile phones and unidentifiable email accounts to contact links in Pakistan. He was also filmed constructing devices out of plastic soft drink bottles and was observed by surveillance officers in an internet cafe researching flight timetables.

Assad Sarwar was twenty-nine when convicted and a married man. He was the quartermaster of the conspiracy and responsible for the purchase, storage and assembly of bomb-making equipment. Unlike Ali, he did not make a suicide video; as the bomb-making expert, he was apparently too valuable a resource to die. He had attended Brunel University, but failed to complete the course.

He met Ali in Pakistan whilst both were engaged in charity work and, together with Ali, he visited refugee camps housing Afghans who had fled the US invasion of their country. Sarwar returned to Britain in May 2003 and worked briefly as a postman, then he went back to Pakistan in October 2005, ostensibly to help survivors of the earthquake in Kashmir. In 2006, he visited Ali's flat in Walthamstow and, according to Sarwar, they discussed UK foreign policy before deciding to stage a publicity stunt.

The third member of the inner circle was Tanvir Hussain, aged twenty-eight. After several unproductive years at college, he worked at a sexual health clinic. In 2005, he became a devout Muslim after entering into an arranged marriage. He came to the attention of the surveillance team when he and Ali applied for fast-track passports purporting to have lost the originals, which contained Pakistani visas. Officers followed him as he bought equipment, including surgical needles and syringes used to feed and extract liquid into and out of sealed bottles. He spent many hours with Ali in the Walthamstow flat, used as the bomb factory.

On 3 August, a surveillance camera in the flat recorded Ali and Tanvir Hussain drilling a hole in the bottom of a soft drinks bottle, in order to empty the bottle and replace its contents with liquid explosives without breaking the seal on the cap, thus making it look as if it had not been tampered with. They could be heard talking about batteries and 'HP', meaning Hydrogen Peroxide.

Later that evening, Ali and Hussain discussed the American cities New York, Miami, Philadelphia, Washington DC, Dallas, Chicago, and Los Angeles. One said, 'I wanted to find out from the travel agent the ten most popular places what British people holiday.' Tanvir Hussain was Ali's right-hand man. He carried out research, helped with communication, and participated in the making of martyrdom videos.

The arrests of the defendants was a major operation in itself. Twenty-four people were arrested and eight were later charged with Conspiracy to Murder. Sixty-nine properties in all were searched, and some 400 computers and 200 mobile phones were seized. The most significant find was a memory stick in Ali's pocket containing details of the targeted flights and a diary with similar details and entries in Ali's handwriting.

Upon receiving the papers in the case and upon reading the proposed opening speech for the prosecution, I found it difficult to comprehend the basis upon which the previous jury failed to convict Ali, Sarwar, and Hussain of targeting aircraft. The evidence was extremely strong, if not over-whelming. The only rational basis might possibly have been that a conspiracy requires a minimum of two conspirators. It may be that at least three jurors were of the view that Ali may not have disclosed his ambition to blow up aircraft to any other alleged conspirator.

There was, however, further evidence now available in the form of a series of emails in which code words were used to discuss plans with an al-Qaeda member in Pakistan. These emails disclosed, using code, not only that the plot was nearing execution, but also that there was no question of an innocuous political stunt.

On 4 July 2006, Ali emailed, 'I got all my bits and bobs, I'm just waiting for lights. They should be here in a couple of days.' Sarwar emailed the same contact in Pakistan on 19 July, saying, 'I've found fifteen suppliers who can get me nice Calvin Klein designer aftershave.' On 3 August, Ali wrote in an email, 'By the way, I've set up my mobile shop now. Now I only need to sort out an opening time.' The following day he sent an email to Pakistan, saying, 'I've done my prep. All I have to do is sort out opening timetable and bookings. That should take a couple of days.'

It was on 6 August that Ali was observed in an internet cafe researching flight times of transatlantic aircraft. On 9 August, Ali was recorded in the flat, speaking of a two-week time frame and discussing taking his child on the suicide mission. He made a suicide video with a co-accused in which these words were spoken: 'Martyrdom operations upon martyrdom operations will keep on raining on these Kuffar.'

There was the closest cooperation between countries, and the initial decision to intervene is said to have been taken by President Bush, who having been informed of the two-week time frame, decided that he could wait no longer and thus ordered the arrest of Rashid Rauf, Ali's contact in Pakistan. This was not the choice of Scotland Yard, who would have waited and secured even more evidence. The suspects were under the closest possible surveillance, and there were no circumstances in which they could possibly board flights with the bombs, which were located in the flat in Walthamstow. However, once Rauf was arrested in Pakistan, there was immediate urgency to make arrests here.

The police were able to arrest Ali and Sarwar together in a car park near Waltham Forest Town Hall, and Ali was found to be in possession of several suicide videos. In all twenty-four suspects were arrested. Nevertheless, there can be no doubt that but for the decision to arrest Rauf, a delay would have permitted several more conspirators to have been arrested and successfully prosecuted. Ideally, arrests would have been made on the day of the proposed airline attack, as the suicide bombers made their way to the airport with liquid bombs in their bags. The only consolation is that the prime movers were brought to justice.

The trial proceeded in a seamless manner. There came a moment, however, that will remain in the memory of all present in court. Essential to the defence of all was the assertion that the plot alleged by the prosecution was simply not feasible. It was submitted that these little bottles of chemicals when mixed together could not possibly blow an airliner out of the sky. The defence argument went that the counter-terrorist officials had been watching too many action movies.

It was being said that the defendants were planning to use TATP, or triacetone triperoxide, a high explosive that supposedly can be made from common household chemicals. However, several difficulties would have rendered the plan unworkable, or so the defendants hoped to establish. The hydrogen peroxide solution has to be concentrated by boiling off the water and that is no easy task. The peroxide and acetone can be mixed and put in one container, but then it must remain cool. Once on the plane, the acid would need to be added drop by drop whilst stirring constantly, or so the narrative was supposed to go.

Whilst it is no defence to a charge of conspiracy that the intended purpose was impossible, the asserted lack of feasibility supported the contention that only land-based, minor explosions were intended.

The prosecution, in dramatic manner, put an end to this line of argument. They filmed a disused passenger aircraft. They formulated the mixture using Sarwar's exact formula, placed it within the aircraft and activated it. The jury were able to observe a gaping hole blasted in the side of the plane. There was no mistaking the power of the explosion, nor its ability to bring down an aircraft.

The trial itself involved the prosecution leading a vast amount of evidence that was not susceptible to any form of effective challenge. Activity in the Walthamstow flat had been recorded. Chemicals, bomb-making equipment, bottles, syringes, emails, computers and mobile phones, together with Ali's memory stick and diary detailing the transatlantic flights selected for obliteration, all comprehensively proved the guilt of the inner circle. The jury were not sure that the foot soldiers knew the full extent of the plot, and that was a reasonable and fair conclusion.

Ali's performance in the witness box was memorable. Faced with a mountain of incontrovertible evidence, he faced up to the challenge, undaunted, fluent, at times even commanding. Peter Wright QC, senior Treasury counsel, was no easy adversary. I had led him ten years earlier in the prosecution of Dr Shipman, as I have described earlier, when his nickname was Biffer, conveying his forceful talent as a cross-examiner. He was not short of ammunition and yet Ali kept going under relentless, yet proper pressure.

The beneficiaries of this performance were the foot soldiers. Ali was a dominant figure and an individual with considerable leadership skills. The recorded conversations gave an insight into his role in the conspiracy: he was the leader of 'this blessed plot', Sarwar was the expert chemist, and Hussain was Ali's right-hand man. The remainder were willing recruits, given a role and told what to say as their suicide videos were recorded.

Sentencing of Ali, Sarwar and Hussain was far from straightforward. Life sentences with long minimum terms were inevitable, and there was some guidance. The four London bombers who perpetrated the failed attacks at Warren Street, Bethnal Green, Shepherd's Bush and the Oval Underground stations were sentenced to life imprisonment with minimum terms of forty years. Each of those offenders had taken the final step in their plot; but as a balancing factor, I concluded that the airline plot was more likely to have succeeded, if not for intervention, and was more likely to have caused a massive loss of life.

The defendants received life sentences with minimum terms of forty years, thirty-six years and thirty-two years, with twenty years for three foot soldiers, convicted of the general conspiracy to murder, accurately reflecting their respective criminality and danger to the public. The Court of Appeal endorsed the accuracy of the sentences.

I am reminded of this case whenever travelling by air. Every deposit of liquids, every queue, and every search are the direct consequence of this airline plot. Thirteen years on, there appears to be no relaxation of airport security, nor should there be. I reflect in every queue upon the devastation that a liquid bomb can cause, so dramatically and effectively demonstrated to this jury.

# Chapter 16

## The Appeal of Kenneth Noye

O N 9 MARCH 2011, I sat with the Lord Chief Justice, Lord
Judge, and with Mr Justice Davis, hearing the appeal of
Kenneth Noye, the conviction having been referred to the Court
of Appeal (Criminal Division) by the Criminal Cases Review
Commission.

The appellant had an unusual criminal past. In 1985, Kenneth
Noye was suspected of involvement in, or connection with,
the spectacular Brink's-Mat gold bullion robbery. He came
under police surveillance, and PC Fordham, camouflaged and
wearing a balaclava at night, entered Noye's garden. The appellant confronted him and there was a violent struggle, during
which Noye stabbed the officer a number of times, killing
him.

When tried for murder, Noye contended that he was acting
in self-defence and was acquitted. In 1986, he was convicted of
handling a proportion of the proceeds of the robbery and was
sentenced to fourteen years' imprisonment. He served his
sentence and was released.

At lunchtime on 19 May 1996, on a roundabout at the M25/
A20 interchange in Kent, twenty-one-year-old Stephen Cameron
was a passenger in a Bedford van being driven by his seventeen-
year-old girlfriend, Danielle Cable. The appellant was on the
same roundabout driving his Land Rover Discovery. He overtook
the Bedford van and stopped in front of it, believing erroneously,
as he contended at trial, that he recognised the driver of the

van. The appellant got out of his vehicle and walked towards the van. He had a knife in his jeans pocket.

Stephen Cameron got out of the van as the appellant approached and a fight followed. During the fight, at a stage when the appellant may have been losing, or believed he was losing, he produced a knife and inflicted two deliberate stabbing wounds to Stephen Cameron in the chest. The second blow concluded the fight and ended Stephen Cameron's life. The appellant made off, disposed of the knife, and left the country by private helicopter on the day after the killing. He flew to a golf course in Normandy, and on the following day he flew by private jet from Paris to Madrid.

He was arrested in Spain on 28 August 1998, having been unlawfully at large for well over two years. He contested extradition proceedings. An order for extradition was made in February 1999, but appealed against unsuccessfully, and he was extradited from Spain some nine months after his arrest in May 1999.

When tried for murder at the Old Bailey in April 2000, Noye denied his guilt, asserting that the use of the knife was in lawful self-defence. He explained that he carried the knife for protection against the risk of kidnapping, or criminal activities by others seeking to learn the whereabouts of the as-yet-undiscovered substantial amount of the Brink's-Mat gold. When he used the knife on Mr Cameron, he believed himself to be in a situation of extreme danger, confronted by a man attacking him in a furious temper, who was threatening to kill him.

He thought the fight might end with Mr Cameron throwing him over the bridge on to the road beneath, or if Mr Cameron knocked him out, he would remove the knife from him and use it on him. The appellant agreed when cross-examined that he realised that to thrust a knife with a four-inch blade into somebody's chest could kill, and that he struck out with the knife deliberately. The jury convicted the appellant and thus were sure that he did not act in reasonable and necessary self-defence. Noye was sentenced to life imprisonment and the minimum term recommended by the judge was sixteen years.

The CCRC had referred Noye's conviction to our court on two grounds:

(a) New evidence that is capable of significantly undermining the credibility of a prosecution expert, Dr Heath, and the evidence he gave at trial.

(b) New evidence that there was bruising to Mr Cameron's knuckles and new evidence that he would not necessarily have sustained bruising to his knuckles.

When Dr Heath gave evidence for the prosecution at trial, he was a most experienced and respected Home Office pathologist. Unfortunately, in the meantime, his reputation and standing had been severely damaged by reason of a number of complaints and adverse findings by the Home Office Tribunal, culminating in Dr Heath resigning from the Register of Home Office Pathologists.

A number of successful appeals against conviction followed, in which Dr Heath had given seriously flawed evidence. The prosecution now accepted that on a number of occasions, Dr Heath had given 'unreliable over-dogmatic evidence and had provided unreasonably deduced conclusions from evidence that did not enable other possibilities to be excluded'.

In this trial, Dr Heath's evidence was disputed by two Home Office pathologists, Dr Jerreat and Dr Djurovic, who were called by the defence. It did not necessarily follow that because Dr Heath was now a discredited witness, and his evidence was disputed at trial, that the conviction in the present case should automatically be considered by us to be unsafe. A rigorous examination of the pathological evidence was called for.

Significant parts of the pathologist's evidence were not in dispute. Dr Heath, however, believed that both wounds were caused by the knife being driven in up to the hilt. Both defence pathologists disputed this. Dr Heath stated that the level of force required to deliver the blows would be considerable, beyond severe; his colleagues believed that moderate force was required. The fatal wound to the chest described as the big wound was 45 degrees horizontal, angled 45 degrees upwards. The depth was approximately 16 centimetres.

The second wound was the subject of dispute. It was further to the left side of the chest, again at 45 degrees both angled upwards and inwards, according to Dr Heath, culling across the top of the liver and creating a slice. Both pathologists called by the defence disputed the angle described by Dr Heath. They believed the knife entered at exactly the same angle and plane as the first wound. If so, it was a shorter wound than that described by Dr Heath. The essence of the dispute centred on the possibility that the two wounds had been inflicted by a single stabbing motion in the course of the fight.

We heard evidence from a fourth pathologist, Dr Cary, also a Home Office accredited pathologist, who had been consulted by the CCRC. His opinions had changed in a number of respects between his initial meeting with the CCRC and giving oral testimony before us. Whilst consistently critical of Dr Heath as to the deductions made relating to the force used and also the direction of the tracts of the wounds, he initially indicated that in his opinion the most likely scenario was that one wound incised the liver, whilst the other wound punctured the heart.

He indicated that 'there may have been a double penetrating action with the penetrations occurring in rapid succession. This could in effect amount to one overall action.' This was the high point of the appellant's case and the apparent basis of the referral by the CCRC. If there was but one single stabbing action, it was arguable that it would be consistent with a shorter knife than that postulated by Dr Heath before the jury, and the knife may also have been delivered with less force than contended for by Dr Heath.

Dr Cary asserted that Dr Heath was 'quite erroneous' when he concluded that the presence of two blunt ends in one of the stab wounds indicated penetration up to the hilt. Dr Cary agreed with Drs Jerreat and Djurovic that the force used to inflict the wounds might well have been moderate, as no bone was penetrated. His final conclusion appeared to be that one stab wound incised the liver and punctured the heart, whilst the other stab wound merely penetrated the abdomen with no further damage.

Dr Cary expressed concern that by using the word 'severe' in relation to force, Dr Heath may have misled the jury into concluding that the appellant's act or acts were intentional. Accordingly, Dr Cary raised two apparent issues. Was it reasonably possible that one single stabbing motion inflicted both wounds, and may the jury have been misled by Dr Heath into concluding that the actions of the appellant were deliberate.

The answer to these apparent issues lay in the evidence of the appellant when he gave evidence before the jury. The transcript read as follows:

Q: And it was a deliberate striking out with the knife?
A: Yes.
Q: So, did you strike out with the knife deliberately?
A: Yes.
Q: It would appear, Mr Noye, that you did it twice, as the result of the wounds found on Stephen Cameron, yes?
A: Yes.
Q: Can we take it that the second blow was equally deliberate?
A: I can't remember honestly doing the second blow, but I accept it, there's two, yes.

Q: There is no question of you suggesting in this case to this
    jury that it was all an accident, are you?

A: Well, no, it wasn't an accident. I struck out in panic, because
    I thought if he'd got the knife off of me, he'd use it.

Q: Right.

A: He was in such a rage that I just . . .

Q: We have reached this point, Mr Noye, that you admit do
    you not, deliberately stabbing this man twice? You admit
    that?

A: Yes.

It follows that there was the clearest evidence, irrespective of
any inaccuracy on the part of Dr Heath, that the appellant had
delivered two blows with the knife and that both blows were
deliberately inflicted.

Turning to the CCRC's second ground that there was a note
of bruising to Mr Cameron's knuckles, which was not adduced
before the jury. There was clear evidence before the jury that
Mr Cameron had punched the appellant. Indeed, it was never
contended by the prosecution that Mr Cameron had not punched
the appellant; the jury could see abrasions to Mr Cameron's
knuckles on the photographs before them. Dr Cary indicated
that some of the abrasions may have been caused when a wounded
Mr Cameron fell to the ground, but there was nothing in this
point, described by Lord Judge as trivial.

It was a pleasure listening to Clare Montgomery QC appearing
for Mr Noye. She had appeared before me on a number of
occasions and demonstrated great ability. Her only arguable point
was that Dr Heath's inaccuracies, not least his exaggeration of
the force necessarily deployed in the use of the knife, must have
had an adverse impact on the jury's view of her client's credibility and the reasonableness of his actions in stabbing Mr
Cameron.

She made reference to the statements of a large number of

eyewitnesses, contending for a scenario in which the appellant was under attack and fearing for his life, either by being thrown over the bridge, or by being disarmed by Mr Cameron who would then use the knife. In panic, he produced and then used the knife in lawful and necessary self-defence. Dr Heath's flawed evidence, she contended, may well have unfairly and improperly contributed to the finding of guilt.

Miss Montgomery had a second point, which she sought to deploy cumulatively with the attack on Dr Heath's evidence. The point had cut no ice with this court when first raised in 2001. The point relied on the non-disclosure of the background and antecedent history of an important eyewitness, who immediately called the police on his mobile phone.

Mr De Cabral was on the roundabout driving a blue Rolls-Royce. He described the appellant coming around the back of the Land Rover and standing in front of it as Mr Cameron tried to get back into his van. There was a tussle and punches were thrown. Mr Cameron hit the appellant first and then it was 'tit for tat'. The appellant then took a flick knife from the front right-hand pocket of his jeans and put his hand behind his back as if to hide the knife.

The appellant then ran at Mr Cameron, who kicked at him. The appellant then lunged forward with the knife towards the sternum of Mr Cameron, who staggered back. As the appellant passed Mr De Cabral, the expression on his face was as though he was saying, 'That's sorted you out. You've got yours, mate.' Mr De Cabral then followed the Land Rover and called the police, saying, 'I've just seen somebody stabbed.'

Shortly before the stabbing, the police had seized a Mercedes motor car, in the possession of Mr De Cabral, which had a secret compartment in its petrol tank specially created for criminal activity. The police seized £120,000 and confiscated it. Shortly after the trial, Mrs De Cabral informed the police that her husband was engaged in dealing in drugs, including cocaine, in a substantial way. Not long after the trial, he was murdered.

At trial, Mr De Cabral must have appeared as a man of substance whose conduct was beyond reproach. Miss Montgomery contended, as had been claimed in the earlier appeal, that there had been material non-disclosure. Mr De Cabral was in fact a villain with an interest in ingratiating himself with the police. A jury properly informed would inevitably place less reliance on him had they known of his criminal lifestyle. The non-disclosure in relation to him coupled with Dr Heath's misleading and inaccurate evidence, she argued, rendered this conviction unsafe.

This argument, elegantly advanced, did not persuade us to interfere with the verdict of the jury. As the appellant himself admitted in the witness box, this was the deliberate use of a knife and two blows were struck, one of which caused the death of Mr Cameron. What the appellant did was not in dispute. The jury had to consider firstly, whether the appellant was or may have been in mortal fear, and if so, was the use of the knife a reasonable response or was it wholly disproportionate. Dr Heath's evidence did not touch upon those issues.

As for the non-disclosure of Mr De Cabral's criminality, this was a wholly separate non-cumulative issue and did not in any way support, endorse or amplify the complaint made concerning Dr Heath's evidence. Whilst Mr De Cabral gave a more detailed account of the stabbing than any other witness, he made concessions to the appellant, and his account at the conclusion of his evidence was no more damaging to the appellant's case than the appellant's own version of the facts, admitting as he did two deliberate stabs.

We were abundantly satisfied that the conviction for murder was safe. There was no possible justification for the appellant, in these circumstances, to produce a knife and to use it as he did. This was a wholly disproportionate response. The type of knife, the length of blade, the angle of the wounds and the length of the tract, were all irrelevant to the verdict, as was Mr De Cabral's criminality.

It is interesting to note that had this offence been committed after 2 April 2010, a twenty-five-year starting point would have been applicable. It would almost certainly have been imposed.

# Chapter 17

## The Review of Operation Midland

THIS REVIEW DISCLOSED the most significant and shocking failings of two elements of the criminal justice process. A grossly incompetent investigation and the misleading of a district judge by the Metropolitan Police Service (MPS) exposed men who had demonstrated the very highest standards in public life to the most vile accusations fabricated by a liar and fantasist. The conduct of police officers resulted in one award of compensation in the sum of £500,000, together with costs of £400,000, and two awards of £100,000.

Far more significant than the financial consequence to the MPS was the misery and distress heaped upon those falsely accused and their families. Five officers were referred to the IPCC/IOPC by the MPS for possible misconduct. After an investigation lasting for almost three years, all five officers were exonerated.

It was in February 2016, and in retirement, that I was painting the garden benches when Lord Thomas, Lord Chief Justice, telephoned. After friendly pleasantries, he told me that the Commissioner for Metropolitan Police, Sir Bernard Hogan-Howe, wished to appoint a senior or retired judge to conduct a review of Operation Midland. Ten days later, I was at New Scotland Yard with Sir Bernard.

I had asked that Louise Oakley should be instructed to assist me. We had previously worked on a report together for the Director of Public Prosecutions. She has a formidable practice at the criminal Bar and was happy to assist in the conduct of the review, whilst the conclusions would necessarily be mine. I agreed not only to review the conduct of Operation Midland by the MPS, but also their handling of non-recent sexual offence allegations against persons of public prominence. I agreed to complete the review within six months of receiving the documentation.

There was inevitably some delay between our meeting at New Scotland Yard and my receiving the volumes of documentation involved. In that time, I read three books written by accused persons in cases that I was to review, namely *Credible and True* by Harvey Proctor, *Love* by Paul Gambaccini, and *No Further Action* by Jim Davidson. All three authors had individually been falsely accused of sexual offences and in Harvey Proctor's case, three cases of murder. All had remained under investigation for a lengthy period. The books, written in very different styles, communicated identical emotions of anger, frustration and despair at their prolonged ordeal.

Within days or even hours of receiving the documentation in Operation Midland, it was obvious that 'Nick', as Carl Beech was then known, was a serial liar and that his allegations were not only false but manifestly incredible. The question in my mind was simply: 'How is it possible that the investigators came to believe him?'

## The Allegation

In a nutshell, 'Nick' had alleged that between the ages of seven and sixteen, on numerous occasions, he had been collected by car from his schools, first in Wiltshire, then Oxfordshire and finally Surrey, and driven to London, where he and other young boys were anally raped, burned, stabbed and tortured by a circle of abusers including Sir Edward Heath; Lord Brittan, former Home Secretary; Lord Bramall, former Chief of General Staff;

Maurice Oldfield, former head of MI6; Sir Michael Hanley, former Director-General of MI5; General Sir Hugh Beach, Master-General of the Ordnance; Lord Janner, a former Labour MP; Jimmy Savile; his stepfather Major Ray Beech; and Harvey Proctor, who allegedly murdered two children in Nick's presence and organised the killing of the third.

Most of the offences were allegedly committed in the Carlton Club, or in the apartment block called Dolphin Square, which has an indoor swimming pool. After serial abuse and on occasions bleeding, 'Nick' would be returned by car to his home, where he lived alone with his mother.

## The Investigation

MPS officers had available to them interviews of 'Nick' conducted in December 2012 by Wiltshire Police, and the blogs written and published by him between May and October 2014. They also had a statement from Nick's mother, dated 16 April 2013 and provided by Wiltshire Police, in which she stated that she had no knowledge of any unauthorised absence from school. She had never seen any bloodstained underwear from him or similar sign of sexual abuse. 'Nick' had told her in a letter in 1986 that he had been abused by her ex-husband, but he mentioned no other accuser. The officers interviewing 'Nick' were not provided with the earlier interviews, or with his blogs.

There were numerous inconsistencies between Nick's allegations made to Wiltshire Police and his allegations made to the MPS, of which the most obvious were:

- He told Wiltshire Police that the first time he was raped, the offender was an unnamed Lieutenant-Colonel. He told the MPS that the first person who raped him was his stepfather.
- He told Wiltshire Police that he was buggered a couple of

times a week by his stepfather. He told the MPS that it was 'not that often'.

- To Wiltshire Police he made no allegation of physical violence against his stepfather. To the MPS he alleged his stepfather used a lot of violence to him and inflicted visible bruises seen by his mother. His mother denied seeing any such bruising in her statement.

- To the Wiltshire Police he stated that the first Army officer who raped him was an unnamed Lieutenant-Colonel. To the MPS he said the first Army officer who raped him was General Bramall.

- To the Wiltshire Police he said that names were never used and named no individual except his deceased stepfather. To the MPS he named nine individuals by name.

- To the Wiltshire Police he said that his abusers were 'a group about twenty in number and included one Middle Eastern person, one American/Canadian and one man called Pete'. To the MPS he alleged that he was raped on numerous occasions by eminent politicians and civil servants whom he named.

- To the Wiltshire Police he stated that he had been taken to different hotels, 'the Hilton on Park Lane and one not far from Oxford Street'. To the MPS he stated that he had been raped on numerous occasions in Dolphin Square and in the Carlton Club.

- To the Wiltshire Police he made no mention of any murder or of Harvey Proctor. To the MPS he described three child murders allegedly committed by Harvey Proctor.

In my judgement, these inconsistencies alone rendered Nick's allegations incredible. There were also numerous inconsistencies between his blogs and his account to the MPS. The investigation however progressed in disordered and chaotic manner, littered with mistakes.

Senior officers overlooked the fact that the Wiltshire Police had doubted Nick's credibility, describing it as 'all a bit odd' and 'it all sounds a bit *Spooks*.'

They caused 'Nick' to be interviewed by officers with no knowledge of his Wiltshire interviews or his blogs.

They failed to arrange any further interview to deal with the numerous inconsistencies between the MPS interviews and the Wiltshire interviews until January 2016.

They delayed visiting Nick's mother for approximately six months.

They failed to trace a friend of 'Nick', named 'Aubrey', asserted by 'Nick' to have been present during acts of sexual abuse until October 2015.

They failed to enquire of the Criminal Injuries Compensation Authority whether 'Nick' had made a claim, before learning of it in February 2015.

Having learned that 'Nick' had made a claim, they failed to ask for details of the claim and thereafter assisted 'Nick' to process his claim during the currency of the claim.

They failed to ask 'Nick' to consent to a medical examination until January 2016, notwithstanding his allegations that he had been stabbed, burned and forcefully anally raped.

They ignored the fact that his medical records obtained in December 2014 disclosed no injury consistent with his allegations.

They ignored the fact that Nick's blog of 19 June 2014 asserted that he was regularly injured, bled into both his underpants and school pants, his feet were stabbed and burned, poppies were pinned to his bare chest, and numerous bones were broken; an assertion entirely contrary both to his medical records and his mother's statement to the Wiltshire Police.

They ignored the fact that 'Nick' asserted in his blog of 18 August 2014 that he *could be gone from anywhere from a few hours to a few days*, which was entirely contrary to his mother's statement to the Wiltshire Police.

They failed to ask 'Nick' for his computers and his mobile phone.

They had no regard to the inherent improbability of men of the highest standing and impeccable character having behaved in the manner alleged.

## Credible and True

On 18 December 2014, no progress having been made with the investigation, DAC Rodhouse, the Gold Commander of Operation Midland, decided to hold a national media briefing asking for further witnesses. His written decision contained these words: 'If asked, we will say we believe "Nick".'

As an immediate consequence of that decision, DSU McDonald announced to the media and the public outside New Scotland Yard, '"Nick" has been spoken to by officers from the murder command. They and I believe that what "Nick" is saying is to be (*sic*) credible and true and as such with those allegations we will investigate them.'

The statement by DSU McDonald that he believed Nick's allegations to be both credible and true should never have been made. DSU McDonald himself has admitted that the words were inappropriate, asserting that he selected the wrong words in the heat of an interview. Assistant Commissioner Dick, as she then was, heard the words 'credible and true' on the radio and instantly realised that they should not have been used.

She was DAC Rodhouse's immediate superior. Significantly, there was no correction for many months, by which time two completely bogus potential witnesses had come forth with a pack of lies purporting to support 'Nick'. Their accounts were so wide of the mark that they were quite correctly rejected. I advised that they should be investigated by an independent force, with a view to their being prosecuted for perverting the course of justice and wasting police time. No decision was ever made and that failure has now been reported to the IOPC.

For my part, I remain at a loss to understand how Messrs Rodhouse and McDonald could possibly have believed 'Nick' on 18 December 2014. Neither Rodhouse nor McDonald had ever met 'Nick', and in Rodhouse's case, he had not himself read either Nick's Wiltshire interviews, or his MPS interviews or his blogs. Further in the same decision log, in which Rodhouse wrote, 'If asked, we will say we do believe "Nick",' he also wrote that 'a full investigation was required to establish the credibility of Nick as a witness.'

It follows that Nick's credibility had not been established and yet the public were being told that he was credible. Whilst neither Rodhouse nor McDonald were referred to the IOPC for having authorised or having used the words 'credible and true', the IOPC have expressed the view that 'there was no basis for an investigation'.

A contrary view appears to be tenable. Nick's allegations were neither credible nor true and there was no sound basis for either authorising the use of the words or for speaking them. Nick's credibility had not been established, as the log confirms, and there was not a scintilla of evidence to confirm or support his allegations in any material particular. The use of the expression 'credible and true' implies that there existed some independent source of information in the possession of the police that confirmed Nick's allegations. There was nothing to their knowledge that could possibly confirm that 'Nick' had told the truth. Nevertheless, McDonald used the expression 'credible and true' a second time, in response to a question from a BBC interviewer.

Both officers have conceded that the words should not have been spoken. On 11 February 2016, in a BBC Radio 4 *Today* programme, Sir Bernard stated that the words were misspoken, and Dame Cressida has very recently stated that the use of the words was wrong. It remains a matter of considerable regret that such an obvious error was not corrected for a period of some fourteen months, despite full knowledge and comprehension of the 'misspeak' by the most senior officers.

## The Application for Search Warrants

On 2 March 2015, an application was made to senior district judge Howard Riddle for warrants to search the homes of Lord Bramall, Lord Brittan (recently deceased), and Harvey Proctor. DAC Rodhouse had authorised the making of the applications. I am in no doubt that these applications should never have been authorised; I stated in my review that the warrants were obtained unlawfully and that Judge Riddle was misled. The judge has since confirmed that he was indeed misled.

In order to obtain warrants, the MPS had to satisfy the judge that *there are reasonable grounds for believing that an indictable offence has been committed*. The applications contained the following:

> *The victim in this matter has been interviewed at length by experienced officers from the child abuse investigation team. His account has remained consistent and he is felt to be a witness who is telling the truth.*

The application failed to disclose the existence of either the Wiltshire interviews or Nick's blogs. 'Nick' was demonstrably inconsistent in his accounts to the Wiltshire Police and the MPS and similarly inconsistent in his blogs, when contrasted with his accounts to either police force. It is simply unarguable that 'Nick' had been consistent. His first abusers were different, the locations were different, his alleged injuries were different, the group of abusers was different.

Aware that there was no corroboration or confirmation of Nick's allegations, the application for the warrants continued:

> *Prior to police involvement, these allegations were detailed to an independent counsellor by the victim who also supports this account as being credible. At the request of police, a qualified consultant Dr Elly Hanson was asked to give an opinion if the counsellor was able to make an accurate judgement of the victim's credibility. Dr Hanson's views were that she felt the counsellor was able to make an accurate judgment of the victim's credibility.*

I interviewed Dr Hanson and she informed me that she was only provided with a fraction of the MPS interviews of 'Nick', had not had time to read them all, had viewed none of the videos of the interviews, had not been given either Nick's blogs or his Wiltshire interviews, or indeed even been informed of their existence.

Her report commenced, 'In this report I provide a brief assessment and opinion on the credibility of the witness "Nick".' Having been given a small fraction of the source material and never having spoken to 'Nick', her opinion was valueless. The provision of such limited material was a matter that should in due course have been considered by the IOPC.

The application forms contain a paragraph headed 'Duty of Disclosure'. It reads:

> *Is there anything of which you are aware that might reasonably be considered capable of undermining any of the grounds of this application, or which for some other reason might affect the court's decision? Include anything that might call into question the credibility of information you have received, and explain why you have decided that the information still can be relied on.*

The letters N/A appeared in the box beneath those words. The failure to disclose the following undermining factors constituted a gross failure of duty to the court:

1. Nick's mother's statement to the Wiltshire Police undermined his complaint that he had been removed from school, injured, made to bleed, soiled his clothing, and been absent from home.

2. No supporting witness had come forward despite extensive media coverage.

3. There was no evidence that 'Fred', asserted by 'Nick' to be his companion at times of abuse, had ever existed.

4. There was no record in existence in any public document of any fatal accident outside Nick's then primary school, alleged by Nick to be a murder in which Harvey Proctor was complicit.

5. Every boy named 'Scott' at Nick's then primary school, alleged by 'Nick' to have been the victim of a murder in which Harvey Proctor was complicit, had been found alive.

6. No victim of any murder alleged by 'Nick' to have been carried out by Harvey Proctor had been either identified or proven to have existed.

7. Nick's interviews with the Wiltshire Police were inconsistent with, and thus undermined, his interviews with the MPS.

8. Nick's blogs were inconsistent with, and thus undermined, both sets of interviews.

At the conclusion of the form, these words are written:

*To the best of my knowledge and belief this application discloses all the information that is material to what the court must decide including anything that might reasonably be considered capable of undermining any of the grounds of the application.*

It is significant that DAC Rodhouse, in written submissions to me, conceded that some five of the above undermining factors should have been disclosed on the form presented to the district judge. He also wrote, 'before applying for the warrants, we fully recognised aspects of the investigation were not borne out by

our investigation.' It is also significant that in granting the applications, the judge wrote on the form: 'This has been considered
at DAC level.'

Authority to make these applications for warrants should never
have been given by DAC Rodhouse. He was fully appraised of
every undermining factor and must have known that in the
event of a full disclosure of undermining factors, no fully
informed district judge could possibly grant the applications.
Notwithstanding Sir Bernard's decision to refer him to the
IPCC/IOPC, they found that he had no case to answer and
exonerated him without interview.

I am quite satisfied not only that there were no reasonable
grounds for believing that an indictable offence had been
committed, but also that senior officers did not believe that
reasonable grounds existed. Had the officers believed that reasonable grounds did exist, I have no doubt that Harvey Proctor
would have been arrested. He was allegedly a serial child murderer
at large.

Five officers were referred to the IPCC/IOPC and all exonerated, in a case in which a district judge was misled and there
was significant non-disclosure.

DAC Rodhouse and DSU McDonald were exonerated
without interview after a short period, it being said that there
was no case to answer.

Whilst under investigation, DCI Tudway, the senior investigating officer (SIO), was promoted to the rank of Superintendent.
When interviewed by the IOPC, she was unable to recall what
information was available to her at what time. When interviewed
by me, she agreed that she had read the Wiltshire interviews,
the MPS interviews, the blogs, and the applications. It is difficult to see how she could believe that 'Nick' had been consistent
and that there were no undermining factors. The other officers
referred were unable to recall what information was available to
them.

The IOPC investigation lasted for almost three years. I was not approached for some twenty months. The lead investigator had no education in or sufficient knowledge of the criminal law.

I remain firmly of the view that one or more of the officers have either perverted the course of justice and/or committed misconduct in public office in the obtaining of the search warrants. I had called for 'a rigorous investigation'. The two most senior officers were never investigated. The process was unreasonably protracted and reached a conclusion that no competent tribunal could have reached.

## The Execution of the Warrants

Prior to the execution of the warrants, the names of those named by 'Nick' had not been published. On 4 March 2015, simultaneous searches took place at five properties, namely, Lord Bramall's home in Farnham, at Lady Brittan's home in Westminster and at her country home in Leyburn, at Mr Proctor's home in Grantham and at his office on the Belvoir Estate.

Shortly before, or as the searches commenced, Nick's family liaison officer contacted him and informed him of the pending searches. Within forty-eight hours of the searches taking place, they had become public knowledge and the shattering ordeal for Lord Bramall, Lady Brittan and Harvey Proctor began.

DAC Rodhouse sought to justify informing 'Nick' of the searches, stating that it would have been a serious blow to the relationship with 'Nick', had he learned of the searches by other means. That observation overlooks the very grave, indeed life-changing consequence of losing anonymity.

In a log dated 11 November 2014, DAC Rodhouse had earlier written: *If the subjects were placed in the public domain, it would cause significant damage to their reputation and distress to them and their families.* He nevertheless authorised the applications. He subsequently conceded that: *It was recognised that informing 'Nick' of the searches could lead to him informing the media.* The decision to inform 'Nick' of the searches has been the immediate cause of much distress.

The searches were exceptionally painful for those whose homes were searched. Full details appear in my review. Lord Bramall was ninety-one years of age and his wife was terminally ill at the time. Twenty-two officers spent ten hours in their home. Lord Bramall was told that the warrant was to search for material relating to the abuse of children, and his wife was moved from room to room during the search. Nothing of significance was found.

Lady Brittan found the search at her London home most distressing. Her husband had died only weeks earlier. She was never told that the search was in relation to the possible prosecution of others, and was given no information as to the purpose of the search, nor was she informed of any rights she had in relation to other people. Nothing of significance was found.

Her home in Leyburn was simultaneously searched. Officers showed particular interest in the garden and grassed areas, conveying the impression to the housekeeper that a body or body parts had been buried therein. Some property not covered by the warrant was seized. Nothing of significance was found.

Harvey Proctor's home was searched by fifteen officers for some fifteen hours. Nothing of significance was found. A large number of laptop computers, hard drives, DVDs and other materials were seized, but a promised list of property was not forthcoming. His office was also searched with nothing of significance found. The decision to search Harvey Proctor's home and office caused him to lose both his home and his employment.

## The Emergence of A and B

In September 2015, two potential witnesses, known as A and B, came forward. There was plainly no truth in their allegations and I do not propose to repeat what were clearly lies. It is by no means unusual for liars to appear in response to public appeals by police for information or further complaints. The process initiated by the 'credible and true' pronouncement on the steps of New Scotland Yard doubtless played a part in producing A and B.

As to witness A, a senior clinical therapist reported that A had admitted giving false information in the past about being systematically sexually abused over a period of time by a paedophile ring. A manager of a clinic wrote to the Probation Service and stated that A 'spent a long period of time giving misinformation and my suspicion is that whether consciously or not, he has a need to be mischievous.'

It was believed that A had done significant levels of internet research about the matters that he had reported. Whilst being interviewed by another force, A had disclosed that he had spent twenty years 'hunting' for information on places such as Dolphin Square and the Paedophile Information Exchange. Witness A spoke about trawling the internet to find out everything about a suspect in this case and 'still with that mentality that I'm going to fuck them all up.' A has a history of criminal offending, including sexual offences against children, numerous fraud and theft offences and, very recently, he made a false claim to the police concerning alleged threats. His evidence given to Operation Midland was manifestly worthless and fraudulent.

B has convictions for theft, fraud and violence. He has a brother in the Church, who states that B is a prolific liar, who has told various untruths about money and property that he has claimed to own. He had invented an allegation of being approached by a paedophile when, in fact, it had been his brother. B alleged that he had been abused by a priest at a named cathedral when he, B, was seven years old, but when enquiries were made, the priest accused did not move to that cathedral until seven years later. When Midland officers showed an album of photos to B, he was unable to identify any suspect, but did select other photos chosen at random.

I studied B's evidence with care and it was plainly worthless. Operation Midland officers readily agreed that neither A nor B could possibly be relied upon and that both had deliberately lied. Accordingly, I recommended in my review that another police force should be asked to carry out investigations into possible offences of attempting to pervert the course of justice by both A and B. I have heard nothing since from the MPS on the subject. I have been informed by the BBC that a decision was made to take no action but never recorded in due form. The MPS has since reported itself to the IOPC.

I am unable to comprehend the decision-making behind taking no action against A and B, as they were apparently attempting to do exactly what 'Nick' had done. The sentence of eighteen years passed on Carl Beech underlines the gravity of this form of conduct. If there exists a sound basis for taking no action against A or B, I have yet to hear it.

## The Investigation Continued

As the months passed and further information was obtained, the mendacity of 'Nick' became increasingly obvious. A shameful low point in the investigation was the interview of Lord Bramall under caution in a police station on 30 April 2015. In the view of many, the most distinguished living Englishman, yet he was treated as a suspected common criminal on the conflicted word of a single individual.

As I watched the video recording of that interview, I was angered and saddened in equal measure. Angered that our criminal justice process could treat this man such a way, when it was blindingly obvious that 'Nick' was a liar. Saddened that such a fine man in his ninety-second year should be exposed to such a degrading ordeal, having given so much for his country.

A rifleman in 1942, he landed on the Normandy beaches, and was awarded the Military Cross in 1945; he was later Staff Officer to Lord Mountbatten in 1965, invested as Knight Commander in 1974, promoted to General in 1976, invested with the Knight Grand Cross in 1979, Field Marshall 1982, Chief of Defence Staff 1982–85, Head of the British Armed Forces 1982, Justice of the Peace, Baron Bramall 1987, Knight of the Garter 1990, Lord Lieutenant of Greater London 1986–88 and Past President of MCC.

He now faced interrogation for one hour and forty-four minutes.

I include two short passages from an interview in which Lord Bramall's innocence was graphically demonstrated:

> Well, I'm absolutely astonished, amazed and bemused. I mean not only do I deny absolutely any of these things but we will do that in more detail, but I find it quite incredible that someone of my career, standing and integrity should have been capable of any of these things, including things like torture, which are unbelievable.

Lord Bramall concluded thus:

> I would ask that as soon as possible I am removed from the investigation and a public statement made to that effect. I can then get on with ensuring that my reputation and my honour is publicly restated, which is not only important to me and my family but to the proud name and standing of the British Army as well and I would be very grateful if you would ensure that your most senior managers are made aware of that statement.

On 20 May 2015, over six months after the investigation was opened, a statement was most belatedly taken from Nick's mother. In it she said that she had no impression that her son was unhappy or that anything was wrong with him. She did not remember ever seeing her son inexplicably dishevelled, dirty or smelly. If he had been taken away by men for any period of time and abused and returned a matter of hours later, she was surprised that she would not have smelled it or sensed it on him. The only injury spoken of in her statement was her son chipping a bone in his ankle on a skiing holiday. The first she heard of any Westminster paedophile ring was when she saw a profile of 'Nick' on television in November 2014.

It struck me as absurd that interviewing Lord Bramall under caution had taken precedence over interviewing Nick's mother.

On 18 June 2015, Harvey Proctor was interviewed under caution. When the officers turned to Nick's allegations he said:

> What this amounts to is a heinous calumny. These allegations are just about the worst allegations you could throw at any other human being. When are you going to prosecute 'Nick', if he exists, for making these false allegations? At what stage do you wake up and find you are being taken for a ride?

The remainder of the interview constituted a most strenuous and determined denial of guilt.

On 28 July 2015, Sir Hugh Beach, a retired general, was interviewed as a potential witness. 'Nick' had named him as being present on occasions when sexual abuse had taken place, without asserting that he was a participant. Shortly after Nick's interviews in November 2014, Sir Hugh was designated a suspect. On 11 June 2015, however, the SIO decided he should no longer be named as a suspect, but interviewed as a potential witness. He was ninety-one years of age at the time of the interview and the urgency of interviewing a potential witness appears to have been lost upon these officers.

When he was interviewed, he said of Lord Bramall: 'I cannot pick a man, a more upright man, a man I admire more for his moral character.' He described the allegation against Lord Bramall as a 'total fairy tale'. He had never been to the Carlton Club or to Dolphin Square.

On 31 July, Lord Bramall was again interviewed and pointed out to the interviewing officers that in relation to the alleged abuse within the barracks, his military assistant and ADC and personal staff would be able to say quite categorically that the alleged offence never happened. He supplied details of his military assistant and his ADC at the time. He told the officers that his reputation was being damaged on Google and it was not fair at his time of life.

It was not until 24 November 2015 that officers even made the decision to trace Lord Bramall's aide-de-camp, a decision most unreasonably delayed in all the circumstances of this investigation.

On 24 August 2015, Harvey Proctor was again interviewed and shown a penknife. The proposition was put to him that he had threatened to cut Nick's genitals with the knife and that Edward Heath had intervened and said 'no'. Mr Proctor told the officers that 'the fantasy gets bigger by the minute'. He told them that they had been taken for a ride.

The next day, Harvey Proctor held a press conference at the St Ermin's hotel, close to New Scotland Yard, as it was then situated. He pointed out that it was most unlikely that he and Edward Heath would be involved in any joint activity. They were not on speaking terms, had opposing political views, and ignored one another within the House of Commons. He questioned how any sex party could ever take place in Edward Heath's home with CCTV, housekeeper, private secretary, chauffeur, police and private detectives assigned to former prime ministers. Mr Proctor proclaimed his innocence in the most strident terms and called for Nick to be prosecuted.

On 11 September 2015, the SIO decided not to ask 'Nick' if officers could examine his computer to see if he had researched any of the information contained in his allegations. She believed such a request 'would cause "Nick" to disengage'. She did not want to do this too early as 'it may damage our relationship'.

This decision was plainly wrong and delayed the closure of this investigation by several months. If 'Nick' was genuine and truthful, he would surely have no objection to his computer being examined.

On 5 October 2015, the police found Aubrey. 'Nick' had told Wiltshire Police that a friend Aubrey was present when he was abused and they were friends from Bicester. Aubrey had not seen anything sexual. 'Nick' subsequently said that he had used the name Aubrey in place of the real victim, Fred. There then followed complex steps taken to trace Fred.

On 6 November, plans were outlined for house-to-house enquiries in Pimlico and Victoria to identify information on suspicious sexual activity that took place around the time of Nick's allegations. In my review, I concluded and maintain that these steps bordered on the hysterical and were disproportionate, having regard to the state of Nick's credibility. He had misled officers concerning Aubrey and no Scott had ever been killed or seriously injured. Nick's evidence was wholly inconsistent with his mother's and was inconsistent with his own earlier statements.

By 17 December, the investigation was in its final days, limping to its death. 'Nick' cancelled appointments with officers for 23 and 30 November and 5 December; then on 21 January, officers learned that 'Nick' had received £22,000 criminal injuries compensation. The SIO continued to argue against asking 'Nick' to permit inspection of his computer and likewise argued against a medical examination, pleading that 'an intimate examination was too intrusive when balanced against the benefit of this from an evidential perspective.'

A report from an eminent psychologist, Professor Andrews, commissioned by MPS, was now to hand; it was critical of the interviewing technique of the interviewing officer, stating that there appeared to be a number of leading questions and that the general thrust of the questioning was to wholeheartedly endorse Nick's account. The CPS were also now involved and indicated that 'they were highly unlikely to bring any prosecution as a result of Nick's allegations as a result of Professor Andrews' report.' DAC Rodhouse questioned whether this was simply Professor Andrews' opinion.

In January 2016, house-to-house enquiries continued and officers carried on investigating the allegations made by A and B. On 11 January, the final interview of 'Nick' took place, but he discontinued at an early stage pleading illness. When asked why he did not mention Lord Bramall's name to the Wiltshire Police, he said that he thought they would find out and he did not want to be the one that gave them that name. As soon as the topic turned to Middle Eastern, Saudi and American diplomats, 'Nick' said that he was ill.

Regardless of Nick's obviously hopeless predicament, the SIO took the view that he should be further interviewed at a later date. He agreed to return three days later, but cancelled the day before, pleading work commitments.

On 14 January 2016, the inevitable decision was made to discontinue against Lord Bramall, but at the same time an extraordinary decision was taken to continue the investigation against Harvey Proctor. This decision ignored the advice of the CPS, namely that if 'Nick' was incredible in the case of one, he was incredible in the case of the other.

On 9 February, a discussion took place regarding bringing Operation Midland to a close, but DAC Rodhouse stressed that this would not be brought forward prematurely: 'The SIO takes a very firm view that we should not ask "Nick" for his computer. This will set a dangerous precedent for victims.'

Previously the SIO had declined to ask 'Nick' for his computer on the grounds that he might lose confidence in her and disengage. However, he had now disengaged and was no longer cooperative. She knew that 'Nick' had received £22,000 and it appears remarkable that she did not contemplate the possibility that 'Nick' had perpetrated a fraud.

## Operation Midland Is Closed

On 21 March 2016, the MPS issued a press statement stating: 'In the course of the investigation officers have not found evidence to prove that they were knowingly misled by a complainant. The MPS does not investigate complaints simply on the basis that their allegations have not been corroborated.'

I wrote in my review that this statement was unfair to every one of those persons named by 'Nick' and their families. It was especially unfair to Lord Bramall and to Harvey Proctor, who had to live through the ordeal of facing these shocking allegations over a prolonged period. The Northumbria Police had little difficulty in finding evidence that the MSP had been misled. There was in fact an abundance of evidence available at the date of closure that the MPS had been misled.

'Nick' had given two different accounts to two different police forces. He lied about Aubrey from Bicester having been sexually assaulted at sex parties. He invented Scott's murder and fabricated numerous injuries. This was 'evidence that they were knowingly misled by a complainant.'

I have subsequently been informed that at a presentation to the press shortly after closure, DAC Rodhouse stated that there were three complainants in Operation Midland, without making it abundantly clear that A and B were regarded by MPS as fraudsters and that both were prolific liars. Informing the public via the press that there were three complainants in Operation Midland may have been linguistically accurate. In the context and without qualification, it gave a most unhappy impression conveying the real possibility that Nick's complaints may well have been true. The statement that there was no evidence that the MPS had been misled by 'Nick' was simply false. This was a shabby end to a reprehensible investigation.

## Why Did They Believe 'Nick' ?

On 16 August 2016, I interviewed collectively the DAC, the SIO, Nick's interviewing officer and two of the officers concerned in the warrant applications. Every officer even at that late date stated, 'I believe "Nick".' It was not within my remit to interview officers individually or to apportion blame to any individual. I was concerned with the performance of the MPS and I could not treat my review as a form of disciplinary hearing. The question remains, 'How was it possible to believe "Nick"?'

It has been said that he was a good liar. He was not a good liar. He could not remember when being interviewed by the MPS what he had told Wiltshire. His blogs were at odds with his interviews and he told lies that would unravel. He told Wiltshire Police that he was hospitalised after an attack by his stepfather; he was not. His Wiltshire abusers were not his MPS abusers and the locations of abuse were not West End hotels. This was not, as the SIO asserted, a 'progressive disclosure', but the inconsistency of a bad serial liar.

He was only a good liar if the MPS interviews are read in total isolation. I agree with Professor Andrews' criticism of the interview technique: 'Nick' was never challenged on any statement of fact. That was not the interviewer's fault, as he had not been supplied with the Wiltshire interviews. The fault lies with officers who had the Wiltshire interviews and the blogs, but did not sufficiently contrast the two, if at all. The only sense in which 'Nick' was a good liar was that he used both the internet and his contact with investigating journalists, in particular Exaro, to obtain information that he drip-fed into the MPS interviews. This ploy simply exaggerated the difference between the two sets of interviews.

The DAC informed me that he did not read the Wiltshire interviews, but was informed of their content by more junior officers. I have been told that is standard and accepted practice within the MPS, but I cannot accept that it is good practice. Never once as junior counsel did a leader ask me what was in the police interviews and likewise, I never once made such enquiry of a junior. Had DAC Rodhouse read the Wiltshire interviews himself, I am quite sure this investigation would have been short-lived.

Another explanation floated in newspapers is that Tom Watson MP's influence played a significant role in causing officers to believe 'Nick'. In October 2012, the then deputy leader of the Labour Party asked a question of David Cameron about clear intelligence suggesting a powerful paedophile network linked to Parliament and Number 10. This was described by Stephen Wright of the *Daily Mail* as: 'The beginning of another high-profile personal crusade for Watson.'

Tom Watson was canvassing for complaints of sexual abuse and referring them to the police. He was receiving information from various sources and a former child protection officer, Peter McKelvie, had seen a tweet on the internet from 'Nick'. He arranged for him to meet Watson.

In an interview with the *Guardian*, Tom Watson spoke about the meeting:

It was a very traumatic and difficult conversation, as you would imagine. He only told me about one murder. He spoke very intermittently and I didn't need to hear any more. What I am certain is, that he is not delusional. He is either telling the truth or he's made up a meticulous and elaborate story. It's not for me to judge. What I was hoping to do was build a relationship with him and get him back into the system, so he could make the allegations to the police.

'Nick' did not name any abuser and according to Watson, they met only once and he sent 'Nick' to the police.

Nick's version of his relationship with Watson was somewhat different. In his first interview with the MPS on 22 October 2014, 'Nick' said, 'Peter McKelvie and Tom Watson then formed a little group that supported me. They did a piece on Dolphin Square. I talked to Tom at some length.'

Critics of Tom Watson point to his simultaneous interest in and involvement in Operation Vincente, an allegation of rape against Lord Brittan dating back to 1967 when he was a student. On 28 April 2014, Tom Watson wrote a letter on House of Commons notepaper to the Director of Public Prosecutions, complaining that the case against Lord Brittan had been dropped before the suspect was interviewed, a decision he described as 'highly irregular and shocking in itself'. The letter was published on the Exaro website.

On 7 July 2014, Lord Brittan was named in the press in connection with a rape allegation in 1967 and on that same date DAC Rodhouse was appointed Gold Commander Operation Vincente. Full details of my review of that Operation can be read on the internet. Suffice it to say that I concluded, as did the CPS on several occasions, that the Full Code Test had not been met. There was no prospect of a conviction, the allegation was politically motivated by a Labour Party activist against a Conservative Home Secretary, and quite properly Lord Brittan was never charged.

Watson's intervention, however, caused Lord Brittan to be interviewed when he was terminally ill, further weakening a hopeless prosecution case. A decision was made to take no further action, but quite disgracefully that decision was never communicated to him and Lord Brittan died unaware of that decision.

Four days after Lord Brittan died, on 25 January 2015, Watson quoted an unnamed survivor of child abuse as having described Lord Brittan as being 'as close to evil as a human being could get'. Watson added, 'Former Home Secretary Leon Brittan stands accused of multiple child rape. Many others knew of these allegations and chose to remain silent. I will not. The police must continue their investigations.'

Uniquely in my experience, DAC Rodhouse sought even after Lord Brittan's death to persuade the CPS to review the case against Lord Brittan. A deceased person can never be tried for any crime and it was not until 24 June 2015 that the CPS released a statement that the police had taken the decision in 2013 to take no further action against Lord Brittan. Finally, on 6 October 2015, nine months after Lord Brittan's death, DAC Rodhouse wrote to Lady Brittan's solicitors confirming that 'unless further evidence had become available no further action would have been taken in respect of this allegation.'

The extent to which DAC Rodhouse was influenced by Watson's exhortation can be only a matter of speculation. There was an abundance of evidence from the very outset of Operation Midland that Nick was an uncorroborated liar, who could not be believed. The length of this enquiry and the manner in which it was conducted cannot be laid at Tom Watson's door.

Three years ago, I put the many failures in this case down to poor judgement and a failure to evaluate known facts accurately. I found that the most significant error was the deception of the district judge and I called for a rigorous investigation by a person or body with the appropriate powers of investigation, which I lacked. I was assured by Sir Bernard that this aspect of the case would be referred to the IPCC, as it then was, and handed my review to him confident that a full and proper investigation would take place.

No such investigation was ever attempted. No single question was asked of the officer authorising the warrants. Now it is said that the officers cannot be investigated, because a statutory investigation has taken place exonerating them. Those named by Carl Beech and their families and the public deserve better. There are reasonable grounds to believe that a criminal offence has been committed.

# Chapter 18

## The Future of the Judiciary

As I depart the criminal courts that have given me such interest and satisfaction both at the Bar and on the Bench, I make ten suggestions for the sole purpose of improving our criminal justice process. Before doing so, I take this opportunity to defend two vital pillars of our constitution that have recently attracted comment, if not criticism.

In the 2019 general election, the Conservative Party manifesto stated: 'After Brexit we need to look at the broader aspects of our constitution: the relationship between the Government, Parliament and the courts.' This has been taken by many as a call for a codified constitution and also as an ambition to select judges of the Supreme Court with a political bias favouring the government.

It may be little more than petulant foot-stamping in the immediate aftermath of Gina Miller's two successes against the government in the Supreme Court, but to dismiss the possibility so lightly would fail to reflect the support in some circles for radical reform and to acknowledge that Parliament is sovereign; with a substantial government majority, such reform could well take place.

My belief is that such reform would be a grave mistake. Our constitution may not be in a single document. It can, however, be found in statutes, case law and the conventions that form our common law. Perusal of the judgments in the Miller cases demonstrates the very existence of a constitution. Creating a single document encapsulating every established principle, rule and convention would both deprive future generations of the flexibility and power of development provided by the common law and also give birth to volumes of interpretation.

I find it unthinkable that judges at any level might be selected for their bias and not on merit. I would anticipate uniform hostility to any such proposal by the existing Bench. The independence of the judiciary is as fundamental as the sovereignty of Parliament. Judicial bias is the enemy of justice. We are proud of our system and the resentment at the imposition of an American-style constitutional arrangement would be enormous.

I turn to measures that I believe would command greater, if not total, support.

## 1. The Lord Chancellor and Secretary of State for Justice must be a lawyer.

In my five decades in the law, I have observed and even participated in a shocking decline in the performance of our criminal justice process. In part only, a lack of adequate funding has been responsible. The serving judiciary are constrained in their complaints by their obligation to maintain the confidence of the public in the system over which they preside. They soldier on with muted voice whilst the public are distracted by the inadequacies of other public services.

The groundbreaking and excellent book *The Secret Barrister* has highlighted: 'The wrongful convictions, collapsing prosecutions, investigative failings, underfunded defences, abiding delays, repetitive adjournments, errors in disclosure and institutional insouciance.' No judge could effectively challenge this portrayal of a process that once commanded global admiration. It requires far more than a concluding chapter to analyse the numerous contributing factors in this sad decline. Much needs to be done.

The Constitutional Reform Act 2005 'modified' the role of

Lord Chancellor, providing that the office holder can no longer act both as a government minister and as a judge. The Act also created the Judicial Appointments Commission now responsible for appointing judges, a responsibility previously vested in the Lord Chancellor. The new title is that of Lord Chancellor and Secretary of State for Justice.

The office remains of critical importance, both to the functioning and morale of the judiciary. The Minister is responsible for the working conditions, salaries and pensions of the judiciary, for legal aid, for the efficient functioning of the courts, prisons, probation service and of recent importance, protecting the independence of the judiciary. The Minister also has a significant role in the appointment of Supreme Court judges, Appeal Court judges and in particular, the Lord Chief Justice.

Prior to the 2005 Act, I had admired several fine Lord Chancellors, in particular Lords Hailsham, Elwyn-Jones, Mackay, Irvine and Falconer, all men of the highest calibre, learned in the law and much respected amongst both lawyers and politicians. None was ever accused of political bias in judicial appointments.

In 2007, Jack Straw was appointed as the first Lord Chancellor and Secretary of State for Justice, a member of the Bar, a former Home Secretary and Foreign Secretary and thus impeccably qualified for the role. He was succeeded in May 2010 by Kenneth Clarke QC, a former Chancellor of the Exchequer, Home Secretary and Secretary of State for Education and Science, also eminently well qualified and quite delighted to be so appointed, according to his memoir.

Both these appointments ensured not only a practical working knowledge of our criminal justice process including the judiciary, but also preserved the status of the office at the Cabinet table. Both were respected heavyweights, well versed in political and legal manoeuvres. The judiciary were well represented.

Between September 2012 and January 2018, four appointments

were made to this office, namely Chris Grayling, Michael Gove, Liz Truss, and David Lidington. None of them were lawyers, none were educated in the law and none had the experience, background or learning necessary to serve or represent the judiciary. One of the great Offices of State had been demoted to a comparatively minor seat in Cabinet.

Chris Grayling was appointed in September 2012, becoming the first non-lawyer to serve as Lord Chancellor for at least 440 years. Lord Pannick described Grayling's performance as 'notable only for his attempts to restrict judicial reviews and human rights, his failure to protect the judiciary against criticism from his colleagues, and the reduction of legal aid to the bare minimum.'*

His predecessor Ken Clarke QC was no less critical: 'He was not at all interested in reforming the prison system in a liberal direction, nor in reducing the prison population. Inevitably therefore he had to return to seek more savings from the legal aid system. He revived the disastrous proposals for criminal legal aid, which dragged him into prolonged and unsuccessful controversy during much of his term of office.'†

Grayling's ban on books being sent into prison was widely criticised and eventually ruled illegal by the High Court. He was severely criticised by HM Inspector of Prisons for interfering with the contents of reports and for using financial controls to influence what was inspected, thereby undermining the independence of the inspector's role. He was criticised by the National Audit Office for a 'rushed implementation' of reforms of the probation system at a cost of £467 million higher than predicted. A subsequent study of Grayling's privatisation of the probation system was described by the British Sociological Association as an 'unmitigated disaster'.

Grayling was criticised by the Justice Select Committee for

* Lord Pannick QC, *Independent*, 25 July 2016.
† Ken Clarke, *Kind of Blue; A Political Memoir*, Macmillan, 2016, p.447.

reducing prison officer numbers from 23,000 in 2012 to 18,000 in 2015 and contributing to a 38 per cent rise in prison deaths in that period, stating that efficiency savings and staff shortages had made 'a significant contribution to the deterioration in safety' in prisons.

Grayling's proposed cuts to legal aid were also widely criticised by the legal profession. Ninety QCs signed and published a letter branding the cuts 'unjust' as they would seriously undermine the rule of law. In 2015, he introduced mandatory court charges ranging from £150 in the magistrates' courts for a guilty plea to £1,200 in the Crown Court for a trial, a measure described by the President of the Law Society as a threat to fair trials, thus causing innocent defendants to plead guilty to avoid swingeing court fees.

In May 2015, Michael Gove replaced Grayling after the general election. His immediate concern was to repair the damage caused by his predecessor. He scrapped the court fees introduced by him and removed the limit on books in prison. Within three months of taking office, he attempted to reduce legal aid fees resulting in the Criminal Bar Association voting to refuse to accept work at the lower proposed rate, thus causing Gove to back down.

In July 2016, Liz Truss was appointed in Theresa May's first government. She was the first woman to hold either office. The Minister of State for Justice, Lord Faulks, resigned from the government doubting that Truss had the clout to be able to stand up to the prime minister when necessary on behalf of judges.★

Truss's novice status was amply demonstrated by her failure to respond to an attack upon the judiciary by the press, when the Divisional Court was described by the *Daily Mail* as the 'Enemies of the People', and in similar terms by others, for

★ Lord Faulks QC, quoted by Frances Gibb, *The Times*, 19 July 2016.

ruling that Parliament – and not the prime minister by use of prerogative powers – would need to trigger Article 50 to start the UK's exit from the European Union. Having initially failed to defend the judges, she later said that the judiciary was robust enough to withstand attack by the *Daily Telegraph* and *Daily Mail*.★

This response caused the Lord Chief Justice, Lord Thomas, to tell the House of Lords constitution select committee that Truss was 'completely and utterly wrong in failing to criticise the media and had taken a position that was wrong constitutionally, absolutely wrong.' She faced a barrage of criticism, not least from a former Lord Chancellor, Lord Falconer, who suggested that, like her predecessors Chris Grayling and Michael Gove, she lacked the essential legal expertise that the constitution requires. He called for her to be sacked, as her perceived inadequate response signalled to the judges that they had lost their constitutional protector.

Her lack of understanding of the judiciary was fully demonstrated when she declared that upon Lord Thomas's retirement, any successor must be under sixty-five or younger in order to navigate Brexit. This edict excluded two outstanding candidates, namely Sir Brian Leveson and Dame Heather Hallett, and was much criticised in legal circles. This observation implies no criticism of Lord Burnett, whose appointment was fully merited. After only eleven months, Liz Truss was moved to the Treasury as Chief Secretary.

David Lidington was appointed in June 2017 and remained in office for six months. He faced criticism for voting against civil partnerships and for contending 'that marriage was for the procreation of children'.

As will be clear, the appointment of four consecutive non-lawyers to this office was a lamentable failure, reflecting not only

★ Liz Truss, *The Times*, 10 November 2016.

upon the decision to appoint them, but demonstrating the necessity for the incumbent to have some background in the law. I well recollect the several meetings between Lord Falconer and Lord Woolf when a 'concordat' was reached between them, in which the responsibilities of the two principle offices were specified. I very much doubt that either envisaged the appointment of a series of non-lawyers. There was much criticism of the legislation at the time. There was neither a Green Paper nor a White Paper and talk was of the Act being drafted on the back of a cigarette packet.

I propose that the Constitutional Reform Act 2005 be amended to provide that the Lord Chancellor must have experience as a qualifying practitioner as defined in s2(3) of the Act. At present the prime minister may take into account experience as a member of either House of Parliament or experience as a minister of the Crown, or experience that the prime minister considers relevant. The four non-lawyers will have qualified for appointment under one or more of those heads. They have cumulatively demonstrated the necessity for a legal qualification.

## 2. High Court judges should be selected for appointment not only by the Judicial Appointments Commission, but also by invitation of the Lord Chief Justice in consultation with the heads of divisions.

Since 2007, the Judicial Appointments Commission (JAC) has been unable to select sufficient candidates of appropriate calibre for appointment to the High Court. In consequence, there has been a continuing shortage of appointed High Court judges, numbering at present approximately twelve. This shortage places a burden upon serving judges and necessarily involves the use of retired judges and deputies, and produces delays.

The nub of the problem is that many good candidates, particularly the leading practitioners, are reluctant to apply to the JAC, but if approached by the head of the judiciary, either flattery or a sense of public duty may overcome the natural resistance to a substantial diminution in income or the fear of rejection. A sound selection process must attract the highest calibre of candidates and at present the leading practitioners are choosing to continue in practice.

This proposed twin selection process would add flexibility to the JAC system by creating an ability to react swiftly to unanticipated vacancies. At all times the High Court must have respected experts in every field in order to function satisfactorily. Promotions, death or premature retirements cannot be anticipated or reacted to in an effective manner by the present system, where the initiative lies exclusively with the applicants and the process is necessarily a lengthy one. A proactive form of headhunting is vital to any well-managed organisation.

It is hoped that recent salary increases will solve the recruitment problem. The Lord Chief Justice, Lord Burnett, and Senior President of Tribunals, Sir Ernest Ryder, in a joint statement said that the proposed 25 per cent increase in salaries would have a significant effect on addressing critical shortages in the judiciary. Whilst the increase in salary will undoubtedly increase the number of applicants, the most able and talented practitioners, in my view, will remain resistant to the present application process.

Leading commercial practitioners in both professions earn well in excess of one million pounds a year. 'Magic Circle' solicitors publish dozens of partners' earnings in that bracket. Applications to reduce earnings by more than two-thirds to £236,000 a year will be limited. A tap on the shoulder by the head of the judiciary, however, can be most persuasive. No large organisation can realistically progress without the ability to recruit positively by way of approach to identified suitable candidates.

## 3. An independent review of the Judicial Appointments Commission should take place.

The JAC has been selecting candidates for appointment to the judiciary since 2007. There are fifteen commissioners and a full-time staff of around fifty public servants. The JAC was created by the Constitutional Reform Act 2005 and took the responsibility for selecting candidates for judicial office out of the hands of the Lord Chancellor. Any selection process will necessarily attract criticism from those not selected, but I find it impossible to attend any legal function without hearing vociferous and disturbing criticism of both the methods and results of the selection process.

The clamour commences with news of the latest star rejected by the JAC after a telephone interview, followed by complaints that a complete duffer has received numerous expensive coaching sessions, had an application form drafted by a tutor, been taught how to demonstrate competencies, and learned of the problems posed in interview from a member of chambers who attended three days earlier, and thus was selected.

I took part in the selection process of circuit judges in 2017. I was one of a panel of three interviewing candidates who would, if appointed, sit in crime. The other two members were human resource specialists with backgrounds outside the law, but with considerable experience in interviewing candidates for the judiciary. They were extremely proficient and I could not fault their judgement.

We were one of three panels interviewing for criminal appointments. Other panels were interviewing for civil appointments and for family appointments. Every candidate to sit in crime was given a written invented scenario containing some practical problems, a sentencing exercise with the appropriate reference books, and a limited time to research the exercise. On attending before the panel, they were asked a number of questions arising

from the exercise and then asked to demonstrate certain competencies. We marked the candidates A, B, C, or D. The exercise
was well set and I am confident that we accurately assessed the
candidates on their performance.

A number of problems occurred to me at the time. The
exercise mainly involved the sentencing of a number of drug
dealers. A candidate with a general criminal practice would have
found the task comparatively simple. A candidate specialising in
fraud or homicide would have been handicapped. We had no
background on any candidate.

One problem involved a juror attending wearing a full-face
veil, a niqab. The defendant objected to her serving. We were
told that any candidate who discharged the juror was to be
assessed as a D. Many candidates will have encountered this
situation and have known how to deal with it, but others will
have come to it for the first time.

After the problem scenario, candidates were required to give
examples from their own experiences demonstrating specified
competencies, for example, exercising judgement, possessing and
building knowledge, assimilating and clarifying information,
working under pressure, or managing work efficiently. As I
listened to the responses, I was conscious that tutoring or group
rehearsing may have assisted some candidates. We were not told
whether the candidate had previously applied and a serial applicant would have had an advantage.

At the conclusion of the process, I believed that we had
selected the best candidates. However, I was very much involved
in the selection process as circuit leader and as a presiding judge.
The Lord Chancellor and his officials were in possession of far
more detailed knowledge under the earlier process. Presiding
judges, circuit judges and circuit leaders were interviewed on a
regular basis, and both competencies and failings were recorded.
Under the present system, candidates select their referees, thus
minimising adverse comment in their contemplation. Short

temper, drink and bad behaviour are as relevant to the appointment process as any competence.

On any view the JAC, with its several Commissioners and
large staff, is by some distance more expensive than the Lord
Chancellor's Department. It complies with existing public
service standards, is transparent and avoids 'tap on the shoulder'
criticism. However, it does not appear to command the respect
of the legal profession, nor is it attracting the very best candidates to its process. Of particular practical concern, from my
own observation, was the fact that a large number of candidates
were out of their depth and within minutes of the interview
had demonstrated their unsuitability. Such interviews continued
to their conclusion and thus cumulatively wasted many hours
of panel time.

Just as the best candidates are not applying to be appointed
to the High Court, there is evidence that many leading
practitioners prefer not to expose themselves to a selection
process that attracts persistent criticism. Numerically, it will be
said in defence of the JAC that there is no shortage of applicants. It will also be said that those appointed are good quality
candidates. My own observations indicate that the highest
quality candidates are not applying, and as in the case of High
Court judges, an approach from a senior judge might well
attract an otherwise reluctant candidate. A review of the practices and efficacy of the JAC would, I am sure, be welcomed
by the professions.

## 4. A Criminal Division of the High Court should be created.

There are three Divisions of the High Court, namely the Queen's
Bench Division (QBD), the Chancery Division, and the Family
Division. Judges of the QBD try the most serious criminal cases.
Historically, every judge of the QBD was well schooled in the

criminal law, and when I was called to the Bar in 1967, almost every murder was tried by a High Court judge (HCJ). They also tried many other serious criminal cases, such as rape and incest.

Over the last fifty years, the deployment of HCJs has altered. The demands of the Administrative Courts and the Commercial Courts and several more divisions of the Court of Appeal (Criminal Division) have left many fewer HCJs available for deployment in the criminal courts. The consequence is that most murders are now tried by senior circuit judges. The only criminal trials presided over by HCJs are cases of special complexity and/or seriousness and/or public importance; for example, the highest profile murders, terrorist trials, extraordinary frauds and cases involving MPs.

The task of deploying appropriate HCJs can be extremely difficult and is made more so by the fact that some of the HCJs most experienced in criminal cases may be committed to civil cases. The criminal law has become far more complex in recent years, whilst both legal professions have become far more specialised. Criminal cases tried by HCJs should be tried by those with specialised knowledge and experience of the criminal law; but there are instances of newly appointed HCJs out on circuit trying difficult criminal cases with only limited experience of serious crime. It also happens that HCJs who have spent their careers at the Bar in criminal courts find themselves trying civil actions with minimal experience in that field.

The creation of a Criminal Division of the High Court will absolve members from trying non-criminal cases and ensure that the most serious criminal trials are tried by experts in the field. If at any time there are insufficient HCJs available, experienced circuit judges, deputy HCJs, or recently retired HCJs can be seconded, as happens at present in the Court of Appeal (Criminal Division). In that court, HCJs with limited experience of crime also frequently sit.

Whilst it may be justified as a form of education, the public, including appellants, are entitled to expect three judges learned in the criminal law to be sitting in that court. I would propose that only members of the Criminal Division or suitably qualified deputies sit in this court, together with an Appeal Court judge. The importance of work in this court cannot be overestimated. For appellants, it is almost always the last chance saloon. The most serious and demanding criminal cases must surely be tried by those with proven expertise in the criminal law.

## 5. A unified Criminal Court should be created.

In 2001, Sir Robin Auld wrote that the practices, procedures, management and funding of the two systems (Crown Courts and magistrates' courts) and their respective administrative cultures were inefficient and harmfully divisive. In his 'Review of the Criminal Courts', he recommended a unified criminal court, which might be called simply the Criminal Court, in which professional judges and lay magistrates would sit at their different levels, all as judges of the same court. His recommendation has not been implemented.

In June 2013, in a paper 'Transforming the CJS', the Ministry of Justice identified numerous aspects of the summary justice process that are working inefficiently.

In January 2015, Sir Brian Leveson concluded in his 'Review of Efficiency in Criminal Proceedings' that the lack of a single IT system and the 'very distinct physical estates' of the two jurisdictions were holding back any move to a unified court. Neither impediment is insuperable. As to the estates, Sir Brian observed: 'A unified criminal court does not mean a concentration of all courts in present Crown Court centres or magistrates' court centres. Instead, it means an examination of what other estate is held by statutory agencies within a given local area and a creative consideration of how these combined assets could be used more flexibly.'

Nothing in Sir Brian's review indicates any long-term opposition to a unified criminal court. For my part, I have long queried the sense in a single prosecution case necessarily visiting two courts, whilst inevitably achieving nothing in the lower court save passage to the higher court. Short-term expenditure in effecting a transition to a unified court would produce significant long-term savings and increased efficiency.

Registrars with appropriate judicial status and powers would exercise administrative case management by fixing trial dates, tribunal and venue, bail, giving and varying directions, acting as case progression officers, and ensuring that cases were ready for trial or plea of guilty. All such pretrial administration would be carried out by internet, avoiding the numerous court appearances and delay that presently beset our criminal justice process.

## 6. In summary jurisdiction, the most demanding cases should be reserved to district judges.

I have already commented upon the inefficiencies in summary justice, readily acknowledged by the Ministry of Justice. As the criminal law has become increasingly sophisticated, so too have the demands made of the lay judiciary. Lack of expertise in disclosure issues was highlighted in Sir Brian's review. An inability of some justices to deliver an articulate and reasoned extempore judgment, and lack of knowledge of the Criminal Procedure Rules, Police and Criminal Evidence Act, Codes of Practice, the Criminal Justice Act 2003, the Human Rights Act, and numerous other enactments crucial to the application of the criminal law, may all be cited in criticism of a volunteer judiciary.

The necessary learning is far too extensive to be gained at weekend seminars and the presence in court of legal advisors is no substitute for legal knowledge. An increased availability of district judges to try the more complex cases must be initiated in order to alleviate public concern. As Sir Robin observed in 2001, 'District judges because of their legal knowledge and experience and because they sit alone, are significantly faster and otherwise more efficient than magistrates.' However, the contribution of the lay judiciary to criminal justice cannot be overstated and was fully appreciated by both Sir Robin and Sir Brian. They deal with a vast amount of work in a most commendable manner.

At present, it often appears to be a matter of chance as to whether magistrates or district judges try a case. Generally, efforts are made to ensure that district judges try the most complex or demanding cases, with no certainty that any such aim will succeed. There has been a constant resistance on the part of the lay magistracy to any defined system that appears to promote district judges, whilst relegating lay magistrates to less important and less interesting work.

I have no doubt that the time has come when certain cases must be reserved to district judges and to them alone. Examples may well be: extradition, cases involving consideration of public safety, public interest immunity claims, child pornography offences, insolvency offences, financial services offences, terrorist offences, immigration offences, insider dealing offences, Official Secrets Acts offences, revenue and customs offences, serious fraud offences, and cases involving complex points of law or evidence, procedural issues or length.

Great care would need to be taken compiling such list. This should not be seen as any insult to the lay Bench, but as a response to the increased complexity of our criminal law and a desire to deploy the skills of district judges to the greatest public advantage.

## 7. Serious fraud trials should be tried either by a judge alone, or by a judge sitting with two assessors.

There have been repeated calls for complex fraud trials to be tried by judge alone or by a judge sitting with expert assessors. Lord Roskill, in 1986, chaired a Fraud Trial Committee, and concluded that juries should be replaced. In 2001, Sir Robin Auld concluded that juries, in such cases, should be replaced by a tribunal of a judge and two expert members. In 2003, legislation was passed implementing such recommendation, but requiring affirmative resolutions that were not forthcoming, and thus the legislation was repealed.

I have spent a significant proportion of my life, possibly as much as anyone alive, either addressing juries as an advocate or directing them as a judge. From time to time, it will be obvious that a particular juror or jurors are not able to follow the evidence. A good judge will be aware of such a danger to the trial process and will swiftly intervene in an attempt to clarify any apparent difficulty. There are cases, however, which are simply too difficult by reason of complexity for a jury to try.

Commercial and international fraud has become increasingly sophisticated and way beyond the comprehension of the majority of our community. Counsel have the task of continuously translating financial terms in an endeavour to assist jurors. This is not only time-consuming, but often destined to fail. Trials that could be concluded in days before a judge and assessors take weeks before a jury, or if triable within weeks, take months with corresponding public expenditure. The duration of many fraud trials are impossible to estimate.

Where a jury has not comprehended an allegation, or worse still a defence, the chances of a miscarriage of justice are greatly amplified, but both branches of the legal profession tend to oppose any change to the present system out of self-interest. Lengthy fraud trials generate exceptional fees.

I am in no doubt that out of fairness to prosecutors, defendants and jurors themselves, serious fraud trials of exceptional complexity should be tried by a judge, or a judge and two expert assessors.

## 8. Defendants in the Crown Court should have a right to elect trial by judge alone.

On a recent visit to Canada, I was impressed with a provision that is fair to defendants, saves time and money, and is increasing in use. It is also widely used in the United States, New Zealand and Australia, with certain restrictions in the most serious cases. A defendant has the right to be tried by judge alone, rather than by a jury. It is easy to see that defendants charged with violence or sexual offences particularly offensive to the public, or from abused minorities, may have greater confidence in a judge trying a case alone. They may also, particularly if innocent, wish to receive a fully reasoned written judgment. A defendant adversely affected by hostile publicity may also seek to be tried by a judge alone. It is widely believed that judges are more responsive to defence submissions in cases based on identification evidence, or reliant upon a questionable confession. An innocent person, albeit with a technical but sound defence, would be well advised to be tried by a judge alone.

## 9. Sentences passed in court should accurately state the length of time that the defendant is actually to serve in custody.

A sentence of sixteen years, for example, may sound to all who hear it passed, or read of it, to be a long sentence. It sounds a long sentence even to the judge passing it. In reality, the defendant will serve very much less, either one half or two-thirds of the sentence actually announced. Sir Harry Ognall, the retired High Court judge, described in his memoirs the practice as 'involving the judiciary being required to lend themselves to a highly publicised con trick'.

A newspaper columnist in the aftermath of the Usman Khan tragedy, when the convicted terrorist on early release stabbed two people to death on London Bridge, described the practice as 'a lie, a deliberate deception, a pretence that criminals – not just terrorists – will serve the full sentence handed down by the courts.'

To meet this criticism, the defendant, victims and the public are entitled to know exactly how long the defendant will actually serve in custody as the law at that time stands. At present nobody, often including the judge, really knows. Many members of the public fail to distinguish between minimum terms, which are actually served in full, and other sentences of which half or even less are served.

In the case of Bright in 2008, it was said by the Appeal Court that: 'The judge determines the length of the sentence, not how long the defendant will spend in custody.' The fact that the judge's explanation as to the time to be served was inaccurate was not a ground for saying that the sentence was wrong in principle, or manifestly excessive. In several reported cases, judges have given inaccurate explanations as to the effect of the sentence they were in the process of passing.

The obligatory task of explaining the effect of a sentence can be exceptionally difficult and often impossible. Over the last two decades or more, there have been numerous changes in sentencing law, included in dozens of statutes.

Mr Justice Mitting, a judge of great experience and ability, in a judgment in the Administrative Court, made it clear that the statutory obligation to explain the effect of consecutive sentences accurately was impossible, saying, 'Indeed, so impossible is it that it has taken from 12 noon until 12 minutes to 5, with a slightly longer short adjournment than usual for reading purposes, to explain the relevant statutory provisions to me, a professional judge . . . It is simply impossible to discern from statutory provisions what a sentence means in practice.'

Having quoted that passage in his review, Sir Brian Leveson indicated that the time had arrived for a comprehensive consolidation of sentencing practice and procedure, bringing every statutory provision into a single code. That is one critical step towards accurately explaining sentences. The other must be an obligation to state the precise time the defendant must actually serve in custody, as the law stands, as opposed to the inflated and misleading figures that have been announced in open court for generations.

## 10. Increased funding of the criminal justice system is essential.

Both branches of the legal profession, the judiciary, defendants, the Crown Prosecution Service (CPS) and the public have suffered from underfunding over the last decade. In May 2016, the House of Commons Public Accounts Committee published a report into 'Efficiency in the Criminal Justice System', commencing with the words, 'The criminal justice system is close to breaking point.'

Since 2010 half of the magistrates' courts in England and Wales have closed, forcing defendants, witnesses, police, lawyers and magistrates to travel sometimes more than fifty miles to access local justice. In Lancashire, towns as large as Chorley and Fleetwood no longer have a criminal court. As Sir Lindsay Hoyle MP stated, 'Once justice is moved away, there is a complete disconnect between the public and law and order.'

Legal aid rates of remuneration have so disadvantaged criminal practitioners that outstanding talent is instantly diverted to more fertile work. In earlier generations, the finest lawyers began their careers in the criminal courts. Tom Denning, as he then was, received his first brief for the prosecution at Winchester Quarter Sessions; Tom Bingham, as he then was, regularly prosecuted shoplifters for Marks and Spencer; and when I first entered the robing room at Blackpool Quarter Sessions, I was confronted by Sandy Temple, Christopher Rose, and George Carman. Talent still exists and thrives at the criminal bar, but those dedicated to the most interesting of pursuits will suffer financially.

The Bar Council figures indicate that the Ministry of Justice had sustained 27 per cent cuts in real terms over a decade and the CPS 34 per cent. It is fanciful to contemplate that this has been without adverse consequence. Crimes are not being detected, and when detected, not being prosecuted. It was not without significance that when both leading political parties announced the proposed increase of 20,000 police officers, no plans were disclosed by either party to deal with any consequence to the criminal justice system arising from such a measure. More police will presumably increase the number of arrests, thereby increasing the business of the criminal courts, already stretched way beyond efficiency.

Justice Secretaries lacking legal education have presided over the closure of some 300 courts and reduced sitting days by some 15 per cent. Bizarrely, they have contended that reducing sitting days saves money. It saves on advocates' fees, judges' salaries, court staff, and so on. Whilst the argument is sound in the very short term, it ignores the fact that the delayed trials still have to be heard at a future date.

The policy has succeeded in creating a shameful and scandalous backlog of criminal cases. Some quite shocking figures have recently been published showing average waiting times between the date of the offence and sentence averaging 533 days, and over 750 days in the worst performing courts. Witnesses forget, victims are unable to put their ordeal behind them, with a significant number disengaging, and innocent accused suffer unimaginable anguish, graphically described by Paul Gambaccini and Harvey Proctor in their respective books.

Our present Justice Secretary, Robert Buckland, is to be congratulated on reinstating some 700 sitting days scheduled to be cut. He has many years' experience in the Crown Court and sits as a recorder. He is well regarded and doubtless very aware of the flawed policies of his predecessors. I question, however, whether he can possibly have the clout of a Hailsham or a Mackay, an Irvine or a Falconer in his dealings with the Treasury or Number 10.

My message to the Justice Secretary is this. Estimates of the cost of HS2 vary between £56 billion, the original 2015 price tag, and £106 billion, the latest published estimate. A mere three billion pounds could in short time repair our fractured, once-envied and now much-criticised system. Reopen some of those closed courts; recorders await, trials are ready to be heard. Unlike the NHS, we have the infrastructure and the manpower and given funds can instantly respond.

Increase legal aid rates, resource a forensic science service, and match the proposed increase in police numbers with an increase in CPS numbers, probation officers and prison officers; permit acquitted defendants to recover their costs, and impose time limits across the board. For example, a maximum of one hundred days for suspects under investigation extendable only by application to a district judge, and fifty days for the CPS to make a charging decision; reduce the custody time limit from 182 days, and all criminal trials to commence within twelve months of charge. These are aspirations, but so much needs urgent attention.

In December 2019, the newly elected prime minister announced: 'My ministers will establish a Royal Commission to review and improve the efficiency and effectiveness of the criminal justice process.' The Runciman Commission on Criminal Justice was established in March 1991 and did not report to Parliament until July 1993. The total expenditure was much criticised.

For my part, I can see what needs to be done without the delay and attendant expenditure. A decade of austerity and incompetence necessitates immediate investment and innovation. Justice delayed is justice denied.

# Acknowledgements

My sincere thanks to all who have assisted me in the production of this book and, in particular, the following:

Rupert Lancaster, my editor, and his most professional team at Hodder & Stoughton for turning a self-indulgent memoir into a serious book.

Martin Redfern, my literary agent, and his dynamic team at Northbank Talent for their enthusiasm and much-needed guidance.

My senior Bar clerks, Bill Blood, Jack Pickles, Joe Pattison, Trevor Doyle and Terri Creathorn; all clerks but in reality, advisers, agents and confidants.

My two judge's clerks, Don McKenzie and Daniel Worker, invaluable companions and now lifelong friends.

My companions at the Bar, mostly fellow members of the Northern Circuit, for their banter, talent, integrity and companionship, which so enriched my professional life.

My family, my wife Toni, David and Daniel, for providing a loving environment that inspired me to progress from criminal hack to the High Court.

I also wish to thank my late parents for providing every possible support from cradle to Bench.

# Index